D1523384

Poetical Works

THE POETICAL WORKS

OF

LORD BYRON.

THE

POETICAL WORKS

OF

LORD BYRON.

IN SIX VOLUMES.—VOL III.

A NEW EDITION.

LONDON:

JOHN MURRAY, ALBEMARLE STREET.

1879

LONDON
BRADBURY, AGNEW, & CO, PRINTERS, WHITEFRIARS

CONTENTS.

THE GIAOUR:

A FRAGMENT OF A TURKISH TALE.

"One fatal remembrance—one sorrow that throws
Its bleak shade alike o'er our joys and our woes—
To which Life nothing darker nor brighter can bring,
For which joy hath no balm—and affliction no sting"—MOORE.

TO

SAMUEL ROGERS, ESQ

AS A SLIGHT BUT MOST SINCERE TOKEN OF

ADMIRATION FOR HIS GENIUS, RESPECT FOR HIS CHARACTER,

AND GRATITUDE FOR HIS FRIENDSHIP,

𝔗𝔥𝔦𝔰 𝔓𝔯𝔬𝔡𝔲𝔠𝔱𝔦𝔬𝔫 𝔦𝔰 𝔍𝔫𝔰𝔠𝔯𝔦𝔟𝔢𝔡,

BY HIS OBLIGED AND AFFECTIONATE SERVANT,

BYRON.

LONDON, *May*, 1818.

B 2

ADVERTISEMENT.

THE tale which these disjointed fragments present, is founded upon circumstances now less common in the East than formerly; either because the ladies are more circumspect than in the "olden time," or because the Christians have better fortune, or less enterprise. The story, when entire, contained the adventures of a female slave, who was thrown, in the Mussulman manner, into the sea for infidelity, and avenged by a young Venetian, her lover, at the time the Seven Islands were possessed by the Republic of Venice, and soon after the Arnauts were beaten back from the Morea, which they had ravaged for some time subsequent to the Russian invasion. The desertion of the Mainotes, on being refused the plunder of Misitra, led to the abandonment of that enterprise, and to the desolation of the Morea, during which the cruelty exercised on all sides was unparalleled even in the annals of the faithful.

INTRODUCTION TO THE GIAOUR.

In the "Hints from Horace," written in 1811, Lord Byron expressed his preference for the octosyllabic metre —

> "Though at first view eight feet may seem in vain
> Form'd, save in ode, to bear a serious strain,
> Yet Scott has shown our wondering isle of late
> This measure shrinks not from a theme of weight
> And, varied skilfully, surpasses far
> Heroic rhyme, but most in love and war,
> Whose fluctuations, tender or sublime,
> Are curb'd too much by long recurring rhyme "

With this opinion of the merits of the measure—which he admits that he borrowed from Scott, as Scott, in his turn, confessed to have derived it from the "Christabel" of Coleridge—Lord Byron naturally tested its compass in his earliest tale   The fragmentary form of the composition was suggested by the then new "Columbus" of Rogers   As to the scene, it was not his recent travels alone that recommended it to Byron, for he had always dwelt fondly upon Eastern subjects, of which the realities harmonised with his imaginative dreams. "Old Knolles," he said, at Missolonghi, "was one of the first books that gave me pleasure when a child , and I believe it had much influence on my future wishes to visit the Levant, and gave, perhaps, the Oriental colouring which is observed in my poetry."   An incident which occurred while the author was at Athens was the foundation of the "Giaour"   His Turkish servant tampered with a female slave, and, on his return from bathing, Lord Byron met an escort who carried the girl, sewn up in a sack, to throw her into the sea. He afterwards said, "that to describe the feelings of the situation was impossible and that to recollect them even, was icy "   Happily the catastrophe was not as tragical as in the tale   He threatened to shoot the leader of the band unless they took back their victim to the governor's house, where, by a combination of menaces, entreaties, and bribery, he obtained her release.   The first draught of the poem was the work of a week , but it then consisted of only four hundred lines, which, in the process of printing, and in future editions, grew to fourteen hundred.   When once the vein of sentiment was opened, he found it hard to check the flow   "I have," he wrote to Mr Murray, during the progress of the fifth edition. " but with some difficulty, *not* added any more to this snake of a poem, which has been lengthening its rattles every month "   It was published in May, 1813, and was in the fifth edition by September. The sensation created by the "Pilgrimage" was abundantly sustained.   The comparison between ancient and modern Greece—now softly pathetic, and now fiercely indignant—the terrible conflicts of a mind torn by passion, revenge, and remorse, were set forth with an eloquence and intensity of description which had a contagious effect. On the copy sent to Scott, Lord Byron inscribed—"To the Monarch of Parnassus, from one of his subjects;" and Scott, on the other hand, observed to Ballantyne, "Byron hits the mark where I don't pretend to fledge my arrow" With his usual manliness he hastened to acknowledge, that, from the publication of "Childe Harold," his star had paled before the lurid light of this flaming meteor. While the Tales of Scott had lost the freshness of novelty, and his later performances had not kept to the pitch of his earlier pieces, Lord Byron was displaying the first-fruits of a genius that in poetic power was the superior of the two. In the prodigality of his images, in the luxuriance, vigour, and polish of his style; in the thrilling representation of agonising passion; Lord Byron was unapproached by the Minstrel of the North But by no one was he welcomed more warmly to the course, and with heart and hand Scott joined with the public to place the chaplet from his own brow on the head of his rival. Lord Byron disposed of the copyright of the "Giaour" for 500 guineas.

THE GIAOUR.

No breath of air to break the wave
That rolls below the Athenian's grave,
That tomb[1] which, gleaming o'er the cliff,
First greets the homeward-veering skiff,
High o'er the land he saved in vain;
When shall such hero live again?

* * * * *

Fair clime! where every season smiles
Benignant o'er those blessed isles,
Which, seen from far Colonna's heignt,
Make glad the heart that hails the sight,
And lend to loneliness delight.
There mildly dimpling, Ocean's cheek
Reflects the tints of many a peak
Caught by the laughing tides that lave
These Edens of the eastern wave:
And if at times a transient breeze
Break the blue crystal of the seas,
Or sweep one blossom from the trees,
How welcome is each gentle air
That wakes and wafts the odours there![2]

---

[1] A tomb above the rocks on the promontory, by some supposed the sepulchre of Themistocles.

[2] ["There *shine the bright abodes ye seek,*
Like dimples upon Ocean's cheek,
So smiling round the waters lave
These Edens of the eastern wave.

For there the Rose. o'er crag or vale,
Sultana of the Nightingale,[3]
    The maid for whom his melody,
    His thousand songs are heard on high,
Blooms blushing to her lover's tale:
His queen, the garden queen, his Rose,
Unbent by winds, unchill'd by snows,
Far from the winters of the west,
By every breeze and season blest,
Returns the sweets by nature given
In softest incense back to heaven;
And grateful yields that smiling sky
Her fairest hue and fragrant sigh.
And many a summer flower is there,
And many a shade that love might share,
And many a grotto, meant for rest,
That holds the pirate for a guest;
Whose bark in sheltering cove below
Lurks for the passing peaceful prow,
Till the gay mariner's guitar[4]
Is heard, and seen the evening star;
Then stealing with the muffled oar,
Far shaded by the rocky shore,
Rush the night-prowlers on the prey,
And turn to groans his roundelay.
Strange—that where Nature loved to trace,
As if for Gods, a dwelling place,
And every charm and grace hath mix'd
Within the paradise she fix'd,
There man, enamour'd of distress,
Should mar it into wilderness,

> Or if, at times, the transient breeze
> Break the *smooth* crystal of the seas,
> Or *brush* one blossom from the trees,
> How *grateful* is the gentle air
> That waves and wafts the *fragrance* there."—MS.

The whole of this passage, from line 7 down to line 167, "Who heard it first had cause to grieve," was not in the first edition.]

[3] The attachment of the nightingale to the rose is a well-known Persian fable. If I mistake not, the "Bulbul of a thousand tales" is one of his appellations.

[4] The guitar is the constant amusement of the Greek sailor by night; with a steady fair wind, and during a calm, it is accompanied always by the voice, and often by dancing.

And trample, brute-like, o'er each flower
That tasks not one laborious hour;
Nor claims the culture of his hand
To bloom along the fairy land,
But springs as to preclude his care,
And sweetly woos him—but to spare !
Strange—that where all is peace beside,
There passion riots in her pride,
And lust and rapine wildly reign
To darken o'er the fair domain.
It is as though the fiends prevail'd
Against the seraphs they assail'd,
And, fix'd on heavenly thrones, should dwell
The freed inheritors of hell ;
So soft the scene, so form'd for joy,
So curst the tyrants that destroy !

He who hath bent him o'er the dead
Ere the first day of death is fled,
The first dark day of nothingness,
The last of danger and distress,
(Before Decay's effacing fingers
Have swept the lines where beauty lingers,)
And mark'd the mild angelic air,
The rapture of repose that's there,[5]
The fix'd yet tender traits that streak
The languor of the placid cheek,
And—but for that sad shrouded eye,
    That fires not, wins not, weeps not, now,
    And but for that chill, changeless brow,
Where cold Obstruction's apathy[6]
Appals the gazing mourner's heart,[7]
As if to him it could impart

---

[5] ["And mark'd the almost dreaming air,
    Which speaks the sweet repose that's there."—MS.]

[6] " Ay, but to die and go we know not where,
    To lye in cold obstruction ? "
                    Measure for Measure, Act iii. sc. 2.

[7] ["Whose touch thrills with mortality,
    And curdles at the gazer's heart "—MS]

The doom he dreads, yet dwells upon;
Yes, but for these and these alone,
(Some moments, ay, one treacherous hour,
He still might doubt the tyrant's power;
So fair, so calm, so softly seal'd,
The first, last look by death reveal'd!*
Such is the aspect of this shore;
'Tis Greece, but living Greece no more!
So coldly sweet, so deadly fair,
We start, for soul is wanting there.
Hers is the loveliness in death,
That parts not quite with parting breath;)
But beauty with that fearful bloom,
That hue which haunts it to the tomb,
Expression's last receding ray,
A gilded halo hovering round decay,
The farewell beam of Feeling past away!
Spark of that flame, perchance of heavenly birth,
Which gleams, but warms no more its cherish'd earth!*

(Clime of the unforgotten brave!¹
Whose land from plain to mountain-cave
Was Freedom's home or Glory's grave!
Shrine of the mighty! can it be,
That this is all remains of thee?)
Approach, thou craven crouching slave:
Say, is not this Thermopylæ?

⁸ I trust that few of my readers have ever had an opportunity of witnessing what is here attempted in description; but those who have will probably retain a painful remembrance of that singular beauty which pervades, with few exceptions, the features of the dead, a few hours, and but for a few hours, after "the spirit is not there." It is to be remarked in cases of violent death by gun-shot wounds, the expression is always that of languor, whatever the natural energy of the sufferer's character; but in death from a stab the countenance preserves its traits of feeling or ferocity, and the mind its bias, to the last.

⁹ [There is infinite beauty and effect, though of a painful and almost oppressive character, in this extraordinary passage; in which the author has illustrated the beautiful, but still and melancholy aspect of the once busy and glorious shores of Greece, by an image more true, more mournful, and more exquisitely finished, than any that we can recollect in the whole compass of poetry.—JEFFREY.]

¹ [From hence to the conclusion of the paragraph, the MS. is written in a hurried and almost illegible hand, as if these splendid lines had been poured forth in one continuous burst of poetic feeling, which would hardly allow time for the pen to follow the imagination.]

These waters blue that round you lave,—
  ᶜOh servile offspring of the free ⌐
Pronounce what sea, what shore is this?
The gulf, the rock of Salamis!
These scenes, their story not unknown,
Arise, and make again your own;
⟨ Snatch from the ashes of your sires
  The embers of their former fires; ⌐
And he who in the strife expires
Will add to theirs a name of fear
That Tyranny shall quake to hear,
And leave his sons a hope, a fame,
They too will rather die than shame:[2]
For Freedom's battle once begun,
Bequeath'd by bleeding Sire to Son,
Though baffled oft is ever won.   ⟨ I must pass ⟩ᶜ
Bear witness, Greece, thy living page!
Attest it many a deathless age!
While kings, in dusty darkness hid,
Have left a nameless pyramid,
Thy heroes, though the general doom
Hath swept the column from their tomb,
A mightier monument command,
The mountains of their native land!
There points thy Muse to stranger's eye
The graves of those that cannot die!
ᶜ 'Twere long to tell, and sad to trace,
  Each step from splendour to disgrace;
Enough—no foreign foe could quell
Thy soul, till from itself it fell; ⌐
Yes! Self-abasement paved the way
To villain-bonds and despot sway.

What can he tell who treads thy shore?
  No legend of thine olden time,
No theme on which the Muse might soar
High as thine own in days of yore,

---

[2] ["And he who in the cause expires,
    Will add a name and fate to them
    Well worthy of his noble stem"—MS.]

When man was worthy of thy clime.
The hearts within thy valleys bred,
The fiery souls that might have led
  Thy sons to deeds sublime,
Now crawl from cradle to the grave,
Slaves—nay, the bondsmen of a slave,[3]
  And callous, save to crime;
Stain'd with each evil that pollutes
Mankind, where least above the brutes;
Without even savage virtue blest,
Without one free or valiant breast,
Still to the neighbouring ports they waft
Proverbial wiles, and ancient craft;
In this the subtle Greek is found,
For this, and this alone, renown'd.
In vain might Liberty invoke
The spirit to its bondage broke,
Or raise the neck that courts the yoke:
No more her sorrows I bewail,
Yet this will be a mournful tale,
And they who listen may believe,
Who heard it first had cause to grieve.

    *   *   *   *   *

  Far, dark, along the blue sea glancing,
The shadows of the rocks advancing
Start on the fisher's eye like boat
Of island-pirate or Mainote;
And fearful for his light caique,
He shuns the near but doubtful creek:
Though worn and weary with his toil,
And cumber'd with his scaly spoil,
Slowly, yet strongly, plies the oar,
Till Port Leone's safer shore
Receives him by the lovely light
That best becomes an Eastern night.

    *   *   *   *   *

[3] Athens is the property of the Kislar Aga (the slave of the seraglio and guardian of the women), who appoints the Waywode A pander and eunuch—these are not polite, yet true appellations—now *governs* the *governor* of Athens !

"Who thundering comes on blackest steed,"
With slacken'd bit and hoof of speed?
Beneath the clattering iron's sound
The cavern'd echoes wake around
In lash for lash, and bound for bound;
The foam that streaks the courser's side
Seems gather'd from the ocean-tide:
Though weary waves are sunk to rest,
There's none within his rider's breast;
And though to-morrow's tempest lower,
'Tis calmer than thy heart, young Giaour!"
I know thee not, I loathe thy race,
But in thy lineaments I trace
What time shall strengthen, not efface:
Though young and pale, that sallow front
Is scathed by fiery passion's brunt;
Though bent on earth thine evil eye,
As meteor-like thou glidest by,
Right well I view and deem thee one
Whom Othman's sons should slay or shun.

On—on he hasten'd, and he drew
My gaze of wonder as he flew:
Though like a demon of the night
He pass'd, and vanish'd from my sight,
His aspect and his air impress'd
A troubled memory on my breast,
And long upon my startled ear
Rung his dark courser's hoofs of fear.
He spurs his steed; he nears the steep,
That, jutting, shadows o'er the deep;
He winds around; he hurries by,
The rock relieves him from mine eye;

[The reciter of the tale is a Turkish fisherman, who has been employed during the day in the gulf of Ægina, and in the evening, apprehensive of the Mainote pirates who infest the coast of Attica, lands with his boat on the harbour of Port Leone, the ancient Piræus. He becomes the eye-witness of nearly all the incidents in the story, and in one of them is a principal agent It is to his feelings, and particularly to his religious prejudices, that we are indebted for some of the most forcible and splendid parts of the poem.—GEORGE ELLIS.]

5 [In Dr. Clarke's Travels, this word, which means *Infidel*, is always written according to its English pronunciation, *Djour* Lord Byron adopted the Italian spelling usual among the Franks of the Levant.]

For well I ween unwelcome he
Whose glance is fix'd on those that flee;
And not a star but shines too bright
On him who takes such timeless flight.
He wound along; but ere he pass'd
One glance he snatch'd, as if his last, ↄ
A moment check'd his wheeling steed,
A moment breathed him from his speed,
A moment on his stirrup stood—
[Why looks he o'er the olive wood?] ᶜˣᵗ ₙₐₜ ⁿ
The crescent glimmers on the hill,
The Mosque's high lamps are quivering still
Though too remote for sound to wake
In echoes of the far tophaike,⁶
The flashes of each joyous peal
Are seen to prove the Moslem's zeal.
To-night, set Rhamazani's sun;
To-night, the Bairam feast's begun;
To-night—but who and what art thou
Of foreign garb and fearful brow?
And what are these to thine or thee,
That thou shouldst either pause or flee?

He stood—some dread was on his face,
Soon Hatred settled in its place:
It rose not with the reddening flush
Of transient Anger's hasty blush,
But pale as marble o'er the tomb,
Whose ghastly whiteness aids its gloom.
His brow was bent, his eye was glazed;
He raised his arm, and fiercely raised,
And sternly shook his hand on high,
As doubting to return or fly;
Impatient of his flight delay'd,
Here loud his raven charger neigh'd—
Down glanced that hand, and grasp'd his blade;⁷

⁶ "Tophaike," musket. The Bairam is announced by the cannon at sunset: the illumination of the mosques, and the firing of all kinds of small arms, loaded with *ball*, proclaim it during the night

⁷   ["Then turn'd it swiftly to his blade,
               As loud his raven charger neigh'd "—MS]

That sound had burst his waking dream,
As Slumber starts at owlet's scream.
The spur hath lanced his courser's sides ;
Away, away, for life he rides :   ·
Swift as the hurl'd on high jerreed [8]
Springs to the touch his startled steed ;
The rock is doubled, and the shore
Shakes with the clattering tramp no more ;
The crag is won, no more is seen
His Christian crest and haughty mien.
'Twas but an instant he restrain'd
That fiery barb so sternly rein'd ; [9]
'Twas but a moment that he stood,
Then sped as if by death pursued ;
But in that instant o'er his soul
Winters of Memory seem'd to roll,
And gather in that drop of time
A life of pain, an age of crime.
O'er him who loves, or hates, or fears,
Such moment pours the grief of years :
What felt *he* then, at once opprest
By all that most distracts the breast ?
That pause, which ponder'd o'er his fate,
Oh, who its dreary length shall date !
Though in Time's record nearly nought,
It was Eternity to Thought !
For infinite as boundless space
The thought that Conscience must embrace,
Which in itself can comprehend
Woe without name, or hope, or end.

The hour is past, the Giaour is gone ;
And did he fly or fall alone ? [1]

---

[8] Jerreed, or Djerrid, a blunted Turkish javelin, which is darted from horseback with great force and precision It is a favourite exercise of the Mussulmans , but I know not if it can be called a *manly* one, since the most expert in the art are the Black Eunuchs of Constantinople. I think, next to these, a Mamlouk at Smyrna was the most skilful that came within my observation

[9]   ["Twas but an instant, though so long
        When thus dilated in my song "—MS.]

[1]   ["But neither fled nor fell alone "— MS]

Woe to that hour he came or went !
The curse for Hassan's sin was sent
To turn a palace to a tomb;
He came, he went, like the simoom,[2]
That harbinger of fate and gloom,
Beneath whose widely-wasting breath
The very cypress droops to death—
Dark tree, still sad when others' grief is fled,
The only constant mourner o'er the dead !

The steed is vanish'd from the stall;
No serf is seen in Hassan's hall;
The lonely spider's thin gray pall
Waves slowly widening o'er the wall;[3]
The bat builds in his haram bower,
And in the fortress of his power
The owl usurps the beacon-tower;
The wild-dog howls o'er the fountain's brim,
With baffled thirst, and famine, grim;[4]
For the stream has shrunk from its marble bed,
Where the weeds and the desolate dust are spread.
'Twas sweet of yore to see it play
And chase the sultriness of day,
As springing high the silver dew
In whirls fantastically flew,
And flung luxurious coolness round
The air, and verdure o'er the ground.
'Twas sweet, when cloudless stars were bright,
To view the wave of watery light,
And hear its melody by night.

---

[2] The blast of the desert, fatal to everything living, and often alluded to in Eastern poetry.

[When the wind blows over the burning desert it gets heated in its passage, and carries with it also the finer particles of sand. The air parches the throat and skin, and, if the face is uncovered, the sand blinds and chokes. But though the simoom is often debilitating, and occasionally fatal, modern travellers attest that its effects have been grossly exaggerated]

[3]   ["The lonely spider's thin gray pall
                Is curtain'd on the splendid wall."—MS]

[4]   ["The wild-dog howls o'er the fountain's brink,
                But vainly tells his tongue to drink."—MS

And oft had Hassan's Childhood play'd
Around the verge of that cascade;
And oft upon his mother's breast
That sound had harmonized his rest;
And oft had Hassan's Youth along
Its bank been soothed by Beauty's song;
And softer seem'd each melting tone
Of Music mingled with its own.
But ne'er shall Hassan's Age repose
Along the brink at twilight's close :]
The stream that fill'd that font is fled—
The blood that warm'd his heart is shed!'
And here no more shall human voice
Be heard to rage, regret, rejoice.
The last sad note that swell'd the gale
Was woman's wildest funeral wail :
That quench'd in silence, all is still,
But the lattice that flaps when the wind is **shrill**:
Though raves the gust, and floods the rain,
No hand shall close its clasp again.
On desert sands 'twere joy to scan
The rudest steps of fellow man,
So here the very voice of Grief
Might wake an Echo like relief—
At least 'twould say, " All are not gone;
There lingers Life, though but in one "—
For many a gilded chamber's there,
Which Solitude might well forbear ; ⁶
Within that dome as yet Decay
Hath slowly work'd her cankering way—
But gloom is gather'd o'er the gate,
Nor there the Fakir's self will wait;

---

⁵   [" For thirsty fox and jackal gaunt
                    May vainly for its waters pant."—MS]

⁶ [" I have just recollected an alteration you may make in the proof   Among the
lines on Hassan's Serai, is this—'Unmeet for solitude to share '   Now, to share
implies more than one, and Solitude is a single gentleman   it must be thus—

                'For many a gilded chamber's there,
                Which Solitude might well forbear ,'

and so on   Will you adopt this correction ? and pray accept a Stilton cheese from me
for your trouble."—*B. Letters*, Stilton, Oct. 3, 1813.]

Nor there will wandering Dervise stay,
For bounty cheers not his delay;
Nor there will weary stranger halt
To bless the sacred "bread and salt." [7]
{ Alike must Wealth and Poverty
Pass heedless and unheeded by,
For Courtesy and Pity died
With Hassan on the mountain side.}
His roof, that refuge unto men,
Is Desolation's hungry den.
The guest flies the hall, and the vassal from labour,
Since his turban was cleft by the infidel's sabre! [8]

✠   *   *   *   *   *

I hear the sound of coming feet,
But not a voice mine ear to greet;
More near—each turban I can scan,
And silver-sheathed ataghan; [9]
The foremost of the band is seen
An Emir by his garb of green: [1]
"Ho! who art thou?"—"This low salam [2]
Replies of Moslem faith I am.
The burthen ye so gently bear,
Seems one that claims your utmost care,
And, doubtless, holds some precious freight,
My humble bark would gladly wait."
     "Thou speakest sooth: thy skiff unmoor,
And waft us from the silent shore;

---

[7] To partake of food, to break bread and salt with your host, ensures the safety of the guest . even though an enemy, his person from that moment is sacred.

[8] I need hardly observe, that Charity and Hospitality are the first duties enjoined by Mahomet; and to say truth, very generally practised by his disciples The first praise that can be bestowed on a chief, is a panegyric on his bounty; the next, on his valour.

[9] The ataghan, a long dagger worn with pistols in the belt, in a metal scabbard, generally of silver; and, among the wealthier, gilt, or of gold.

[1] Green is the privileged colour of the prophet's numerous pretended descendants; with them, as here, faith (the family inheritance) is supposed to supersede the necessity of good works they are the worst of a very indifferent brood.

[2] "Salam aleikoum ! aleikoum salam !" peace be with you; be with you peace— the salutation reserved for the faithful :—to a Christian, "Urlarula," a good journey; or "saban hiresem, saban serula ," good morn, good even; and sometimes, "may your end be happy;" are the usual salutes.

Nay, leave the sail still furl'd, and ply
The nearest oar that's scatter'd by,
And midway to those rocks where sleep
The channell'd waters dark and deep.
Rest from your task—so—bravely done,
Our course has been right swiftly run;
Yet 'tis the longest voyage, I trow,
That one of— * * * *

* * * * * "

 Sullen it plunged, and slowly sank,
The calm wave rippled to the bank;
I watch'd it as it sank, methought
Some motion from the current caught
Bestirr'd it more,—'twas but the beam
That checker'd o'er the living stream:
I gazed, till vanishing from view,
Like lessening pebble it withdrew;
Still less and less, a speck of white
That gemm'd the tide, then mock'd the sight;
And all its hidden secrets sleep,
Known but to Genii of the deep,
Which, trembling in their coral caves,
They dare not whisper to the waves.

* * * * *

 As rising on its purple wing
The insect-queen ' of eastern spring,
O'er emerald meadows of Kashmeer
Invites the young pursuer near,
And leads him on from flower to flower
A weary chase and wasted hour,
Then leaves him, as it soars on high,
With panting heart and tearful eye:
So Beauty lures the full-grown child,
With hue as bright, and wing as wild:
A chase of idle hopes and fears,
Begun in folly, closed in tears.

' The blue-winged butterfly of Kashmeer, the most rare and beautiful of the species

If won, to equal ills betray'd,[4]
Woe waits the insect and the maid ;
A life of pain, the loss of peace,
From infant's play, and man's caprice :
The lovely toy so fiercely sought
Hath lost its charm by being caught,
For every touch that woo'd its stay
Hath brush'd its brightest hues away,
Till charm, and hue, and beauty gone,
'Tis left to fly or fall alone.
With wounded wing, or bleeding breast,
Ah ! where shall either victim rest ?
Can this with faded pinion soar
From rose to tulip as before ?
Or Beauty, blighted in an hour,
Find joy within her broken bower ?
No : gayer insects fluttering by
Ne'er droop the wing o'er those that die,
And lovelier things have mercy shown
To every failing but their own,
And every woe a tear can claim
Except an erring sister's shame.

*   *   ·*   *   *

The Mind, that broods o'er guilty woes,
    Is like the Scorpion girt by fire ;
In circle narrowing as it glows,[5]
The flames around their captive close,
Till inly search'd by thousand throes,
    And maddening in her ire,
One sad and sole relief she knows,
The sting she nourish'd for her foes,
Whose venom never yet was vain,
Gives but one pang, and cures all pain,
And darts into her desperate brain :
So do the dark in soul expire,
Or live like Scorpion girt by fire ;[6]

[" If caught, to fate alike betray'd "—MS.]
[" The gathering flames around her close."—MS.]
Alluding to the dubious suicide of the scorpion, so placed for experiment by

So writhes the mind Remorse hath riven,'
Unfit for earth, undoom'd for heaven,
Darkness above, despair beneath,
Around it flame, within it death !

*   *   *   *   *

Black Hassan from the Haram flies,
Nor bends on woman's form his eyes ;
The unwonted chase each hour employs,
Yet shares he not the hunter's joys.
Not thus was Hassan wont to fly
When Leila dwelt in his Serai.
Doth Leila there no longer dwell ?
That tale can only Hassan tell :
Strange rumours in our city say
Upon that eve she fled away
When Rhamazan's ° last sun was set,
And flashing from each minaret
Millions of lamps proclaim'd the feast
Of Bairam through the boundless East.
'Twas then she went as to the bath,
Which Hassan vainly search'd in wrath ;
For she was flown her master's rage
In likeness of a Georgian page,
And far beyond the Moslem's power
Had wrong'd him with the faithless Giaour.
Somewhat of this had Hassan deem'd ;
But still so fond, so fair she seem'd,
Too well he trusted to the slave
Whose treachery deserved a grave :
And on that eve had gone to mosque,
And thence to feast in his kiosk.

gentle philosophers   Some maintain that the position of the sting, when turned
towards the head, is merely a convulsive movement ; but others have actually brought
in the verdict "Felo de se." The scorpions are surely interested in a speedy decision of the question ; as, if once fairly established as insect Catos, they will probably
be allowed to live as long as they think proper, without being martyred for the sake
of an hypothesis
    [Lord Byron assured Mr. Dallas that the simile of the scorpion was imagined in his
sleep.]
7   ["So writhes the mind by Conscience riven "—MS.]

° The cannon at sunset close the Rhamazan.

Such is the tale his Nubians tell,
Who did not watch their charge too well;
(But others say, that on that night,
By pale Phingari's* trembling light,
The Giaour upon his jet-black steed
Was seen, but seen alone to speed
With bloody spur along the shore,
Nor maid nor page behind him bore.)

    *   *   *   *   *

[Her eye's dark charm 'twere vain to tell,
But gaze on that of the Gazelle,
It will assist thy fancy well;
As large, as languishingly dark,
But Soul beam'd forth in every spark
That darted from beneath the lid,
Bright as the jewel of Giamschid.¹]
\Yea, *Soul*, and should our prophet say
That form was nought but breathing clay,
By Alla! I would answer nay;]
Though on Al-Sirat's * arch I stood,
Which totters o'er the fiery flood,
With Paradise within my view,
And all his Houris* beckoning through.
Oh! who young Leila's glance could read
And keep that portion of his creed

⁹ Phingari, the moon
¹ The celebrated fabulous ruby of Sultan Giamschid, the embellisher of Istakhar; from its splendour, named Schebgerag, "the torch of night," also "the cup of the sun," &c. In the first edition, "Giamschid" was written as a word of three syllables; so D'Herbelot has it, but I am told Richardson reduces it to a dissyllable, and writes "Jamshid" I have left in the text the orthography of the one with the pronunciation of the other.
[It was to Moore that he owed the correction]
² Al Sirat, the bridge of breath, narrower than the thread of a famished spider, and sharper than the edge of a sword, over which the Mussulmans must *skate* into Paradise, to which it is the only entrance, but this is not the worst, the river beneath being hell itself, into which, as may be expected, the unskilful and tender of foot contrive to tumble with a "facilis descensus Averni," not very pleasing in prospect to the next passenger. There is a shorter cut downwards for the Jews and Christians.
³ [The virgins of Paradise, called, from their large black eyes, *Hur al cyun*. An intercourse with these, according to the institution of Mahomet, is to constitute the principal felicity of the faithful. Not formed of clay like mortal women, they are adorned with unfading charms, and possess the privilege of an eternal youth.]

Which saith that woman is but dust,
A soulless toy for tyrant's lust? [4]
On her might Muftis gaze, and own
That through her eye the Immortal shone;
On her fair cheek's unfading hue
The young pomegranate's [5] blossoms strew
Their bloom in blushes ever new;
Her hair in hyacinthine [6] flow,
When left to roll its folds below,
As midst her handmaids in the hall
She stood superior to them all,
Hath swept the marble where her feet
Gleam'd whiter than the mountain sleet
Ere from the cloud that gave it birth
It fell, and caught one stain of earth.
The cygnet nobly walks the water;
So moved on earth Circassia's daughter,
The loveliest bird of Franguestan! [7]
As rears her crest the ruffled Swan,
    And spurns the wave with wings of pride,
When pass the steps of stranger man
    Along the banks that bound her tide;
Thus rose fair Leila's whiter neck:—
Thus arm'd with beauty would she check
Intrusion's glance, till Folly's gaze
Shrunk from the charms it meant to praise.
Thus high and graceful was her gait;
Her heart as tender to her mate;
Her mate—stern Hassan, who was he?
Alas! that name was not for thee!

*   *   *   *   *

Stern Hassan hath a journey ta'en
With twenty vassals in his train,

[4] A vulgar error: the Koran allots at least a third of Paradise to well-behaved women; but by far the greater number of Mussulmans interpret the text their own way, and exclude their moieties from heaven. Being enemies to Platonics, they cannot discern "any fitness of things" in the souls of the other sex, conceiving them to be superseded by the Houris.
[5] An oriental simile, which may, perhaps, though fairly stolen, be deemed "plus Arabe qu'en Arabie."
[6] Hyacinthine, in Arabic "Sunbul;" as common a thought in the eastern poets as it was among the Greeks.   [7] "Franguestan," Circassia.

Each arm'd, as best becomes a man,
With arquebuss and ataghan;
The chief before, as deck'd for war,
Bears in his belt the scimitar
Stain'd with the best of Arnaut blood,
When in the pass the rebels stood,
And few return'd to tell the tale
Of what befell in Parne's vale.
The pistols which his girdle bore
Were those that once a pasha wore,
Which still, though gemm'd and boss'd with gold,
Even robbers tremble to behold.
{ 'Tis said he goes to woo a bride
More true than her who left his side;
The faithless slave that broke her bower,
And, worse than faithless, for a Giaour ! }

*   *   *   *   *

The sun's last rays are on the hill,
And sparkle in the fountain rill,
Whose welcome waters, cool and clear,
Draw blessings from the mountaineer:
Here may the loitering merchant Greek
Find that repose 'twere vain to seek
In cities lodged too near his lord,
And trembling for his secret hoard—
Here may he rest where none can see,
\In crowds a slave, in deserts free;
And with forbidden wine may stain
The bowl a Moslem must not drain.

*   *   *   *   *

The foremost Tartar's in the gap
Conspicuous by his yellow cap;
The rest in lengthening line the while
Wind slowly through the long defile:
Above, the mountain rears a peak,
Where vultures whet the thirsty beak,
And theirs may be a feast to-night,
Shall tempt them down ere morrow's light;

Beneath, a river's wintry stream
Has shrunk before the summer beam,
And left a channel bleak and bare,
Save shrubs that spring to perish there:
Each side the midway path there lay
Small broken crags of granite gray,
By time, or mountain lightning, riven
From summits clad in mists of heaven;
For where is he that hath beheld
The peak of Liakura unveil'd?

*   *   *   *   *

They reach the grove of pine at last;
"Bismillah!* now the peril's past;
For yonder view the opening plain,
And there we'll prick our steeds amain:"
The Chiaus spake, and as he said,
A bullet whistled o'er his head;
The foremost Tartar bites the ground!
   Scarce had they time to check the rein,
Swift from their steeds the riders bound;
   But three shall never mount again:
Unseen the foes that gave the wound,
   The dying ask revenge in vain.
With steel unsheath'd, and carbine bent,
Some o'er their courser's harness leant,
   Half shelter'd by the steed;
Some fly beneath the nearest rock,
And there await the coming shock,
   Nor tamely stand to bleed
Beneath the shaft of foes unseen,
Who dare not quit their craggy screen.
Stern Hassan only from his horse
Disdains to light, and keeps his course,
   Till fiery flashes in the van
Proclaim too sure the robber-clan
Have well secured the only way
Could now avail the promised prey;

* "In the name of God;" the commencement of all the chapters of the Koran but one, and of prayer and thanksgiving

Then curl'd his very beard[*] with ire,
And glared his eye with fiercer fire ;
"Though far and near the bullets hiss,
I've scaped a bloodier hour than this."
And now the foe their covert quit,
And call his vassals to submit ;
But Hassan's frown and furious word
Are dreaded more than hostile sword,
Nor of his little band a man
Resign'd carbine or ataghan,
Nor raised the craven cry, Amaun![1]
In fuller sight, more near and near,
The lately ambush'd foes appear,
And, issuing from the grove, advance
Some who on battle-charger prance.
Who leads them on with foreign brand
Far flashing in his red right hand ?
" 'Tis he ! 'tis he ! I know him now ;
I know him by his pallid brow ;
I know him by the evil eye[2]
That aids his envious treachery ,
I know him by his jet-black barb ;
Though now array'd in Arnaut garb,
Apostate from his own vile faith,
It shall not save him from the death :
'Tis he ! well met in any hour,
Lost Leila's love, accursed Giaour !")

As rolls the river into ocean,
In sable torrent wildly streaming ;
As the sea-tide's opposing motion,
In azure column proudly gleaming,

---

[*] A phenomenon not uncommon with an angry Mussulman. In 1809, the Capitan Pacha's whiskers at a diplomatic audience were no less lively with indignation than a tiger cat's, to the horror of all the dragomans ; the portentous mustachios twisted, they stood erect of their own accord, and were expected every moment to change their colour, but at last condescended to subside, which, probably, saved more heads than they contained hairs

[1] "Amaun," quarter, pardon.

[2] The "evil eye," a common superstition in the Levant, and of which the imaginary effects are yet very singular on those who conceive themselves affected.

Beats back the current many a rood,
In curling foam and mingling flood,
While eddying whirl, and breaking wave,
Roused by the blast of winter, rave;
Through sparkling spray, in thundering clash,
The lightnings of the waters flash
In awful whiteness o'er the shore,
That shines and shakes beneath the roar;
‹ Thus—as the stream and ocean greet,
With waves that madden as they meet—
Thus join the bands, whom mutual wrong,
And fate, and fury, drive along.
The bickering sabres' shivering jar; ›
    And pealing wide or ringing near
    Its echoes on the throbbing ear,
The deathshot hissing from afar;
The shock, the shout, the groan of war, \
    Reverberate along that vale,
    More suited to the shepherd's tale: |
Though few the numbers—theirs the strife,
That neither spares nor speaks for life![a]
Ah! fondly youthful hearts can press,
To seize and share the dear caress;
But Love itself could never pant
For all that Beauty sighs to grant
With half the fervour Hate bestows
Upon the last embrace of foes,
When grappling in the fight they fold
Those arms that ne'er shall lose their hold:
Friends meet to part; Love laughs at faith,
True foes, once met, are join'd till death!

*   *   *   *   *

With sabre shiver'd to the hilt,
Yet dripping with the blood he spilt;
Yet strain'd within the sever'd hand
Which quivers round that faithless brand;
His turban far behind him roll'd,
And cleft in twain its firmest fold;

[a] ["That neither gives nor asks for life"—MS.]

His flowing robe by falchion torn,
And crimson as those clouds of morn
That, streak'd with dusky red, portend
The day shall have a stormy end;
A stain on every bush that bore
A fragment of his palampore ;⁴
 ⸜His breast with wounds unnumber'd riven,
His back to earth, his face to heaven,
Fall'n Hassan lies—his unclosed eye
Yet lowering on his enemy, ⸝
As if the hour that seal'd his fate
Surviving left his quenchless hate ;
And o'er him bends that foe with brow
As dark as his that bled below.—

        *   *   *   *   *

 ⸜" Yes, Leila sleeps beneath the wave,
But his shall be a redder grave ;
Her spirit pointed well the steel
Which taught that felon heart to feel.
He call'd the Prophet, but his power
Was vain against the vengeful Giaour :⸝
He call'd on Alla, but the word
Arose unheeded or unheard.
Thou Paynim fool ! could Leila's prayer
Be pass'd, and thine accorded there ?
I watch'd my time, I leagued with these,
The traitor in his turn to seize ;
My wrath is wreak'd, the deed is done,
And now I go—but go alone."

        *   *   *   *   *

        *   *   *   *   *

The browsing camels' bells are tinkling :
His mother look'd from her lattice high—⁵

---

⁴ The flowered shawls generally worn by persons of rank.
⁵ ["The mother of Sisera looked out at a window, and cried through the lattice,
Why is his chariot so long in coming ? why tarry the wheels of his chariot "—*Judges*,
ch. v. ver. 28]

She saw the dews of eve besprinkling
The pasture green beneath her eye,
　　She saw the planets faintly twinkling :
" 'Tis twilight—sure his train is nigh."[6]
She could not rest in the garden-bower,
But gazed through the grate of his steepest tower.
" Why comes he not? his steeds are fleet,
Nor shrink they from the summer heat;
Why sends not the Bridegroom his promised gift?
Is his heart more cold, or his barb less swift?
Oh, false reproach ! yon Tartar now
Has gain'd our nearest mountain's brow,
And warily the steep descends,
And now within the valley bends ;
And he bears the gift at his saddle bow—
How could I deem his courser slow?
Right well my largess shall repay
His welcome speed, and weary way."

The Tartar lighted at the gate,
But scarce upheld his fainting weight :[7]
His swarthy visage spake distress,
But this might be from weariness ;
His garb with sanguine spots was dyed,
But these might be from his courser's side ;

[6] [This beautiful passage of thirty-four lines, which first appeared in the fifth edition, opened thus in the original draught—

" His mother look'd from the lattice high,
　　With throbbing heart and eager eye ,
The browsing camel bells are tinkling,
And the last beam of twilight twinkling
　　'Tis eve , his train should now be nigh
She could not rest in her garden bower,
And gazed through the loop of her steepest tower.
' Why comes he not ? his steeds are fleet,
And well are they train'd to the summer's heat ' "

Another copy began—

" The browsing camel bells are tinkling,
And the first beam of evening twinkling ;
His mother looked from her lattice high,
With throbbing breast and eager eye—
' 'Tis twilight—sure his train is nigh ' "]

[7]　　　[" And flung to earth his fainting weight "—MS.]

He drew the token from his vest—
Angel of Death! 'tis Hassan's cloven crest!
His calpac* rent—his caftan red—
"Lady, a fearful bride thy son hath wed:
Me, not from mercy, did they spare,
But this empurpled pledge to bear.
Peace to the brave! whose blood is spilt:
Woe to the Giaour! for his the guilt."

  *   *   *   *   *

A turban* carved in coarsest stone,
A pillar with rank weeds o'ergrown,
Whereon can now be scarcely read
The Koran verse that mourns the dead,
Point out the spot where Hassan fell
A victim in that lonely dell.
There sleeps as true an Osmanlie
As e'er at Mecca bent the knee;
As ever scorn'd forbidden wine,
Or pray'd with face towards the shrine,
In orisons resumed anew
At solemn sound of "Alla Hu!"[1]
Yet died he by a stranger's hand,
And stranger in his native land;
Yet died he as in arms he stood,
And unavenged, at least in blood.
But him the maids of Paradise
 Impatient to their halls invite,
And the dark heaven of Houris' eyes
 On him shall glance for ever bright;

[8] The calpac is the solid cap or centre part of the head-dress; the shawl is wound round it, and forms the turban.

[9] The turban, pillar, and inscriptive verse, decorate the tombs of the Osmanlies, whether in the cemetery or the wilderness In the mountains you frequently pass similar mementos; and on inquiry you are informed that they record some victim of rebellion, plunder, or revenge.

[1] "Alla Hu!" the concluding words of the Muezzin's call to prayer from the highest gallery on the exterior of the Minaret On a still evening, when the Muezzin has a fine voice, which is frequently the case, the effect is solemn and beautiful beyond all the bells in Christendom —[Valid, the son of Abdalmalek, was the first who erected a minaret or turret; and this he placed on the grand mosque at Damascus, for the muezzin or crier to announce from it the hour of prayer.]

They come—their kerchiefs green they wave,[2]
And welcome with a kiss the brave!
Who falls in battle 'gainst a Giaour
Is worthiest an immortal bower.

*   *   *   .   *   *

But thou, false Infidel! shalt writhe
Beneath avenging Monkir's[3] scythe;
And from its torments 'scape alone
To wander round lost Eblis'[4] throne;
And fire unquench'd, unquenchable,
Around, within, thy heart shall dwell;
Nor ear can hear nor tongue can tell
The tortures of that inward hell!
But first, on earth as Vampire[5] sent,
Thy corse shall from its tomb be rent:
Then ghastly haunt thy native place,
And suck the blood of all thy race;
There from thy daughter, sister, wife,
At midnight drain the stream of life;
Yet loathe the banquet which perforce
Must feed thy livid living corse:
Thy victims ere they yet expire
Shall know the demon for their sire,
As cursing thee, thou cursing them,
Thy flowers are wither'd on the stem.

[2] The following is part of a battle-song of the Turks —"I see—I see a dark-eyed girl of Paradise, and she waves a handkerchief, a kerchief of green; and cries aloud, 'Come, kiss me, for I love thee,'" &c.

[3] Monkir and Nekir, are the inquisitors of the dead, before whom the corpse undergoes a slight noviciate and preparatory training for damnation. If the answers are none of the clearest, he is hauled up with a scythe and thumped down with a red-hot mace till properly seasoned, with a variety of subsidiary probations The office of these angels is no sinecure, there are but two, and the number of orthodox deceased being in a small proportion to the remainder, their hands are always full See Relig Ceremon. and Sale's Koran

[4] Eblis, the Oriental Prince of Darkness —[D'Herbelot supposes this title to have been a corruption of the Greek Διαβολος]

[5] The Vampire superstition is still general in the Levant. Honest Tournefort tells a long story, which Mr. Southey, in the notes on Thalaba, quotes about these "Vroucolochas," as he calls them The Romaic term is "Vardoulacha" I recollect a whole family being terrified by the scream of a child, which they imagined must proceed from such a visitation The Greeks never mention the word without horror. I find that "Broucolokas" is an old legitimate Hellenic appellation—at least is so applied to Arsenius, who, according to the Greeks, was after his death animated by the Devil. The moderns, however, use the word I mention.

But one that for thy crime must fall,
The youngest, most beloved of all,
Shall bless thee with a *father's* name—
That word shall wrap thy heart in flame !
Yet must thou end thy task, and mark
Her cheek's last tinge, her eye's last spark,
And the last glassy glance must view
Which freezes o'er its lifeless blue ;
Then with unhallow'd hand shalt tear
The tresses of her yellow hair,
Of which in life a lock when shorn
Affection's fondest pledge was worn,
But now is borne away by thee,
Memorial of thine agony !
Wet with thine own best blood shall drip
Thy gnashing tooth and haggard lip ;[6]
Then stalking to thy sullen grave,
Go—and with Gouls and Afrits rave ;
Till these in horror shrink away
From spectre more accursed than they !'

  *   *   *   *   *

" How name ye yon lone Caloyer ?
 His features I have scann'd before
In mine own land : 'tis many a year,
 Since, dashing by the lonely shore,
I saw him urge as fleet a steed
As ever served a horseman's need.
But once I saw that face, yet then
It was so mark'd with inward pain,
I could not pass it by again ;
It breathes the same dark spirit now,
As death were stamp'd upon his brow.

 " 'Tis twice three years at summer tide
 Since first among our freres he came ;

---

[6] The freshness of the face, and the wetness of the lip with blood, are the never-failing signs of a Vampire. The stories told in Hungary and Greece of these foul feeders are singular, and some of them most *incredibly* attested.
[7] [The imprecations of the Turk against the "accursed Giaour," are introduced with great judgment, and contribute much to the dramatic effect of the narrative.—GEORGE ELLIS.]

And here it soothes him to abide
  For some dark deed he will not name
But never at our vesper prayer,
Nor e'er before confession chair
Kneels he, nor recks he when arise
Incense or anthem to the skies, ⌐
But broods within his cell alone, ⌡
His faith and race alike unknown. ⌡
The sea from Paynim land he crost,
And here ascended from the coast ;
Yet seems he not of Othman race, ⌐
But only Christian in his face :   ⌡
I'd judge him some stray renegade,
Repentant of the change he made,
Save that he shuns our holy shrine,
Nor tastes the sacred bread and wine.
Great largess to these walls he brought,
And thus our abbot's favour bought ;
But were I prior, not a day
Should brook such stranger's further stay,
Or pent within our penance cell
Should doom him there for aye to dwell.
Much in his visions mutters he
Of maiden whelm'd beneath the sea ;[8]
Of sabres clashing, foemen flying,
Wrongs avenged, and Moslem dying.
On cliff he hath been known to stand,
And rave as to some bloody hand
Fresh sever'd from its parent limb,
Invisible to all but him,
Which beckons onward to his grave.
And lures to leap into the wave."

    *   *   *   *   *

    *   *   *   *   *

Dark and unearthly is the scowl[9]
That glares beneath his dusky cowl.

[8]   ["Of foreign maiden lost at sea."—MS.]
  [9] [The remaining lines, about five hundred in number, were, with the exception of the last sixteen, added to the poem, during its first progress through the press, or in subsequent editions]

The flash of that dilating eye
Reveals too much of times gone by
Though varying, indistinct its hue,
Oft will his glance the gazer rue,
For in it lurks that nameless spell,
Which speaks, itself unspeakable,
A spirit yet unquell'd and high,
That claims and keeps ascendancy ;
And like the bird whose pinions quake,
But cannot fly the gazing snake,
Will others quail beneath his look,
Nor 'scape the glance they scarce can brook.
From him the half-affrighted Friar
When met alone would fain retire,
As if that eye and bitter smile
Transferr'd to others fear and guile :
Not oft to smile descendeth he,
And when he doth 'tis sad to see
That he but mocks at Misery.
How that pale lip will curl and quiver !
Then fix once more as if for ever ;
As if his sorrow or disdain
Forbade him e'er to smile again.
Well were it so—such ghastly mirth
From joyaunce ne'er derived its birth.
But sadder still it were to trace
What once were feelings in that face :
Time hath not yet the features fix'd,
But brighter traits with evil mix'd ;
And there are hues not always faded,
Which speak a mind not all degraded
Even by the crimes through which it waded :
The common crowd but see the gloom
Of wayward deeds, and fitting doom ;
The close observer can espy
A noble soul, and lineage high :
Alas ! though both bestow'd in vain,
Which Grief could change, and Guilt could stain,
It was no vulgar tenement
To which such lofty gifts were lent,

And still with little less than dread
On such the sight is riveted.
The roofless cot, decay'd and rent,
   Will scarce delay the passer-by;
The tower by war or tempest bent,
While yet may frown one battlement,
   Demands and daunts the stranger's eye;
Each ivied arch, and pillar lone,
Pleads haughtily for glories gone!

" His floating robe around him folding,
   Slow sweeps he through the column'd aisle,
With dread beheld, with gloom beholding
   The rites that sanctify the pile.
But when the anthem shakes the choir,
And kneel the monks, his steps retire
By yonder lone and wavering torch
His aspect glares within the porch;
There will he pause till all is done—
And hear the prayer, but utter none.
See—by the half-illumined wall [1]
His hood fly back, his dark hair fall,
That pale brow wildly wreathing round,
As if the Gorgon there had bound
The sablest of the serpent-braid
That o'er her fearful forehead stray'd:
For he declines the convent oath,
And leaves those locks unhallow'd growth,
But wears our garb in all beside;
And, not from piety but pride,
Gives wealth to walls that never heard
Of his one holy vow nor word.
Lo!—mark ye, as the harmony
Peals louder praises to the sky,
That livid cheek, that stony air
Of mix'd defiance and despair!
Saint Francis, keep him from the shrine!
Else may we dread the wrath divine
Made manifest by awful sign.

   [1] [" Behold—as turns he from the wall."— MS.]

If ever evil angel bore
The form of mortal, such he wore;
By all my hope of sins forgiven,
Such looks are not of earth nor heaven!"

To love the softest hearts are prone,
But such can ne'er be all his own;
Too timid in his woes to share,
Too meek to meet, or brave despair;
And sterner hearts alone may feel
The wound that time can never heal.
The rugged metal of the mine
Must burn before its surface shine,[2]
But plunged within the furnace-flame,
It bends and melts—though still the same
Then temper'd to thy want, or will,
'Twill serve thee to defend or kill;
A breast-plate for thine hour of need,
Or blade to bid thy foeman bleed;
But if a dagger's form it bear,
Let those who shape its edge, beware!
Thus passion's fire, and woman's art,
Can turn and tame the sterner heart;
From these its form and tone are ta'en,
And what they make it, must remain,
But break—before it bend again.

    *   *   *   *   *
    *   *   *   *   *

If solitude succeed to grief,
Release from pain is slight relief;
The vacant bosom's wilderness
Might thank the pang that made it less.
We loathe what none are left to share ·
Even bliss—'twere woe alone to bear:
The heart once left thus desolate
Must fly at last for ease—to hate.

[2] ["Must burn before it smite or shine."—MS.]

It is as if the dead could feel
The icy worm around them steal,
And shudder, as the reptiles creep
To revel o'er their rotting sleep,
Without the power to scare away
The cold consumers of their clay !
It is as if the desert bird,[3]
   Whose beak unlocks her bosom's stream
   To still her famish'd nestlings' scream,
Nor mourns a life to them transferr'd,
Should rend her rash devoted breast,
And find them flown her empty nest.
The keenest pangs the wretched find
   Are rapture to the dreary void,
The leafless desert of the mind,
   The waste of feelings unemploy'd.
Who would be doom'd to gaze upon
A sky without a cloud or sun ?
Less hideous far the tempest's roar,
Than ne'er to brave the billows more—
Thrown, when the war of winds is o'er,
A lonely wreck on Fortune's shore,
'Mid sullen calm, and silent bay,
Unseen to drop by dull decay ;—
Better to sink beneath the shock
Than moulder piecemeal on the rock !

    *   *   *   *   *

"Father ! thy days have pass'd in peace,
   'Mid counted beads, and countless prayer;
To bid the sins of others cease,
   Thyself without a crime or care,
Save transient ills that all must bear,
Has been thy lot from youth to age;
And thou wilt bless thee from the rage
Of passions fierce and uncontroll'd,
Such as thy penitents unfold,

[3] The pelican is, I believe, the bird so libelled, by the imputation of feeding
her chickens with her blood.

Whose secret sins and sorrows rest
Within thy pure and pitying breast.
My days, though few, have pass'd below
In much of joy, but more of woe;
Yet still in hours of love or strife,
I've 'scaped the weariness of life:
Now leagued with friends, now girt by foes,
I loathed the languor of repose.
Now nothing left to love or hate,
No more with hope or pride elate,
I'd rather be the thing that crawls
Most noxious o'er a dungeon's walls,
Than pass my dull, unvarying days,
Condemn'd to meditate and gaze.
Yet, lurks a wish within my breast
For rest—but not to feel 'tis rest.
Soon shall my fate that wish fulfil;
   And I shall sleep without the dream
Of what I was, and would be still,
   Dark as to thee my deeds may seem:[4]
My memory now is but the tomb
Of joys long dead; my hope, their doom:
Though better to have died with those
Than bear a life of lingering woes.
My spirit shrunk not to sustain
The searching throes of ceaseless pain;
Nor sought the self-accorded grave
Of ancient fool and modern knave:
Yet death I have not fear'd to meet;
And in the field it had been sweet,
Had danger woo'd me on to move
The slave of glory, not of love.
I've braved it—not for honour's boast;
I smile at laurels won or lost;
To such let others carve their way,
For high renown, or hireling pay:
But place again before my eyes
Aught that I deem a worthy prize—

[4] ["Though hope hath long withdrawn her beam."—MS.]

The maid I love, the man I hate—
And I will hunt the steps of fate,
To save or slay, as these require,
Through rending steel, and rolling fire:
Nor needst thou doubt this speech from one
Who would but do—what he *hath* done.
Death is but what the haughty brave,
The weak must bear, the wretch must crave;
Then let life go to Him who gave:
I have not quail'd to danger's brow
When high and happy—need I *now?*

*   *   *   *   *

"I loved her, Friar! nay, adored—
   But these are words that all can use—
I proved it more in deed than word;
There's blood upon that dinted sword,
   A stain its steel can never lose:
'Twas shed for her, who died for me,
   It warm'd the heart of one abhorr'd:
Nay, start not—no—nor bend thy knee,
   Nor midst my sin such act record;
Thou wilt absolve me from the deed,
For he was hostile to thy creed!
The very name of Nazarene
Was wormwood to his Paynim spleen.
Ungrateful fool! since but for brands
Well wielded in some hardy hands,
And wounds by Galileans given,
The surest pass to Turkish heaven,
For him his Houris still might wait
Impatient at the Prophet's gate.
I loved her—love will find its way
Through paths where wolves would fear to prey;
And if it dares enough, 'twere hard
If passion met not some reward—
No matter how, or where, or why,
I did not vainly seek, nor sigh:
Yet sometimes, with remorse, in vain
I wish she had not loved again.

She died—I dare not tell thee how,
But look—'tis written on my brow!
There read of Cain the curse and crime,
In characters unworn by time:
Still, ere thou dost condemn me, pause;
Not mine the act, though I the cause.
Yet did he but what I had done
Had she been false to more than one.
Faithless to him, he gave the blow;
But true to me, I laid him low:
Howe'er deserved her doom might be,
Her treachery was truth to me;
To me she gave her heart, that all
Which tyranny can ne'er enthrall;
And I, alas! too late to save!
Yet all I then could give, I gave,
'Twas some relief, our foe a grave.
His death sits lightly; but her fate
Has made me—what thou well mayst hate.

   His doom was seal'd—he knew it well,
Warn'd by the voice of stern Taheer,
Deep in whose darkly boding ear*
The deathshot peal'd of murder near
   As filed the troop to where they fell!

* This superstition of a second-hearing (for I never met with downright second-sight in the East) fell once under my own observation. On my third journey to Cape Colonna, early in 1811, as we passed through the defile that leads from the hamlet between Keratia and Colonna, I observed Dervish Tahiri riding rather out of the path and leaning his head upon his hand, as if in pain. I rode up and inquired. "We are in peril," he answered. "What peril? we are not now in Albania, nor in the passes to Ephesus, Messalunghi, or Lepanto, there are plenty of us, well armed, and the Choriates have not courage to be thieves"—"True, Affendi, but nevertheless the shot is ringing in my ears."—"The shot! not a tophaike has been fired this morning"—"I hear it notwithstanding—Bom—Bom—as plainly as I hear your voice."—"Psha!"—"As you please, Affendi, if it is written, so will it be."—I left this quick-eared predestinarian, and rode up to Basili, his Christian compatriot, whose ears though not at all prophetic, by no means relished the intelligence. We all arrived at Colonna, remained some hours, and returned leisurely, saying a variety of brilliant things, in more languages than spoiled the building of Babel, upon the mistaken seer. Romaic, Arnaout, Turkish, Italian, and English were all exercised, in various conceits, upon the unfortunate Mussulman. While we were contemplating the beautiful prospect, Dervish was occupied about the columns. I thought he was deranged into an antiquarian, and asked him if he had become a "Palaocastro" man? "No," said he, "but these pillars will be useful in making a stand;" and added other remarks, which at least evinced his own belief in his troublesome faculty of *forehearing*. On our return to Athens we heard from Leoné (a prisoner set ashore some days after) of the intended

He died too in the battle broil,
A time that heeds nor pain nor toil;
One cry to Mahomet for aid,
One prayer to Alla all he made:
He knew and cross'd me in the fray—
I gazed upon him where he lay,
And watch'd his spirit ebb away:
Though pierced like pard by hunter's steel,
He felt not half that now I feel.
I search'd, but vainly search'd, to find
The workings of a wounded mind;
Each feature of that sullen corse
Betray'd his rage, but no remorse.
Oh, what had Vengeance given to trace
Despair upon his dying face!
The late repentance of that hour
When Penitence hath lost her power
To tear one terror from the grave,
And will not soothe, and cannot save.

*   *   *   *   *

"The cold in clime are cold in blood,
Their love can scarce deserve the name;
But mine was like the lava flood
    That boils in Ætna's breast of flame.
I cannot prate in puling strain
Of ladye-love, and beauty's chain:

attack of the Mainotes, mentioned, with the cause of its not taking place, in the notes to Childe Harold, Canto 2nd   I was at some pains to question the man, and he described the dresses, arms, and marks of the horses of our party, so accurately, that, with other circumstances, we could not doubt of *his* having been in "villanous company," and ourselves in a bad neighbourhood.   Dervish became a soothsayer for life, and I dare say is now hearing more musketry than ever will be fired, to the great refreshment of the Arnaouts of Berat, and his native mountains —I shall mention one trait more of this singular race.   In March, 1811, a remarkably stout and active Arnaout came (I believe the fiftieth on the same errand) to offer himself as an attendant, which was declined: "Well, Affendi," quoth he, "may you live!—you would have found me useful   I shall leave the town for the hills to-morrow; in the winter I return, perhaps you will then receive me "—Dervish, who was present, remarked as a thing of course, and of no consequence, "in the mean time he will join the Klephtes" (robbers), which was true to the letter.   If not cut off, they come down in the winter, and pass it unmolested in some town, where they are often as well known as their exploits

If changing cheek, and scorching vein,⁶
Lips taught to writhe, but not complain,
If bursting heart, and madd'ning brain,
And daring deed, and vengeful steel,
And all that I have felt, and feel,
Betoken love—that love was mine,
And shown by many a bitter sign.
'Tis true, I could not whine nor sigh,
I knew but to obtain or die.
I die—but first I have possess'd,
And come what may, I *have been* bless'd.
Shall I the doom I sought upbraid?
No—reft of all, yet undismay'd'
But for the thought of Leila slain,
Give me the pleasure with the pain,
So would I live and love again.
I grieve, but not, my holy guide!
For him who dies, but her who died:
She sleeps beneath the wandering wave—
Ah! had she but an earthly grave,
This breaking heart and throbbing head
Should seek and share her narrow bed.
She was a form of life and light,
That, seen, became a part of sight;
And rose, where'er I turn'd mine eye,
The Morning-star of Memory!

" Yes, Love indeed is light from heaven;⁸
    A spark of that immortal fire
With angels shared, by Alla given,
    To lift from earth our low desire.

["I cannot prate in puling strain
Of bursting heart and madd'ning brain,
And fire that raged in every vein."—MS]

["Even now alone yet undismay'd,—
I know no friend, and ask no aid."—MS.]

⁸ [The hundred and twenty-six lines which follow, down to "Tell me no more of fancy's gleam," first appeared in the fifth edition In returning the proof to Mr. Murray, Lord Byron says —"The last lines Hodgson likes It is not often he does; and when he don't, he tells me with great energy, and I fret, and alter. I have thrown them in to soften the ferocity of our infidel , and, for a dying man, have given him a

Devotion wafts the mind above,
But Heaven itself descends in love;
A feeling from the Godhead caught,
To wean from self each sordid thought;
A Ray of him who form'd the whole;
A Glory circling round the soul!
I grant *my* love imperfect, all.
That mortals by the name miscall;
Then deem it evil, what thou wilt;
But say, oh say, *hers* was not guilt!
She was my life's unerring light:
That quench'd, what beam shall break my night? ⁹
Oh! would it shone to lead me still,
Although to death or deadliest ill!
Why marvel ye, if they who lose
  This present joy, this future hope,
  No more with sorrow meekly cope;
In phrensy then their fate accuse;
In madness do those fearful deeds
  That seem to add but guilt to woe?

good deal to say for himself." Among the Giaour MSS. is the first draught of this
passage, which we subjoin:

"Yes ⎱
    ⎰ Love indeed ⎰ doth spring ⎱ from heaven:
If ⎰   ⎱ descend ⎰
              be born

                 immortal
    A spark of that ⎰ eternal ⎱ fire,
               celestial
To human hearts in mercy given,
  To lift from earth our low desire.
A feeling from the Godhead caught,
To wean from self ⎰ each ⎱ sordid thought;
            our
  Devotion sends the soul above,
  But Heaven itself descends to love.
Yet marvel not, if they who love
  This present joy, this future hope,
  Which taught them with all ill to cope,
In madness, then, their fate accuse—
  In madness do those fearful deeds
That seem ⎰ to add but guilt to ⎱ woe.
         but to augment their ⎰
    Alas! the ⎰ breast ⎱ that inly bleeds,
           heart ⎰
Has nought to dread from outward foe," &c.]

["That quench'd, I wander'd far in night."

Or,   "'Tis quench'd, and I am lost in night."—MS.

Alas ! the breast that inly bleeds
   Hath nought to dread from outward blow
Who falls from all he knows of bliss,
Cares little into what abyss.
Fierce as the gloomy vulture's now
   To thee, old man, my deeds appear:
I read abhorrence on thy brow,
   And this too was I born to bear!
'Tis true, that, like that bird of prey,
With havock have I mark'd my way:
But this was taught me by the dove,
To die—and know no second love.
This lesson yet hath man to learn,
Taught by the thing he dares to spurn:
The bird that sings within the brake,
The swan that swims upon the lake,
One mate, and one alone, will take.
And let the fool still prone to range,[1]
And sneer on all who cannot change,
Partake his jest with boasting boys;
I envy not his varied joys,
But deem such feeble, heartless man,
Less than yon solitary swan;
Far, far beneath the shallow maid
He left believing and betray'd.
Such shame at least was never mine—
Leila ! each thought was only thine !
My good, my guilt, my weal, my woe,
My hope on high—my all below.
Earth holds no other like to thee,
Or, if it doth, in vain for me :
For worlds I dare not view the dame
Resembling thee, yet not the same.
The very crimes that mar my youth,
This bed of death—attest my truth !
'Tis all too late—thou wert, thou art
The cherish'd madness of my heart !

---

[1] [" And let the light, inconstant fool
    That sneers his coxcomb ridicule."—MS.]

"And she was lost—and yet I breathed,
  But not the breath of human life :
A serpent round my heart was wreathed,
  And stung my every thought to strife.
Alike all time, abhorr'd all place,
Shuddering I shrank from Nature's face,
Where every hue that charm'd before
The blackness of my bosom wore.
The rest thou dost already know,
And all my sins, and half my woe.
But talk no more of penitence ;
Thou seest I soon shall part from hence :
And if thy holy tale were true,
The deed that's done canst *thou* undo ?
Think me not thankless—but this grief
Looks not to priesthood for relief.²
My soul's estate in secret guess:³
But wouldst thou pity more, say less.
When thou canst bid my Leila live,
Then will I sue thee to forgive ;
Then plead my cause in that high place
Where purchased masses proffer grace.
Go, when the hunter's hand hath wrung
From forest-cave her shrieking young,
And calm the lonely lioness :
But soothe not—mock not *my* distress !

  "In earlier days, and calmer hours,
    When heart with heart delights to blend,
  Where bloom my native valley's bowers,⁴
    I had—Ah ! have I now ?—a friend !
  To him this pledge I charge thee send,
    Memorial of a youthful vow ;

---

² The monk's sermon is omitted It seems to have had so little effect upon the
patient, that it could have no hopes from the reader. It may be sufficient to say, that
it was of a customary length (as may be perceived from the interruptions and uneasi-
ness of the patient), and was delivered in the usual tone of all orthodox preachers.

³   [——— "but this grief
          In truth is not for thy relief
          My state thy thought can never guess. —MS.]

⁴   .   ["Where rise my native city's towers "—MS.]

I would remind him of my end: [5]
  Though souls absorb'd like mine allow
Brief thought to distant friendship's claim,
Yet dear to him my blighted name.
'Tis strange—he prophesied my doom,
  And I have smiled—I then could smile—
When Prudence would his voice assume,
  And warn—I reck'd not what—the while
But now remembrance whispers o'er
Those accents scarcely mark'd before.
Say—that his bodings came to pass,
  And he will start to hear their truth,
  And wish his words had not been sooth:
Tell him, unheeding as I was,
  Through many a busy bitter scene
  Of all our golden youth had been,
In pain, my faltering tongue had tried
To bless his memory ere I died;
But Heaven in wrath would turn away,
If Guilt should for the guiltless pray.
I do not ask him not to blame,
Too gentle he to wound my name;
And what have I to do with fame?
I do not ask him not to mourn,
Such cold request might sound like scorn;
And what than friendship's manly tear
May better grace a brother's bier?
But bear this ring, his own of old,
And tell him—what thou dost behold!
The wither'd frame, the ruin'd mind,
The wrack by passion left behind,
A shrivell'd scroll, a scatter'd leaf,
Sear'd by the autumn blast of grief!

    *   *   *   *   *

" Tell me no more of fancy's gleam,
No, father, no, 'twas not a dream;

---

[5] [" I have no heart to love him now,
    And 'tis but to declare my end "—MS.

Alas! the dreamer first must sleep,
I only watch'd, and wish'd to weep;
But could not, for my burning brow
'Throbb'd to the very brain as now:
I wish'd but for a single tear,
As something welcome, new, and dear:
I wish'd it then, I wish it still;
Despair is stronger than my will.
Waste not thine orison, despair*
Is mightier than thy pious prayer:
I would not, if I might, be blest;
I want no paradise, but rest.
'Twas then, I tell thee, father! then
I saw her; yes, she lived again;
And shining in her white symar,'
As through yon pale gray cloud the star
Which now I gaze on, as on her,
Who look'd and looks far lovelier;
Dimly I view its trembling spark;'
To-morrow's night shall be more dark;
And I, before its rays appear,
That lifeless thing the living fear.
I wander, father! for my soul
Is fleeting towards the final goal.
I saw her, friar! and I rose
Forgetful of our former woes;
And rushing from my couch, I dart,
And clasp her to my desperate heart,
I clasp—what is it that I clasp?
No breathing form within my grasp,
No heart that beats reply to mine—
Yet, Leila! yet the form is thine!
And art thou, dearest, changed so much
As meet my eye, yet mock my touch?
Ah! were thy beauties e'er so cold,
I care not so my arms enfold
The all they ever wish'd to hold.

6   ["Nay—kneel not, father, rise—despair," &c.—MS.]
7 "Symar," a shroud.
8   ["Which now I view with trembling spark "—MS.]

Alas! around a shadow prest
They shrink upon my lonely breast;
Yet still 'tis there!   In silence stands,
And beckons with beseeching hands!
With braided hair, and bright-black eye—
I knew 'twas false—she could not die!
But he is dead! within the dell
I saw him buried where he fell;
He comes not, for he cannot break
From earth; why then art thou awake?
They told me wild waves rolled above
The face I view, the form I love;
They told me—'twas a hideous tale!—
I'd tell it, but my tongue would fail:
If true, and from thine ocean-cave
Thou com'st to claim a calmer grave,
Oh! pass thy dewy fingers o'er
This brow that then will burn no more;
Or place them on my hopeless heart:
But, shape or shade! whate'er thou art,
In mercy ne'er again depart!
Or farther with thee bear my soul
Than winds can waft or waters roll!

    *   *   *   *   *

{ "Such is my name, and such my tale.
   Confessor! to thy secret ear
I breathe the sorrows I bewail,
   And thank thee for the generous tear
This glazing eye could never shed.
Then lay me with the humblest dead,
And, save the cross above my head,
Be neither name nor emblem spread,
By prying stranger to be read,
Or stay the passing pilgrim's tread." * }

* The circumstance to which the above story relates was not very uncommon in
Turkey.   A few years ago the wife of Muchtar Pacha complained to his father of his
son's supposed infidelity; he asked with whom, and she had the barbarity to give in
a list of the twelve handsomest women in Yanina.   They were seized, fastened up in
sacks, and drowned in the lake the same night!   One of the guards who was present
informed me, that not one of the victims uttered a cry, or show·d a symptom of terror

(He pass'd—nor of his name and race
Hath left a token or a trace,
Save what the father must not say)
Who shrived him on his dying day :
{ This broken tale was all we knew [1]
Of her he loved, or him he slew.

at so sudden a "wrench from all we know, from all we love" The fate of Phrosine, the fairest of this sacrifice, is the subject of many a Romaic and Arnaout ditty The story in the text is one told of a young Venetian many years ago, and now nearly forgotten I heard it by accident recited by one of the coffee-house story-tellers who abound in the Levant, and sing or recite their narratives The additions and interpolations by the translator will be easily distinguished from the rest, by the want of Eastern imagery , and I regret that my memory has retained so few fragments of the original. For the contents of some of the notes I am indebted partly to D'Herbelot, and partly to that most Eastern, and, as Mr. Weber justly entitles it, "sublime tale," the "Caliph Vathek" I do not know from what source the author of that singular volume may have drawn his materials , some of his incidents are to be found in the "Bibliothèque Orientale," but for correctness of costume, beauty of description, and power of imagination, it far surpasses all European imitations , and bears such marks of originality, that those who have visited the East will find some difficulty in believing it to be more than a translation As an Eastern tale, even Rasselas must bow before it ; his "Happy Valley" will not bear a comparison with the "Hall of Eblis."

[1]   ["Nor whether most he mourn'd none knew,
                           For her he loved or him he slew."—MS]

THE BRIDE OF ABYDOS:

A TURKISH TALE.

"Had we never loved so kindly,
Had we never loved so blindly,
Never met or never parted,
We had ne'er been broken-hearted."—BURNS.

TO

THE RIGHT HON. LORD HOLLAND,

This Tale is Inscribed,

WITH EVERY SENTIMENT OF REGARD AND RESPECT,

BY HIS GRATEFULLY OBLIGED

AND SINCERE FRIEND,

BYRON.

INTRODUCTION TO THE BRIDE OF ABYDOS.

—◆—

The "Bride of Abydos" was written early in November 1813, and was published on the 2nd of December Galt, on its appearance, remarked a coincidence between the first part, and some real event within his own experience, upon which Lord Byron observes that *his* story also was drawn from existence He appears just before to have engaged in one of those feverish attachments which troubled the period of his London reign. The double issue was to make him wretched, and to originate "The Bride." "All convulsions," he says, "end with me in rhyme. It was written to distract my dreams from * * *. Were it not thus, it had never been composed, and had I not done something at that time I must have gone mad by eating my own heart,—bitter diet !" "I am much more indebted to the tale," he records in his Journal, at the period of publication, "than I can ever be to the most important reader, as it wrung my thoughts from reality to imagination; from selfish regrets to vivid recollections, and recalled me to a country replete with the brightest and darkest, but always most lively colours of my memory." There can be no doubt, however, that some of his pent up feelings flowed into the fiction, for he was less accustomed to divert the course of his troubles, than to relieve his heart by giving them utterance "I began a comedy," he says in his Journal of this very period, "and burnt it because the scene ran into *reality;* a novel for the same reason In rhyme, I can keep more away from facts, but the thought always runs through, through . . . yes, yes, through." The tale was struck off in four days, and he composed faster, and for more hours at a time, than in any previous attempt To the original sketch there were added in the printing about two hundred lines, and, as was usual with him, the interpolated passages are among the most splendid in the poem He announced to Mr Murray, during the revisal, that he was doing his best to beat the "Giaour," but in this he considered he had not succeeded, and the public thought so too; though his friend, Mr. Hodgson, maintained that "The Bride" was better versified than "The Fragment," and George Ellis asserted that it was in every respect superior There is nothing in "The Giaour," to answer to the touching and confiding affection of the guileless Zuleika; but, in spite of paragraphs of exceeding beauty, the execution of "The Bride" is decidedly inferior. If the verse is more varied, it wants, in general, the force and finish, the nerve and impetuosity, of the elder tale. The title was a misnomer. Mr. Croker inquired why it was called "The *Bride* of Abydos," since the death of the lovers anticipates the marriage; —and Lord Byron replied, that the question was "unanswerable." "I was a great fool, ' he adds, "to make the *bull*, and am ashamed of not being an Irishman." The opening lines were supposed to have been imitated from a song of Goethe's—

"Kennst du das Land wo die citronen bluhn?"

But the author of "The Bride," could not read German, and if he borrowed the idea, he must, he said, have derived it from Madame de Stael, who copied Goethe in some verses, which Lord Byron, however, was nearly confident he had never seen when he penned his own The resemblance between the French and the English is extremely slight, and is almost confined to the first line,—"Cette terre où les myrtes fleurissent" Lord Byron received 500 guineas for "The Bride."

THE BRIDE OF ABYDOS.

CANTO THE FIRST.

I.

Know ye the land where the cypress and myrtle
  Are emblems of deeds that are done in their clime?
Where the rage of the vulture, the love of the turtle,
  Now melt into sorrow, now madden to crime!
Know ye the land of the cedar and vine,
Where the flowers ever blossom, the beams ever shine;
Where the light wings of Zephyr, oppress'd with perfume
Wax faint o'er the gardens of Gúl[1] in her bloom;
Where the citron and olive are fairest of fruit,
And the voice of the nightingale never is mute:
Where the tints of the earth, and the hues of the sky,
In colour though varied, in beauty may vie,
And the purple of ocean is deepest in dye;
Where the virgins are soft as the roses they twine,
And all, save the spirit of man, is divine?
'Tis the clime of the East; 'tis the land of the Sun—
Can he smile on such deeds as his children have done?[2]
Oh! wild as the accents of lovers' farewell
Are the hearts which they bear, and the tales which they tell.

---

[1] "Gúl," the rose.

[2]   "Souls made of fire, and children of the Sun,
      With whom revenge is virtue."—Young's *Revenge.*

II.

Begirt with many a gallant slave,
Apparell'd as becomes the brave,
Awaiting each his lord's behest
To guide his steps, or guard his rest,
Old Giaffir sate in his Divan:
　Deep thought was in his aged eye;
And though the face of Mussulman
　Not oft betrays to standers by
The mind within, well skill'd to hide
All but unconquerable pride,
His pensive cheek and pondering brow
Did more than he was wont avow.

III

"Let the chamber be clear'd."—The train disappear'd—
　"Now call me the chief of the Haram guard."
With Giaffir is none but his only son,
　And the Nubian awaiting the sire's award.
　"Haroun—when all the crowd that wait
　Are pass'd beyond the outer gate,
　(Woe to the head whose eye beheld
　My child Zuleika's face unveil'd!)
Hence, lead my daughter from her tower,
Her fate is fix'd this very hour:
Yet not to her repeat my thought;
By me alone be duty taught!"

"Pacha! to hear is to obey."
No more must slave to despot say—
Then to the tower had ta'en his way,
But here young Selim silence brake,
　First lowly rendering reverence meet;
And downcast look'd, and gently spake,
　Still standing at the Pacha's feet:
For son of Moslem must expire,
Ere dare to sit before his sire!

"Father! for fear that thou shouldst chide
My sister, or her sable guide,

Know—for the fault, if fault there be,
Was mine, then fall thy frowns on me—
So lovelily the morning shone,
      That—let the old and weary sleep—
I could not; and to view alone
      The fairest scenes of land and deep,
With none to listen and reply
To thoughts with which my heart beat high
Were irksome—for whate'er my mood,
In sooth I love not solitude;
I on Zuleika's slumber broke,
      And, as thou knowest that for me
      Soon turns the Haram's grating key,
Before the guardian slaves awoke
We to the cypress groves had flown,
And made earth, main, and heaven our own!
There linger'd we, beguiled too long
With Mejnoun's tale, or Sadi's song; [3]
Till I, who heard the deep tambour [4]
Beat thy Divan's approaching hour,
To thee, and to my duty true,
Warn'd by the sound, to greet thee flew:
But there Zuleika wanders yet—
Nay, Father, rage not—nor forget
That none can pierce that secret bower
But those who watch the women's tower."

IV

" Son of a slave "—the Pacha said—
" From unbelieving mother bred,
Vain were a father's hope to see
Aught that beseems a man in thee
Thou, when thine arm should bend the bow,
      And hurl the dart, and curb the steed,
      Thou, Greek in soul if not in creed,
Must pore where babbling waters flow,

[3] Mejnoun and Leila, the Romeo and Juliet of the East. Sadi, the moral poet of Persia
[4] Tambour   Turkish drum, which sounds at sunrise, noon, and twilight

And watch unfolding roses blow.
Would that yon orb, whose matin glow
Thy listless eyes so much admire,
Would lend thee something of his fire!
Thou, who wouldst see this battlement
By Christian cannon piecemeal rent;
Nay, tamely view old Stambol's wall
Before the dogs of Moscow fall,
Nor strike one stroke for life and death
Against the curs of Nazareth!
Go—let thy less than woman's hand
Assume the distaff—not the brand.
But, Haroun!—to my daughter speed:
And hark—of thine own head take heed—
If thus Zuleika oft takes wing—
Thou see'st yon bow—it hath a string!"

v.

No sound from Selim's lip was heard,
    At least that met old Giaffir's ear,
But every frown and every word
Pierced keener than a Christian's sword.
    "Son of a slave!—reproach'd with fear!
    Those gibes had cost another dear.
Son of a slave!—and *who* my sire?"
    Thus held his thoughts their dark career;
And glances ev'n of more than ire
    Flash forth, then faintly disappear.
Old Giaffir gazed upon his son
    And started; for within his eye
He read how much his wrath had done;
He saw rebellion there begun:
    "Come hither, boy—what, no reply?
I mark thee—and I know thee too;
But there be deeds thou dar'st not do:
But if thy beard had manlier length,
And if thy hand had skill and strength,
I'd joy to see thee break a lance,
Albeit against my own perchance."

As sneeringly these accents fell,
On Selim's eye he fiercely gazed :
   That eye return'd him glance for glance,
And proudly to his sire's was raised,
   Till Giaffir's quail'd and shrunk askance—
And why—he felt, but durst not tell.
" Much I misdoubt this wayward boy
Will one day work me more annoy :
I never loved him from his birth,
And—but his arm is little worth,
And scarcely in the chase could cope
With timid fawn or antelope,
Far less would venture into strife
Where man contends for fame and life—
I would not trust that look or tone :
No—nor the blood so near my own.
That blood—he hath not heard—no more—
I'll watch him closer than before.
He is an Arab[5] to my sight,
Or Christian crouching in the fight—
But hark !—I hear Zuleika's voice ;
   Like Houris' hymn it meets mine ear :
She is the offspring of my choice ;
   Oh ! more than ev'n her mother dear,
With all to hope, and nought to fear—
My Peri ! ever welcome here !
Sweet, as the desert fountain's wave
To lips just cool'd in time to save—
   Such to my longing sight art thou ;
Nor can they waft to Mecca's shrine
More thanks for life, than I for thine,
   Who blest thy birth and bless thee now."

VI.

Fair, as the first that fell of womankind,
   When on that dread yet lovely serpent smiling,
Whose image then was stamp'd upon her mind—
   But once beguiled—and ever more beguiling ;

[5] The Turks abhor the Arabs (who return the compliment a hundred fold) even
more than they hate the Christians

Dazzling, as that, oh ! too transcendent vision
   To Sorrow's phantom-peopled slumber given,
When heart meets heart again in dreams Elysian,
   And paints the lost on Earth revived in Heaven ;
Soft, as the memory of buried love ;
Pure, as the prayer which Childhood wafts above ;
Was she—the daughter of that rude old Chief,
Who met the maid with tears—but not of grief.

Who hath not proved how feebly words essay [6]
To fix one spark of Beauty's heavenly ray ?
Who doth not feel, until his failing sight
Faints into dimness with its own delight,
His changing cheek, his sinking heart confess
The might, the majesty of Loveliness ?
Such was Zuleika, such around her shone
The nameless charms unmark'd by her alone—
The light of love, the purity of grace,
The mind, the Music [7] breathing from her face,
The heart whose softness harmonized the whole,
And oh ! that eye was in itself a Soul !

Her graceful arms in meekness bending
   Across her gently-budding breast ;

[6] [These twelve fine lines were added in the course of printing]

[7] This expression has met with objections   I will not refer to "Him who hath not Music in his soul," but merely request the reader to recollect, for ten seconds, the features of the woman whom he believes to be the most beautiful , and, if he then does not comprehend fully what is feebly expressed in the above line, I shall be sorry for us both.   For an eloquent passage in the latest work of the first female writer of this, perhaps of any, age, on the analogy (and the immediate comparison excited by that analogy) between "painting and music," see vol iii , cap. 10, DE L'ALLEMAGNE. And is not this connection still stronger with the original than the copy ? with the colouring of Nature than of Art ?   After all, this is rather to be felt than described ; still I think there are some who will understand it, at least they would have done had they beheld the countenance whose speaking harmony suggested the idea , for this passage is not drawn from imagination but memory, that mirror which Affliction dashes to the earth, and looking down upon the fragments, only beholds the reflection multiplied ! [Two versions of the line preceded the one in the text —"Mind on her lip, and music in her face," and "The mind of music breathing in her face."   It was alleged that Lord Byron owed the idea to a line of the lyric poet Lovelace, "The melody and music of her face "   Sir Thomas Browne, too, had written, "There is music even in beauty."   The effect of the appeal to Madame de Stael is thus recorded in "Byron's Diary " of December 7, 1813 —"This morning, a very pretty billet from the Stael.   She has been pleased to be pleased with my slight eulogy in the note annexed to the ' Bride ' "]

At one kind word those arms extending
To clasp the neck of him who blest
His child caressing and carest,
Zuleika came—and Giaffir felt
His purpose half within him melt:
Not that against her fancied weal
His heart though stern could ever feel;
Affection chain'd her to that heart;
Ambition tore the links apart.

VII.

"Zuleika! child of gentleness!
How dear this very day must tell,
When I forget my own distress,
In losing what I love so well,
To bid thee with another dwell:
Another! and a braver man
Was never seen in battle's van.
We Moslem reck not much of blood;
    But yet the line of Carasman[8]
Unchanged, unchangeable hath stood
    First of the bold Timariot bands
That won and well can keep their lands.
Enough that he who comes to woo
Is kinsman of the Bey Oglou
His years need scarce a thought employ;
I would not have thee wed a boy.
And thou shalt have a noble dower:
And his and my united power
Will laugh to scorn the death-firman,
Which others tremble but to scan,
And teach the messenger[9] what fate
The bearer of such boon may wait.

[8] Carasman Oglou, or Kara Osman Oglou, is the principal landholder in Turkey, he governs Magnesia. those who, by a kind of feudal tenure, possess land on condition of service, are called Timariots they serve as Spahis, according to the extent of territory, and bring a certain number into the field, generally cavalry.
[9] When a Pacha is sufficiently strong to resist, the single messenger, who is always the first bearer of the order for his death, is strangled instead, and sometimes five or six, one after the other, on the same errand, by command of the refractory patient, if, on the contrary, he is weak or loyal, he bows, kisses the Sultan's respectable

And now thou know'st thy father's will;
   All that thy sex hath need to know:
'Twas mine to teach obedience still—
   The way to love, thy lord mav show."

VIII

In silence bow'd the virgin's head;
   And if her eye was fill'd with tears
That stifled feeling dare not shed,
And changed her cheek from pale to red,
   And red to pale,,as through her ears
Those winged words like arrows sped,
   What could such be but maiden fears?
So bright the tear in Beauty's eye,
Love half regrets to kiss it dry;
So sweet the blush of Bashfulness,
Even Pity scarce can wish it less!

Whate'er it was the sire forgot;
Or if remember'd, mark'd it not;
Thrice clapp'd his hands, and call'd his steed,[1]
   Resign'd his gem-adorn'd chibouque,[2]
And mounting featly for the mead,
   With Maugrabee[3] and Mamaluke,
   His way amid his Delis took,[4]
To witness many an active deed
With sabie keen, or blunt jerreed.
The Kislar only and his Moors
Watch well the Haram's massy doors.

signature, and is bowstrung with great complacency. In 1810, several of these
presents were exhibited in the niche of the Seraglio gate; among others, the
head of the Pacha of Bagdat, a brave young man, cut off by treachery, after
a desperate resistance.
  [1] Clapping of the hands calls the servants   The Turks hate a superfluous expen-
diture of voice, and they have no bells.
  [2] "Chibouque," the Turkish pipe, of which the amber mouth-piece, and sometimes
the ball which contains the leaf, is adorned with precious stones, if in possession of
the wealthier orders
  [3] "Maugrabee," Moorish mercenaries
  [4] "Delis," bravos who form the forlorn hope of the cavalry, and always begin the
action

IX

His head was leant upon his hand,
　　His eye look'd o'er the dark blue water
That swiftly glides and gently swells
Between the winding Dardanelles;
But yet he saw nor sea nor strand,
Nor even his Pacha's turban'd band
　　Mix in the game of mimic slaughter,
Careering cleave the folded felt [5]
With sabre stroke right sharply dealt;
Nor mark'd the javelin-darting crowd,
Nor heard their Ollahs [6] wild and loud—
　　He thought but of old Giaffir's daughter!

X

No word from Selim's bosom broke;
One sigh Zuleika's thought bespoke:
Still gazed he through the lattice grate,
Pale, mute, and mournfully sedate.
To him Zuleika's eye was turn'd,
But little from his aspect learn'd:
Equal her grief, yet not the same;
Her heart confess'd a gentler flame:
But yet that heart, alarm'd or weak,
She knew not why, forbade to speak.
Yet speak she must—but when essay?
"How strange he thus should turn away!
Not thus we e'er before have met;
Not thus shall be our parting yet."
Thrice paced she slowly through the room,
　　And watch'd his eye—it still was fix'd
　　She snatch'd the urn wherein was mix'd

[5] A twisted fold of *felt* is used for scimitar practice by the Turks, and few but Mussulman arms can cut through it at a single stroke   sometimes a tough turban is used for the same purpose.   The jerreed is a game of blunt javelins, animated and graceful

[6] "Ollahs," Alla il Allah, the "Leilies," as the Spanish poets call them, the sound is Ollah , a cry of which the Turks, for a silent people, are somewhat profuse, particularly during the jerreed, or in the chase, but mostly in battle   Their animation in the field, and gravity in the chamber, with their pipes and comboloios, form an amusing contrast.

The Persian Atar-gul's[7] perfume,
And sprinkled all its odours o'er
The pictured roof[8] and marble floor:
The drops, that through his glittering vest
The playful girl's appeal address'd,
Unheeded o'er his bosom flew,
As if that breast were marble too.
" What, sullen yet? it must not be—
Oh! gentle Selim, this from thee!"
She saw in curious order set
     The fairest flowers of eastern land—
" He loved them once; may touch them yet,
     If offer'd by Zuleika's hand."
The childish thought was hardly breathed
Before the rose was pluck'd and wreathed;
The next fond moment saw her seat
Her fairy form at Selim's feet:
"This rose to calm my brother's cares
A message from the Bulbul[9] bears;
It says to-night he will prolong
For Selim's ear his sweetest song;
And though his note is somewhat sad,
He'll try for once a strain more glad,
With some faint hope his alter'd lay
May sing these gloomy thoughts away.

XI

" What! not receive my foolish flower?
     Nay then I am indeed unblest
On me can thus thy forehead lower?
     And know'st thou not who loves thee best?

[7] "Atar-gul," ottar of roses   The Persian is the finest

[8] The ceiling and wainscots, or rather walls, of the Mussulman apartments are generally painted, in great houses, with one eternal and highly-coloured view of Constantinople, wherein the principal feature is a noble contempt of perspective; below, arms, scimitars, &c, are, in general, fancifully and not inelegantly disposed.

[9] It has been much doubted whether the notes of this "Lover of the rose" are sad or merry; and Mr. Fox's remarks on the subject have provoked some learned controversy as to the opinions of the ancients on the subject   I dare not venture a conjecture on the point, though a little inclined to the "errare mallem," &c, *if* Mr. Fox *was* mistaken

Oh, Selim dear! oh, more than dearest!
Say, is it me thou hat'st or fearest?
Come, lay thy head upon my breast,
And I will kiss thee into rest,
Since words of mine, and songs must fail,
Ev'n from my fabled nightingale.
I knew our sire at times was stern,
But this from thee had yet to learn:
Too well I know he loves thee not;
But is Zuleika's love forgot?
Ah! deem I right? the Pacha's plan—
This kinsman Bey of Carasman
Perhaps may prove some foe of thine.
If so, I swear by Mecca's shrine,—
If shrines that ne'er approach allow
To woman's step admit her vow,—
Without thy free consent, command,
The Sultan should not have my hand!
Think'st thou that I could bear to part
With thee, and learn to halve my heart?
Ah! were I sever'd from thy side,
Where were thy friend—and who my guide?
Years have not seen, Time shall not see,
The hour that tears my soul from thee:
Ev'n Azrael,[1] from his deadly quiver
　　When flies that shaft, and fly it must,
That parts all else, shall doom for ever
　　Our hearts to undivided dust!"

XII.

He lived, he breathed, he moved, he felt;
He raised the maid from where she knelt;
His trance was gone, his keen eye shone
With thoughts that long in darkness dwelt;
With thoughts that burn—in rays that melt.
As the stream late conceal'd
　　By the fringe of its willows,

---

[1] "Azrael," the angel of death.

When it rushes reveal'd
  In the light of its billows;
As the bolt bursts on high
  From the black cloud that bound it,
Flash'd the soul of that eye
  Through the long lashes round it.
A war-horse at the trumpet's sound,
A lion roused by heedless hound,
A tyrant waked to sudden strife
By graze of ill-directed knife,
Starts not to more convulsive life
Than he, who heard that vow, display'd,
And all, before repress'd, betray'd:
" Now thou art mine, for ever mine,
With life to keep, and scarce with life resign;
Now thou art mine, that sacred oath,
Though sworn by one, hath bound us both.
Yes, fondly, wisely hast thou done;
That vow hath saved more heads than one:
But blench not thou—thy simplest tress
Claims more from me than tenderness;
I would not wrong the slenderest hair
That clusters round thy forehead fair,
For all the treasures buried far
Within the caves of Istakar.*
This morning clouds upon me lower'd,
Reproaches on my head were shower'd,
And Giaffir almost call'd me coward !
Now I have motive to be brave;
The son of his neglected slave,
Nay, start not, 'twas the term he gave,
May show, though little apt to vaunt,
A heart his words nor deeds can daunt.
His son, indeed !—yet, thanks to thee,
Perchance I am, at least shall be;
But let our plighted secret vow
Be only known to us as now.
I know the wretch who dares demand
From Giaffir thy reluctant hand;

---

* The treasures of the Pre-Adamite Sultans See D'Herbelot. article *Istakar.*

More ill-got wealth, a meaner soul
Holds not a Musselim's[3] control;
Was he not bred in Egripo?[4]
A viler race let Israel show !
But let that pass—to none be told
Our oath; the rest shall time unfold.
To me and mine leave Osman Bey !
I've partisans for peril's day :
Think not I am what I appear;
I've arms, and friends, and vengeance near."

XIII.

" Think not thou art what thou appearest !
  My Selim, thou art sadly changed :
This morn I saw thee gentlest, dearest;
  But now thou'rt from thyself estranged.
My love thou surely knew'st before,
It ne'er was less, nor can be more.
To see thee, hear thee, near thee stay,
  And hate the night I know not why,
Save that we meet not but by day;
  With thee to live, with thee to die,
I dare not to my hope deny :
Thy cheek, thine eyes, thy lips to kiss,
Like this—and this—no more than this,
For, Allah ! sure thy lips are flame :
  What fever in thy veins is flushing ?
My own have nearly caught the same,
  At least I feel my cheek, too, blushing.
To soothe thy sickness, watch thy health,
Partake, but never waste thy wealth,
Or stand with smiles unmurmuring by,
And lighten half thy poverty,
Do all but close thy dying eye,
For that I could not live to try;

---

  [3] "Musselim," a governor, the next in rank after a Pacha ; a Waywode is the third ; and then come the Agas.
  [4] "Egripo," the Negropont According to the proverb, the Turks of Egripo, the Jews of Salonica, and the Greeks of Athens, are the worst of their respective races.

To these alone my thoughts aspire:
More can I do? or thou require?
But, Selim, thou must answer why
We need so much of mystery?
The cause I cannot dream nor tell,
But be it, since thou say'st 'tis well;
Yet what thou mean'st by 'arms' and 'friends,'
Beyond my weaker sense extends.
I meant that Giaffir should have heard
   The very vow I plighted thee;
His wrath would not revoke my word:
   But surely he would leave me free.
   Can this fond wish seem strange in me,
To be what I have ever been?
What other hath Zuleika seen
From simple childhood's earliest hour?
   What other can she seek to see
Than thee, companion of her bower,
   The partner of her infancy?
These cherish'd thoughts with life begun,
   Say, why must I no more avow?
What change is wrought to make me shun
   The truth; my pride, and thine till now?
To meet the gaze of stranger's eyes
Our law, our creed, our God denies;
Nor shall one wandering thought of mine
At such, our Prophet's will, repine:
No! happier made by that decree,
He left me all in leaving thee.
Deep were my anguish, thus compell'd
To wed with one I ne'er beheld:
This wherefore should I not reveal?
Why wilt thou urge me to conceal?
I know the Pacha's haughty mood
To thee hath never boded good;
And he so often storms at nought,
Allah! forbid that e'er he ought!
And why I know not, but within
My heart concealment weighs like sin.
If then such secrecy be crime,

And such it feels while lurking here;
Oh, Selim! tell me yet in time,
    Nor leave me thus to thoughts of fear.
Ah! yonder see the Tchocadar,[a]
My father leaves the mimic war;
I tremble now to meet his eye—
Say, Selim, canst thou tell me why?"

XIV.

"Zuleika—to thy tower's retreat
Betake thee—Giaffir I can greet:
And now with him I fain must prate
Of firmans, imposts, levies, state.
There's fearful news from Danube's banks,
Our Vizier nobly thins his ranks,
For which the Giaour may give him thanks!
Our Sultan hath a shorter way
Such costly triumph to repay.
But, mark me, when the twilight drum
    Hath warn'd the troops to food and sleep,
Unto thy cell with Selim come;
    Then softly from the Haram creep
    Where we may wander by the deep:
    Our garden battlements are steep;
Nor these will rash intruder climb
To list our words, or stint our time;
And if he doth, I want not steel
Which some have felt, and more may feel.
Then shalt thou learn of Selim more
Than thou hast heard or thought before:
Trust me, Zuleika—fear not me!
Thou know'st I hold a Haram key."

"Fear thee, my Selim! ne'er till now
Did word like this——"
                            "Delay not thou;

---

[a] "Tchocadar"—one of the attendants who precedes a man of authority

I keep the key—and Haroun's guard
Have *some*, and hope of *more* reward.
To-night, Zuleika, thou shalt hear
My tale, my purpose, and my fear:
I am not, love! what I appear."

CANTO THE SECOND.

I.

THE winds are high on Helle's wave,
  As on that night of stormy water
When Love, who sent, forgot to save
The young, the beautiful, the brave,
  The lonely hope of Sestos' daughter.
Oh ! when alone along the sky
Her turret-torch was blazing high,
Though rising gale, and breaking foam,
And shrieking sea-birds warn'd him home;
And clouds aloft and tides below,
With signs and sounds, forbade to go,
He could not see, he would not hear,
Or sound or sign foreboding fear ;
His eye but saw that light of love,
The only star it hail'd above;
His ear but rang with Hero's song,
" Ye waves, divide not lovers long !"—
That tale is old, but love anew
May nerve young hearts to prove as true.

II.

The winds are high and Helle's tide
  Rolls darkly heaving to the main;
And Night's descending shadows hide
  That field with blood bedew'd in vain,
The desert of old Priam's pride;
  The tombs, sole relics of his reign,

All—save immortal dreams that could beguile
The blind old man of Scio's rocky isle!

III

Oh! yet—for there my steps have been ;
   These feet have press'd the sacred shore,
These limbs that buoyant wave hath borne—
Minstrel! with thee to muse, to mourn,
   To trace again those fields of yore,
Believing every hillock green
   Contains no fabled hero's ashes,
And that around the undoubted scene
   Thine own "broad Hellespont"[1] still dashes,
Be long my lot! and cold were he
Who there could gaze denying thee!

IV.

The night hath closed on Helle's stream,
   Nor yet hath risen on Ida's hill
That moon, which shone on his high theme:
No warrior chides her peaceful beam,
   But conscious shepherds bless it still.
Their flocks are grazing on the mound
   Of him who felt the Dardan's arrow:
That mighty heap of gather'd ground
   Which Ammon's son ran proudly round,[2]
By nations raised, by monarchs crown'd,
   Is now a lone and nameless barrow!
Within—thy dwelling-place how narrow!

[1] The wrangling about this epithet, "the broad Hellespont" or the "boundless Hellespont," whether it means one or the other, or what it means at all, has been beyond all possibility of detail. I have even heard it disputed on the spot, and not foreseeing a speedy conclusion to the controversy, amused myself with swimming across it in the mean time ; and probably may again, before the point is settled. Indeed, the question as to the truth of "the tale of Troy divine" still continues, much of it resting upon the talismanic word "ατυρος" probably Homer had the same notion of distance that a coquette has of time ; and when he talks of boundless, means half a mile ; as the latter, by a like figure, when she says *eternal* attachment, simply specifies three weeks.

[2] Before his Persian invasion, and crowned the altar with laurel, &c. He was afterwards imitated by Caracalla in his race. It is believed that the last also poisoned a friend, named Festus, for the sake of new Patroclan games. I have seen the sheep feeding on the tombs of Æsietes and Antilochus. the first is in the centre of the plain.

Without—can only strangers breathe
The name of him that *was* beneath :
Dust long outlasts the storied stone ;
But Thou—thy very dust is gone !

v.

Late, late to-night will Dian cheer
The swain, and chase the boatman's fear ;
Till then—no beacon on the cliff
May shape the course of struggling skiff ;
The scatter'd lights that skirt the bay,
All, one by one, have died away ;
The only lamp of this lone hour
Is glimmering in Zuleika's tower.
Yes ! there is light in that lone chamber,
  And o'er her silken ottoman
Are thrown the fragrant beads of amber,
  O'er which her fairy fingers ran ; [3]
Near these, with emerald rays beset,
(How could she thus that gem forget ?)
Her mother's sainted amulet, [4]
Whereon engraved the Koorsee text,
Could smooth this life, and win the next ;
And by her comboloio [5] lies
A Koran of illumined dyes ;
And many a bright emblazon'd rhyme
· By Persian scribes redeem'd from time ;
And o'er those scrolls, not oft so mute,
Reclines her now neglected lute ;
And round her lamp of fretted gold
Bloom flowers in urns of Cluna's mould ;

[3] When rubbed, the amber is susceptible of a perfume, which is slight, but *not* disagreeable

[4] The belief in amulets engraved on gems, or enclosed in gold boxes, containing scraps from the Koran, worn round the neck, wrist, or arm, is still universal in the East   The Koorsee (throne) verse in the second cap of the Koran describes the attributes of the Most High, and is engraved in this manner, and worn by the pious, as the most esteemed and sublime of all sentences

[5] "Comboloio"—a Turkish rosary   The MSS , particularly those of the Persians, are richly adorned and illuminated   The Greek females are kept in utter ignorance , but many of the Turkish girls are highly accomplished, though not actually qualified for a Christian coterie.   Perhaps some of our own "*blues*" might not be the worse for *bleaching*.

The richest work of Iran's loom,
And Sheeraz' tribute of perfume ;
All that can eye or sense delight
  Are gather'd in that gorgeous room :
  But yet it hath an air of gloom.
She, of this Peri cell the sprite,
What doth she hence, and on so rude a night ?

VI.

Wrapt in the darkest sable vest,
  Which none save noblest Moslem wear,
To guard from winds of heaven the breast
  As heaven itself to Selim dear,
With cautious steps the thicket threading,
  And starting oft, as through the glade
  The gust its hollow moanings made,
Till on the smoother pathway treading,
More free her timid bosom beat,
  The maid pursued her silent guide ;
And though her terror urged retreat,
  How could she quit her Selim's side ?
  How teach her tender lips to chide ?

VII.

They reach'd at length a grotto, hewn
  By nature, but enlarged by art,
Where oft her lute she wont to tune.
  And oft her Koran conn'd apart ;
And oft in youthful reverie
She dream'd what Paradise might be ·
Where woman's parted soul shall go
Her Prophet had disdain'd to show ;
But Selim's mansion was secure,
Nor deem'd she, could he long endure
His bower in other worlds of bliss
Without *her*, most beloved in this !
Oh ! who so dear with him could dwell ?
What Houri soothe him half so well ?

VIII.

Since last she visited the spot
Some change seem'd wrought within the grot:
It might be only that the night
Disguised things seen by better light:
That brazen lamp but dimly threw
A ray of no celestial hue;
But in a nook within the cell
Her eye on stranger objects fell.
There arms were piled, not such as wield
The turban'd Delis in the field;
But brands of foreign blade and hilt,
And one was red—perchance with guilt!
Ah! how without can blood be spilt?
A cup too on the board was set
That did not seem to hold sherbet.
What may this mean? she turn'd to see
Her Selim—"Oh! can this be he?"

IX

His robe of pride was thrown aside,
    His brow no high-crown'd turban bore,
But in its stead a shawl of red,
    Wreathed lightly round, his temples wore:
That dagger, on whose hilt the gem
Were worthy of a diadem,
No longer glitter'd at his waist,
Where pistols unadorn'd were braced;
And from his belt a sabre swung,
And from his shoulder loosely hung
The cloak of white, the thin capote
That decks the wandering Candiote;
Beneath—his golden plated vest
Clung like a cuirass to his breast;
The greaves below his knee that wound
With silvery scales were sheathed and bound.
But were it not that high command
Spake in his eye, and tone, and hand,

All that a careless eye could see
In him was some young Galiongée.[6]

x.

"I said I was not what I seem'd;
    And now thou see'st my words were true:
I have a tale thou hast not dream'd,
    If sooth—its truth must others rue.
My story now 'twere vain to hide,
I must not see thee Osman's bride:
But had not thine own lips declared
How much of that young heart I shared,
I could not, must not, yet have shown
The darker secret of my own.
In this I speak not now of love;
That, let time, truth, and peril prove:
But first—Oh! never wed another—
Zuleika! I am not thy brother!"

xi.

"Oh! not my brother!—yet unsay—
    God! am I left alone on earth
To mourn—I dare not curse—the day[7]
    That saw my solitary birth?
Oh! thou wilt love me now no more!
    My sinking heart foreboded ill;
But know *me* all I was before,
    Thy sister—friend—Zuleika still.
Thou led'st me here perchance to kill;
    If thou hast cause for vengeance, see!
My breast is offer'd—take thy fill!
    Far better with the dead to be
Than live thus nothing now to thee:

[6] "Galiongée"—or Galiongi, a sailor, that is, a Turkish sailor; the Greeks navigate, the Turks work the guns   Their dress is picturesque; and I have seen the Capitan Pacha, more than once, wearing it as a kind of *incog*   Their legs, however, are generally naked   The buskins described in the text as sheathed behind with silver are those of an Arnaut robber, who was my host (he had quitted the profession) at his Pyrgo, near Gastouni in the Morea; they were plated in scales one over the other, like the back of an armadillo.

[7]   ["To curse—if I could curse—the day."—MS.]

Perhaps far worse, for now I know
Why Giaffir always seem'd thy foe;
And I, alas! am Giaffir's child,
For whom thou wert contemn'd, reviled.
If not thy sister—would'st thou save
My life, Oh! bid me be thy slave!"

XII.

"My slave, Zuleika!—nay, I'm thine:
  But, gentle love, this transport calm,
Thy lot shall yet be link'd with mine;
I swear it by our Prophet's shrine,
  And be that thought thy sorrow's balm.
So may the Koran[8] verse display'd
Upon its steel direct my blade,
In danger's hour to guard us both,
As I preserve that awful oath!
The name in which thy heart hath prided
  Must change; but, my Zuleika, know,
That tie is widen'd, not divided,
  Although thy Sire's my deadliest foe.
My father was to Giaffir all
  That Selim late was deem'd to thee;
That brother wrought a brother's fall,
  But spared, at least, my infancy!
And lull'd me with a vain deceit
That yet a like return may meet.
He rear'd me, not with tender help,
  But like the nephew of a Cain;[9]

---

[8] The characters on all Turkish scimitars contain sometimes the name of the place of their manufacture, but more generally a text from the Koran, in letters of gold Amongst those in my possession is one with a blade of singular construction it is very broad, and the edge notched into serpentine curves like the ripple of water, or the wavering of flame. I asked the Armenian who sold it, what possible use such a figure could add he said, in Italian, that he did not know, but the Mussulmans had an idea that those of this form gave a severer wound, and liked it because it was "piu feroce" I did not much admire the reason, but bought it for its peculiarity

[9] It is to be observed, that every allusion to any thing or personage in the Old Testament, such as the Ark, or Cain, is equally the privilege of Mussulman and Jew · indeed, the former profess to be much better acquainted with the lives, true and fabulous, of the patriarchs, than is warranted by our own sacred writ, and not content with Adam, they have a biography of Pre-Adamites Solomon is the monarch of all

He watch'd me like a lion's whelp,
　　That gnaws and yet may break his chain.
　My father's blood in every vein
　Is boiling! but for thy dear sake
　No present vengeance will I take;
　　Though here I must no more remain.
　But first, beloved Zuleika! hear
　How Giaffir wrought this deed of fear.

XIII.

' How first their strife to rancour grew,
　　If love or envy made them foes,
　It matters little if I knew;
　In fiery spirits, slights, though few
　　And thoughtless, will disturb repose.
　In war Abdallah's arm was strong,
　Remember'd yet in Bosniac song,
　And Paswan's' rebel hordes attest
　How little love they bore such guest:
　His death is all I need relate,
　The stern effect of Giaffir's hate;
　And how my birth disclosed to me,
　Whate'er beside it makes, hath made me free.

XIV.

" When Paswan, after years of strife,
　At last for power, but first for life,
　In Widdin's walls too proudly sate,
　Our Pachas rallied round the state;
　Nor last nor least in high command,
　Each brother led a separate band;

necromancy, and Moses a prophet inferior only to Christ and Mahomet　Zuleika is
the Persian name of Potiphar's wife; and her amour with Joseph constitutes one of
the finest poems in their language.　It is, therefore, no violation of costume to put
the names of Cain, or Noah, into the mouth of a Moslem —[Some doubt having been
expressed by Mr. Murray, as to the propriety of making a Mussulman speak of Cain,
Lord Byron sent him the preceding note—"for the benefit of the ignorant "　"I
don't care one lump of sugar," he says, "for my poetry , but for my costume, and
my correctness, on those points, I will combat lustily."]
　[1] Paswan Oglou, the rebel of Widdin ; who, for the last years of his life, set the
whole power of the Porte at defiance

They gave their horse-tails * to the wind,
    And mustering in Sophia's plain
Their tents were pitch'd, their post assign'd;
    To one, alas! assign'd in vain!
What need of words? the deadly bowl,
    By Giaffir's order drugg'd and given,
With venom subtle as his soul,
    Dismiss'd Abdallah's hence to heaven.
Reclined and feverish in the bath,
He, when the hunter's sport was up,
But little deem'd a brother's wrath
    To quench his thirst had such a cup:
The bowl a bribed attendant bore;
He drank one draught,³ nor needed more!
If thou my tale, Zuleika, doubt,
Call Haroun—he can tell it out.

XV.

"The deed once done, and Paswan's feud
In part suppress'd, though ne'er subdued,
    Abdallah's Pachalick was gain'd:—
Thou know'st not what in our Divan
Can wealth procure for worse than man—
    Abdallah's honours were obtain'd
By him a brother's murder stain'd;
'Tis true, the purchase nearly drain'd
His ill-got treasure, soon replaced.
Would'st question whence? Survey the waste,
And ask the squalid peasant how
His gains repay his broiling brow!—
Why me the stern usurper spared,
Why thus with me his palace shared,
I know not. Shame, regret, remorse,
And little fear from infant's force;

---

² "Horse-tail,"—the standard of a Pacha.
    ³ Giaffir, Pacha of Argyro Castro, or Scutari, I am not sure which, was actually taken off by the Albanian Ali, in the manner described in the text. Ali Pacha, while I was in the country, married the daughter of his victim, some years after the event had taken place at a bath in Sophia or Adrianople. The poison was mixed in the cup of coffee, which is presented before the sherbet by the bath keeper, after dressing.

Besides, adoption as a son
By him whom Heaven accorded none,
Or some unknown cabal, caprice,
Preserved me thus :—but not in peace :
He cannot curb his haughty mood,
Nor I forgive a father's blood.

XVI.

" Within thy father's house are foes ;
    Not all who break his bread are true :
To these should I my birth disclose,
    His days, his very hours were few :
They only want a heart to lead,
A hand to point them to the deed.
But Haroun only knows, or knew
    This tale, whose close is almost nigh :
He in Abdallah's palace grew,
    And held that post in his Serai
    Which holds he here—he saw him die ;
But what could single slavery do ?
Avenge his lord ? alas ! too late ;
Or save his son from such a fate ?
He chose the last, and when elate
    With foes subdued, or friends betray'd,
Proud Giaffir in high triumph sate,
He led me helpless to his gate,
    And not in vain it seems essay'd
    To save the life for which he pray'd.
The knowledge of my birth secured
    From all and each, but most from me·
Thus Giaffir's safety was ensured.
    Removed he too from Roumelie
To this our Asiatic side,
Far from our seats by Danube's tide,
    With none but Haroun, who retains
Such knowledge—and that Nubian feels
    A tyrant's secrets are but chains,
From which the captive gladly steals,
And this and more to me reveals :

Such still to guilt just Alla sends—
Slaves, tools, accomplices—no friends!

XVII.

" All this, Zuleika, harshly sounds;
  But harsher still my tale must be:
Howe'er my tongue thy softness wounds,
  Yet I must prove all truth to thee.
  I saw thee start this garb to see,
Yet is it one I oft have worn,
  And long must wear: this Galiongée,
To whom thy plighted vow is sworn,
  Is leader of those pirate hordes,
  Whose laws and lives are on their swords;
To hear whose desolating tale
Would make thy waning cheek more pale:
Those arms thou see'st my band have brought,
The hands that wield are not remote;
This cup too for the rugged knaves
  Is fill'd—once quaff'd, they ne'er repine:
Our Prophet might forgive the slaves;
  They're only infidels in wine.

XVIII.

" What could I be?   Proscribed at home,
And taunted to a wish to roam;
And listless left—for Giaffir's fear
Denied the courser and the spear—
Though oft—Oh, Mahomet! how oft!—
In full Divan the despot scoff'd,
As if my weak unwilling hand
Refused the bridle or the brand:
He ever went to war alone,
And pent me here untried—unknown;
To Haroun's care with women left,
By hope unblest, of fame bereft,
While thou—whose softness long endear'd,
Though it unmann'd me, still had cheer'd—
To Brusa's walls for safety sent,
Awaited'st there the field's event.

Haroun who saw my spirit pining
   Beneath inaction's sluggish yoke,
His captive, though with dread resigning,
   My thraldom for a season broke,
On promise to return before
The day when Giaffir's charge was o'er.
'Tis vain—my tongue can not impart
My almost drunkenness of heart,
When first this liberated eye
Survey'd Earth, Ocean, Sun, and Sky,
As if my spirit pierced them through,
And all their inmost wonders knew!
One word alone can paint to thee
That more than feeling—I was Free!
E'en for thy presence ceased to pine;
The World—nay, Heaven itself was mine!

XIX.

"The shallop of a trusty Moor
Convey'd me from this idle shore;
I long'd to see the isles that gem
Old Ocean's purple diadem:
I sought by turns, and saw them all;[4]
   But when and where I join'd the crew,
With whom I'm pledged to rise or fall,
   When all that we design to do
Is done, 'twill then be time more meet
To tell thee, when the tale's complete.

XX.

" 'Tis true, they are a lawless brood,
But rough in form, nor mild in mood;
And every creed, and every race,
With them hath found—may find a place:
But open speech, and ready hand,
Obedience to their chief's command;
A soul for every enterprise,
That never sees with terror's eyes;

Friendship for each, and faith to all,
And vengeance vow'd for those who fall,
Have made them fitting instruments
For more than ev'n my own intents.
And some—and I have studied all
   Distinguish'd from the vulgar rank,
But chiefly to my council call
   The wisdom of the cautious Frank—
And some to higher thoughts aspire,
   The last of Lambro's[5] patriots there
   Anticipated freedom share;
And oft around the cavern fire
On visionary schemes debate,
To snatch the Rayahs[6] from their fate.
So let them ease their hearts with prate
Of equal rights, which man ne'er knew;
I have a love for freedom too.
Ay! let me like the ocean-Patriarch[7] roam,
Or only know on land the Tartar's home![8]
My tent on shore, my galley on the sea,
Are more than cities and Serais to me:
Borne by my steed, or wafted by my sail,
Across the desert, or before the gale,
Bound where thou wilt, my barb! or glide, my prow!
But be the star that guides the wanderer, Thou!
Thou, my Zuleika, share and bless my bark;
The Dove of peace and promise to mine ark![9]

---

[5] Lambro Canzani, a Greek, famous for his efforts, in 1789-90, for the independence of his country. Abandoned by the Russians, he became a pirate, and the Archipelago was the scene of his enterprises. He is said to be still alive at Petersburgh. He and Riga are the two most celebrated of the Greek revolutionists.

[6] "Rayahs,"—all who pay the capitation tax, called the "Haratch."

[7] This first of voyages is one of the few with which the Mussulmans profess much acquaintance.

[8] The wandering life of the Arabs, Tartars, and Turkomans, will be found well detailed in any book of Eastern travels. That it possesses a charm peculiar to itself, cannot be denied. A young French renegado confessed to Châteaubriand, that he never found himself alone, galloping in the desert, without a sensation approaching to rapture which was indescribable.

[9] [The longest, as well as most splendid, of those passages, with which the perusal of his own strains, during revision, inspired him, was that rich flow of eloquent feeling which follows the couplet,—"Thou, my Zuleika, share and bless my bark," &c.—a strain of poetry, which, for energy and tenderness of thought, for music of versification, and selectness of diction, has, throughout the greater portion of it, but few rivals in either ancient or modern song. —MOORE:]

Or, since that hope denied in worlds of strife,
Be thou the rainbow to the storms of life!
The evening beam that smiles the clouds away,
And tints to-morrow with prophetic ray![1]
Blest—as the Muezzin's strain from Mecca's wall
To pilgrims pure and prostrate at his call;
Soft—as the melody of youthful days,
That steals the trembling tear of speechless praise;
Dear—as his native song to Exile's ears,
Shall sound each tone thy long-loved voice endears.
For thee in those bright isles is built a bower
Blooming as Aden[2] in its earliest hour.
A thousand swords, with Selim's heart and hand,
Wait—wave—defend—destroy—at thy command!
Girt by my band, Zuleika at my side,
The spoil of nations shall bedeck my bride.
The Haram's languid years of listless ease
Are well resign'd for cares—for joys like these:
Not blind to fate, I see, where'er I rove,
Unnumber'd perils,—but one only love!
Yet well my toils shall that fond breast repay,
Though fortune frown, or falser friends betray.
How dear the dream in darkest hours of ill,
Should all be changed, to find thee faithful still!
Be but thy soul, like Selim's firmly shown;
To thee be Selim's tender as thine own;
To soothe each sorrow, share in each delight,
Blend every thought, do all—but disunite!
Once free, 'tis mine our horde again to guide;
Friends to each other, foes to aught beside:

[1] [Originally written thus—

"And tints to-morrow with $\begin{Bmatrix} \text{an airy} \\ \text{a fancied} \end{Bmatrix}$ ray."

Lord Byron bid Mr. Murray choose between "fancied" and "airy;" but later he substituted the felicitous epithet which stands in the text. At the same time he sent two other versions, that Gifford might select that which was "best, or rather not worst—"

"And $\begin{Bmatrix} \text{gilds} \\ \text{tints} \end{Bmatrix}$ the hope of morning with its ray."

"And gilds to-morrow's hope with heavenly ray."]

[2] "Jannat-al-Aden," the perpetual abode, the Mussulman paradise.

Yet there we follow but the bent assign'd
By fatal Nature to man's warring kind .
Mark ! where his carnage and his conquests cease !
He makes a solitude, and calls it—peace ! '
I like the rest must use my skill or strength,
But ask no land beyond my sabre's length :
Power sways but by division—her resource
The blest alternative of fraud or force !
Ours be the last; in time deceit may come
When cities cage us in a social home :
There ev'n thy soul might err—how oft the heart
Corruption shakes which peril could not part !
And woman, more than man, when death or woe,
Or even Disgrace, would lay her lover low,
Sunk in the lap of Luxury will shame—
Away suspicion !—*not* Zuleika's name !
But life is hazard at the best , and here
No more remains to win, and much to fear :
Yes, fear !—the doubt, the dread of losing thee,
By Osman's power, and Giaffir's stern decree.
That dread shall vanish with the favouring gale,
Which Love to-night hath promised to my sail :
No danger daunts the pair his smile hath blest,
Their steps still roving, but their hearts at rest
With thee all toils are sweet, each clime hath charms ;
Earth—sea alike—our world within our arms '
Ay—let the loud winds whistle o'er the deck,
So that those arms cling closer round my neck :
The deepest murmur of this lip shall be,'
No sigh for safety, but a prayer for thee !
The war of elements no fears impart
To Love, whose deadliest bane is human Art :

' [This line, as Lord Byron acknowledged, is taken from Tacitus ·—" Ubi solitu-
dinem faciunt pacem appellant."]

                          [" Then if my lip once murmurs, it must be "—MS.
Lord Byron states that he intended this passage for an imitation of Medea's speech in
the seventh book of Ovid's Metamorphoses ·—

        " My love possest, in Jason's bosom laid,
          Let seas swell high ,—I cannot be dismay'd
          While I infold my husband in my arms
          Or should I fear, I should but fear his harms "
                               SANDYS' *translation.*]

There lie the only rocks our course can check;
Here moments menace—*there* are years of wreck !
But hence ye thoughts that rise in Horror's shape !
This hour bestows, or ever bars escape.
Few words remain of mine my tale to close;
Of thine but *one* to waft us from our foes ;
Yea—foes—to me will Giaffir's hate decline ?
And is not Osman, who would part us, thine ?

XXI.

" His head and faith from doubt and death
   Return'd in time my guard to save;
   Few heard, none told, that o'er the wave
From isle to isle I roved the while:
And since, though parted from my band
Too seldom now I leave the land,
No deed they've done, nor deed shall do,
Ere I have heard and doom'd it too :
I form the plan, decree the spoil,
'Tis fit I oftener share the toil.
But now too long I've held thine ear;
Time presses, floats my bark, and here
We leave behind but hate and fear.
To-morrow Osman with his train
Arrives—to-night must break thy chain :
And would'st thou save that haughty Bey,—
   Perchance *his* life who gave thee thine,—
With me this hour away—away !
   But yet, though thou art plighted mine,
Would'st thou recall thy willing vow,
Appall'd by truths imparted now,
Here rest I—not to see thee wed :
But be that peril on *my* head ! "

XXII.

Zuleika, mute and motionless,
Stood like that statue of distress,
When, her last hope for ever gone,
The mother harden'd into stone ;

All in the maid that eye could see
Was but a younger Niobé.
But ere her lip, or even her eye,
Essay'd to speak, or look reply,
Beneath the garden's wicket porch
Far flash'd on high a blazing torch !
Another—and another—and another—
" Oh ! fly—no more—yet now my more than brother ! "
Far, wide, through every thicket spread
The fearful lights are gleaming red ;
Nor these alone—for each right hand
Is ready with a sheathless brand.
They part, pursue, return, and wheel
With searching flambeau, shining steel ;
And last of all, his sabre waving,
Stern Giaffir in his fury raving :
And now almost they touch the cave—
Oh ! must that grot be Selim's grave ?

XXIII.

Dauntless he stood—" 'Tis come—soon past—
One kiss, Zuleika—'tis my last .
    But yet my band not far from shore
May hear this signal, see the flash ;
Yet now too few—the attempt were rash :
    No matter—yet one effort more."
Forth to the cavern mouth he stept ;
    His pistol's echo rang on high,
Zuleika started not, nor wept,
    Despair benumb'd her breast and eye !—
" They hear me not, or if they ply
Their oars, 'tis but to see me die ;
That sound hath drawn my foes more nigh.
Then forth my father's scimitar,
Thou ne'er hast seen less equal war !
Farewell, Zuleika !—Sweet ! retire :
    Yet stay within—here linger safe,
    At thee his rage will only chafe.
Stir not—lest even to thee perchance
Some erring blade or ball should glance.

Fear'st thou for him?—may I expire
If in this strife I seek thy sire!
No—though by him that poison pour'd;
No—though again he call me coward!
But tamely shall I meet their steel?
No—as each crest save *his* may feel!"

XXIV.

One bound he made, and gain'd the sand:
   Already at his feet hath sunk
The foremost of the prying band,
   A gasping head, a quivering trunk:
Another falls—but round him close
A swarming circle of his foes;
From right to left his path he cleft,
   And almost met the meeting wave:
His boat appears—not five oars' length—
His comrades strain with desperate strength—
   Oh! are they yet in time to save?
   His feet the foremost breakers lave;
His band are plunging in the bay,
Their sabres glitter through the spray;
Wet—wild—unwearied to the strand
They struggle—now they touch the land!
They come—'tis but to add to slaughter—
His heart's best blood is on the water.

XXV.

Escaped from shot, unharm'd by steel,
Or scarcely grazed its force to feel,
Had Selim won, betray'd, beset,
To where the strand and billows met;
There as his last step left the land,
And the last death-blow dealt his hand—
Ah! wherefore did he turn to look
   For her his eye but sought in vain?
That pause, that fatal gaze he took,
   Hath doom'd his death, or fix'd his chain.
Sad proof, in peril and in pain,
How late will Lover's hope remain

His back was to the dashing spray;
Behind, but close, his comrades lay,
When, at the instant, hiss'd the ball—
" So may the foes of Giaffir fall ! "
Whose voice is heard? whose carbine rang?
Whose bullet through the night-air sang,
Too nearly, deadly aim'd to err?
'Tis thine—Abdallah's Murderer !
The father slowly rued thy hate,
The son hath found a quicker fate :
Fast from his breast the blood is bubbling.
The whiteness of the sea-foam troubling—
If aught his lips essay'd to groan,
The rushing billows choked the tone !

XXVI.

Morn slowly rolls the clouds away ;
  Few trophies of the fight are there:
The shouts that shook the midnight-bay
  Are silent; but some signs of fray
    That strand of strife may bear,
And fragments of each shiver'd brand;
Steps stamp'd ; and dash'd into the sand
The print of many a struggling hand
    May there be mark'd; nor far remote
    A broken torch, an oarless boat;
And tangled on the weeds that heap
The beach where shelving to the deep
    There lies a white capote !
'Tis rent in twain—one dark-red stain
The wave yet ripples o'er in vain :
    But where is he who wore?
Ye! who would o'er his relics weep,
Go, seek them where the surges sweep
Their burthen round Sigæum's steep
    And cast on Lemnos' shore:
The sea-birds shriek above the prey,
O'er which their hungry beaks delay,
As shaken on his restless pillow,
His head heaves with the heaving billow ;

That hand, whose motion is not life,
Yet feebly seems to menace strife,
Flung by the tossing tide on high,
　　Then levell'd with the wave—'
What recks it, though that corse shall lie
　　Within a living grave?
The bird that tears that prostrate form
Hath only robb'd the meaner worm;
The only heart, the only eye
Had bled or wept to see him die,
Had seen those scatter'd limbs composed,
　　And mourn'd above his turban-stone,⁶
That heart hath burst—that eye was closed—
　　Yea—closed before his own!

XXVII

By Helle's stream there is a voice of wail!
And woman's eye is wet—man's cheek is pale:
Zuleika! last of Giaffir's race,
　　Thy destin'd lord is come too late:
He sees not—ne'er shall see thy face!
　　　　Can he not hear
The loud Wul-wulleh⁷ warn his distant ear?
　　Thy handmaids weeping at the gate,
　　The Koran-chanters of the hymn of fate,
　　The silent slaves with folded arms that wait,
Sighs in the hall, and shrieks upon the gale,
　　　　Tell him thy tale!
Thou didst not view thy Selim fall!
　　That fearful moment when he left the cave
　　　　Thy heart grew chill:
He was thy hope—thy joy—thy love—thine all,
And that last thought on him thou could'st not save
　　　　Sufficed to kill;

⁵ [The incident here depicted was witnessed by Lord Byron near the Dardanelles. The body of a man, who had been executed, rose and fell with the waves, and several sea-fowl that approached to devour it were scared away by the movement of the arms]

⁶ A turban is carved in stone above the graves of *men* only.

⁷ The death-song of the Turkish women The "silent slaves" are the men, whose notions of decorum forbid complaint in *public*.

Burst forth in one wild cry—and all was still.
Peace to thy broken heart, and virgin grave!
Ah! happy! but of life to lose the worst!
That grief—though deep—though fatal—was thy first!
Thrice happy! ne'er to feel nor fear the force
Of absence, shame, pride, hate, revenge, remorse!
And, oh! that pang where more than Madness lies
The worm that will not sleep—and never dies;
Thought of the gloomy day and ghastly night,
That dreads the darkness, and yet loathes the light,
That winds around, and tears the quivering heart!
Ah! wherefore not consume it—and depart!
Woe to thee, rash and unrelenting chief!
　　Vainly thou heap'st the dust upon thy head,
　　Vainly the sackcloth o'er thy limbs dost spread:
　　By that same hand Abdallah—Selim bled.
Now let it tear thy beard in idle grief:
Thy pride of heart, thy bride for Osman's bed,
She, whom thy sultan had but seen to wed,
　　　　Thy Daughter's dead!
　　Hope of thine age, thy twilight's lonely beam,
　　The Star hath set that shone on Helle's stream.
What quench'd its ray?—the blood that thou hast shed!
Hark! to the hurried question of Despair:
"Where is my child?"—an Echo answers—"Where?" [8]

XXVIII.

Within the place of thousand tombs
　　That shine beneath, while dark above
The sad but living cypress glooms
　　And withers not, though branch and leaf
Are stamp'd with an eternal grief,
　　Like early unrequited Love,
One spot exists, which ever blooms,

---

[8] "I came to the place of my birth, and cried, 'The friends of my youth, where are they?' and an Echo answered, 'Where are they?'"—*From an Arabic MS*　The above quotation (from which the idea in the text is taken) must be already familiar to every reader: it is given in the first annotation, p 67, of "The Pleasures of Memory," a poem so well known as to render a reference almost superfluous　but to whose pages all will be delighted to recur

Ev'n in that deadly grove—
A single rose is shedding there
  Its lonely lustre, meek and pale :
It looks as planted by Despair—
  So white—so faint—the slightest gale
Might whirl the leaves on high;
  And yet, though storms and blight assail,
And hands more rude than wintry sky
  May wring it from the stem—in vain—
  To-morrow sees it bloom again!
The stalk some spirit gently rears,
And waters with celestial tears;
  For well may maids of Helle deem
That this can be no earthly flower,
Which mocks the tempest's withering hour,
And buds unshelter'd by a bower;
Nor droops, though Spring refuse her shower,
  Nor woos the summer beam :
To it the livelong night there sings
  A bird unseen—but not remote :
Invisible his airy wings,
But soft as harp that Houri strings
  His long entrancing note!
It were the Bulbul; but his throat,
  Though mournful, pours not such a strain :
For they who listen cannot leave
The spot, but linger there and grieve,
  As if they loved in vain!
And yet so sweet the tears they shed,
'Tis sorrow so unmix'd with dread,
They scarce can bear the morn to break
  That melancholy spell,
And longer yet would weep and wake,
  He sings so wild and well!
But when the day-blush bursts from high
  Expires that magic melody.
And some have been who could believe,
(So fondly youthful dreams deceive,
  Yet harsh be they that blame,)
That note so piercing and profound

Will shape and syllable[9] its sound
   Into Zuleika's name.
'Tis from her cypress summit heard,
That melts in air the liquid word:
'Tis from her lowly virgin earth
That white rose takes its tender birth.
There late was laid a marble stone;
Eve saw it placed—the Morrow gone!
It was no mortal arm that bore
That deep fixed pillar to the shore;
For there, as Helle's legends tell,
Next morn 'twas found where Selim fell;
Lash'd by the tumbling tide, whose wave
Denied his bones a holier grave
And there by night, reclin'd, 'tis said,
Is seen a ghastly turban'd head:
   And hence extended by the billow,
   'Tis named the "Pirate-phantom's pillow!"
   Where first it lay that mourning flower
   Hath flourish'd; flourisheth this hour,
Alone and dewy, coldly pure and pale,
As weeping Beauty's cheek at Sorrow's tale!

[9] "And airy tongues that *syllable* men's names."—MILTON.

For a belief that the souls of the dead inhabit the form of birds, we need not travel to the East   Lord Lyttleton's ghost story, the belief of the Duchess of Kendal, that George I flew into her window in the shape of a raven (see "Orford's Reminiscences"), and many other instances, bring this superstition nearer home.   The most singular was the whim of a Worcester lady, who, believing her daughter to exist in the shape of a singing bird, literally furnished her pew in the cathedral with cages full of the kind, and as she was rich, and a benefactress in beautifying the church, no objection was made to her harmless folly.   For this anecdote, see "Orford's Letters"

THE CORSAIR:

A TALE

——"I suoi pensieri in lui dormir non ponno "
    TASSO, *Gerusalemme Liberata,* canto x

TO THOMAS MOORE, ESQ.

My dear Moore,

I dedicate to you the last production with which I shall trespass on public patience, and your indulgence, for some years; and I own that I feel anxious to avail myself of this latest and only opportunity of adorning my pages with a name, consecrated by unshaken public principle, and the most undoubted and various talents. While Ireland ranks you among the firmest of her patriots; while you stand alone the first of her bards in her estimation, and Britain repeats and ratifies the decree, permit one, whose only regret, since our first acquaintance, has been the years he had lost before it commenced, to add the humble but sincere suffrage of friendship, to the voice of more than one nation. It will at least prove to you, that I have neither forgotten the gratification derived from your society, nor abandoned the prospect of its renewal, whenever your leisure or inclination allows you to atone to your friends for too long an absence. It is said among those friends, I trust truly, that you are engaged in the composition of a poem whose scene will be laid in the East; none can do those scenes so much justice. The wrongs of your own country,* the

---

* [This political allusion having been objected to by a friend, Lord Byron sent a second dedication to Mr. Moore, with a request that he would "take his choice." It ran as follows :—

"My dear Moore,   *January* 7th, 1814.

"I had written to you a long letter of dedication, which I suppress, because, though it contained something relating to you, which every one had been glad to hear, yet there was too much about politics and poesy, and all things whatsoever, ending with that topic on which most men are fluent, and none very amusing,—*one's self*. It might have been re-written; but to what purpose? My praise could add nothing to your well-earned and firmly established fame; and with my most hearty admiration of your talents, and delight in your conversation, you are already acquainted. In

magnificent and fiery spirit of her sons, the beauty and feeling of her
daughters, may there be found ; and Collins, when he denominated his
Oriental his Irish Eclogues, was not aware how true, at least, was a part
of his parallel. Your imagination will create a warmer sun, and less
clouded sky ; but wildness, tenderness, and originality, are part of your
national claim of oriental descent, to which you have already thus far
proved your title more clearly than the most zealous of your country's
antiquarians.

May I add a few words on a subject on which all men are supposed to
be fluent, and none agreeable ?—Self. I have written much, and published
more than enough to demand a longer silence than I now meditate ; but,
for some years to come, it is my intention to tempt no further the award of
"Gods, men, nor columns." In the present composition I have attempted
not the most difficult, but, perhaps, the best adapted measure to our
language, the good old and now neglected heroic couplet. The stanza
of Spenser is perhaps too slow and dignified for narrative ; though, I
confess, it is the measure most after my own heart ; Scott alone,* of the
present generation, has hitherto completely triumphed over the fatal
facility of the octosyllabic verse ; and this is not the least victory of his
fertile and mighty genius : in blank verse, Milton, Thomson, and our
dramatists, are the beacons that shine along the deep, but warn us from
the rough and barren rock on which they are kindled. The heroic
couplet is not the most popular measure certainly ; but as I did not
deviate into the other from a wish to flatter what is called public opinion,
I shall quit it without further apology, and take my chance once more
with that versification, in which I have hitherto published nothing but
compositions whose former circulation is part of my present, and will be
of my future regret.

With regard to my story, and stories in general, I should have been
glad to have rendered my personages more perfect and amiable, if possible,
inasmuch as I have been sometimes criticised, and considered no less
responsible for their deeds and qualities than if all had been personal.
Be it so—if I have deviated into the gloomy vanity of "drawing from
self," the pictures are probably like, since they are unfavourable : and if

availing myself of your friendly permission to inscribe this poem to you, I can only
wish the offering were as worthy your acceptance, as your regard is dear to

"Yours, most affectionately and faithfully,

"BYRON."]

* [After the words "Scott alone." Lord Byron had inserted, in a parenthesis—
"He will excuse the '*Mr.*'—we do not say *Mr.* Cæsar."]

not, those who know me are undeceived, and those who do not, I have little interest in undeceiving. I have no particular desire that any but my acquaintance should think the author better than the beings of his imagining; but I cannot help a little surprise, and perhaps amusement, at some odd critical exceptions in the present instance, when I see several bards (far more deserving, I allow) in very reputable plight, and quite exempted from all participation in the faults of those heroes, who, nevertheless, might be found with little more morality than "The Giaour," and perhaps—but no—I must admit Childe Harold to be a very repulsive personage; and as to his identity, those who like it must give him whatever "alias" they please.*

If, however, it were worth while to remove the impression, it might be of some service to me, that the man who is alike the delight of his readers and his friends, the poet of all circles, and the idol of his own, permits me here and elsewhere to subscribe myself,

Most truly,

And affectionately,

His obedient servant,

BYRON.

January 2, 1814.

* [It is difficult to say whether we are to receive this passage as an admission or a denial of the opinion to which it refers; but Lord Byron certainly did the public injustice, if he supposed it imputed to him the criminal actions with which many of his heroes were stained. Men no more expected to meet in Lord Byron the Corsair, who "knew himself a villain," than they looked for the hypocrisy of Kehama on the shores of the Derwent Water, or the profligacy of Marmion on the banks of the Tweed.—SIR WALTER SCOTT.]

INTRODUCTION TO THE CORSAIR.

"THE CORSAIR" was completed on the 31st of December, 1813, having been composed in ten days, at the rate of 200 lines a-day. When the wonderful merit of the Tale is considered, the feat is without a parallel in the history of poetry. The only additions to the original draught were the fifth, seventeenth, and twenty-third sections of Canto III   Medora was a portrait of an acquaintance, and is called *Francesca* in the manuscript   Lord Byron had tried the heroic couplet in one of the paragraphs of "The Bride of Abydos," and the admiration lavished upon it, may have induced him to adopt that measure in "The Corsair." Though no metre was so hackneyed, it assumed in his hands a distinctive character.   There are lines which recall his deep study of Pope, but, with much of Pope's terseness, there is far greater freedom; and, with less negligence than Dryden, there is even more than Dryden's ease and spirit   The stream of the narrative bounds along in a rapid and sparkling current; and, notwithstanding the fetters of a monotonous metre, and the exigences of rhyme, all the varieties of incident and emotion assume their natural and ever-changing expression   Without one feeble passage—and hardly a feeble couplet—there are gems which shine conspicuous amid the general blaze.   Myriads of partings have been painted in poetry, but the parting of Conrad and Medora is the master-piece of them all.   Nor can anything be truer to nature than the instant exchange of feminine tenderness for martial enthusiasm in the Pirate's breast, when nearing the vessel he sees his flag, and hears the animating hum of preparation.   The unrivalled scene in which the Corsair throws off his disguise, is needless to be specified, and from the second visit of Gulnare to his cell, up to her final dismissal, is one glorious flow of passionate verse   Lord Byron has informed us that the tale "was written *con amore* and much from *existence* "   A few days later, and he makes in his journal this singular entry .   "Hobhouse told me an odd report,—that *I* am the actual Conrad, the veritable Corsair, and that part of my travels are supposed to have passed in piracy.   Um !—people sometimes hit near the truth, but never the whole truth.   H don't know what I was about the year after he left the Levant , nor does any one—nor—nor—nor—however, it is a lie—but 'I doubt the equivocation of the fiend that lies like truth !' "   He mentioned the report to a female acquaintance, who replied, " I don't wonder, Conrad is so *like,*" upon which he remarks that if *she* knew nothing, no one else could   Whatever may be the meaning of these dark allusions, the figure, the features, and the spare diet of Conrad, had their counterpart in Lord Byron ; and in his supercilious smile, in his haughty and melancholy mien, in his low opinion of mankind, and in his self reproachful and uneasy soul, "that man of loneliness and mystery" was the poet in his sombre and unbending moods.   The success of the poem was immense   Sir James Mackintosh mentioned, as a proof of Lord Byron being *the* author of the time, that 6,000 copies of " The Bride of Abydos" were sold within a month, but of "The Corsair" 14,000 were sold in a day.   Lord Byron presented the copyright to Mr. Dallas, who disposed of it for 500 guineas.

THE CORSAIR.[1]

CANTO THE FIRST.

"———— nessun maggior dolore,
Che ricordarsi del tempo felice
Nella miseria, ————————"—DANTE.

I

"O'ER the glad waters of the dark blue sea,
Our thoughts as boundless, and our souls as free,
Far as the breeze can bear, the billows foam,
Survey our empire, and behold our home!
These are our realms, no limits to their sway—
Our flag the sceptre all who meet obey.
Ours the wild life in tumult still to range
From toil to rest, and joy in every change.
Oh, who can tell? not thou, luxurious slave!
Whose soul would sicken o'er the heaving wave;
Not thou, vain lord of wantonness and ease!
Whom slumber soothes not—pleasure cannot please—
Oh, who can tell, save he whose heart hath tried,
And danced in triumph o'er the waters wide,
The exulting sense—the pulse's maddening play,
That thrills the wanderer of that trackless way?
That for itself can woo the approaching fight,
And turn what some deem danger to delight;

[1] The time in this poem may seem too short for the occurrences, but the whole of the Ægean isles are within a few hours' sail of the continent, and the reader must be kind enough to take the *wind* as I have often found it.

That seeks what cravens shun with more than zeal,
And where the feebler faint can only feel—
Feel—to the rising bosom's inmost core,
Its hope awaken and its spirit soar?
No dread of death if with us die our foes—
Save that it seems even duller than repose;
Come when it will—we snatch the life of life—
When lost—what recks it by disease or strife?
Let him who crawls enamour'd of decay,
Cling to his couch, and sicken years away;
Heave his thick breath, and shake his palsied head;
Ours—the fresh turf, and not the feverish bed,
While gasp by gasp he falters forth his soul,
Ours with one pang—one bound—escapes control.
His corse may boast its urn and narrow cave,
And they who loath'd his life may gild his grave:
Ours are the tears, though few, sincerely shed,
When Ocean shrouds and sepulchres our dead.
For us, even banquets fond regret supply
In the red cup that crowns our memory;
And the brief epitaph in danger's day,
When those who win at length divide the prey,
And cry, Remembrance saddening o'er each brow,
How had the brave who fell exulted *now!*"

II.

Such were the notes that from the Pirate's isle
Around the kindling watch-fire rang the while:
Such were the sounds that thrill'd the rocks along,
And unto ears as rugged seem'd a song!
In scatter'd groups upon the golden sand,
They game—carouse—converse—or whet the brand
Select the arms—to each his blade assign,
And careless eye the blood that dims its shine;
Repair the boat, replace the helm or oar,
While others straggling muse along the shore;
For the wild bird the busy springes set,
Or spread beneath the sun the dripping net:
Gaze where some distant sail a speck supplies,
With all the thirsting eye of Enterprise;

Tell o'er the tales of many a night of toil,
And marvel where they next shall seize a spoil:
No matter where—their chief's allotment this;
Theirs, to believe no prey nor plan amiss.
But who that CHIEF? his name on every shore
Is famed and fear'd—they ask and know no more.
With these he mingles not but to command;
Few are his words, but keen his eye and hand.
Ne'er seasons he with mirth their jovial mess,
But they forgive his silence for success.
Ne'er for his lip the purpling cup they fill,
That goblet passes him untasted still—
And for his fare—the rudest of his crew
Would that, in turn, have pass'd untasted too;
Earth's coarsest bread, the garden's homeliest roots,
And scarce the summer luxury of fruits,
His short repast in humbleness supply
With all a hermit's board would scarce deny.
But while he shuns the grosser joys of sense,
His mind seems nourish'd by that abstinence.
"Steer to that shore!"—they sail. "Do this!"—'tis done:
"Now form and follow me!"—the spoil is won.
Thus prompt his accents and his actions still,
And all obey and few inquire his will;
To such, brief answer and contemptuous eye
Convey reproof, nor further deign reply.

III.

"A sail!—a sail!"—a promised prize to Hope!
Her nation—flag—how speaks the telescope?
No prize, alas! but yet a welcome sail:
The blood-red signal glitters in the gale.
Yes—she is ours—a home-returning bark—
Blow fair, thou breeze!—she anchors ere the dark,
Already doubled is the cape—our bay
Receives that prow which proudly spurns the spray.
How gloriously her gallant course she goes!
Her white wings flying—never from her foes—
She walks the waters like a thing of life,
And seems to dare the elements to strife.

Who would not brave the battle-fire, the wreck,
To move the monarch of her peopled deck!

IV.

Hoarse o'er her side the rustling cable rings;
The sails are furl'd; and anchoring round she swings;
And gathering loiterers on the land discern
Her boat descending from the latticed stern.
'Tis mann'd—the oars keep concert to the strand,
Till grates her keel upon the shallow sand.
Hail to the welcome shout!—the friendly speech!
When hand grasps hand uniting on the beach;
The smile, the question, and the quick reply,
And the heart's promise of festivity!

V.

The tidings spread, and gathering grows the crowd:
The hum of voices, and the laughter loud,
And woman's gentler anxious tone is heard—
Friends', husbands', lovers' names in each dear word:
"Oh! are they safe? we ask not of success—
But shall we see them? will their accents bless?
From where the battle roars, the billows chafe,
They doubtless boldly did—but who are safe?
Here let them haste to gladden and surprise,
And kiss the doubt from these delighted eyes!"

VI.

"Where is our chief? for him we bear report—
And doubt that joy—which hails our coming—short;
Yet thus sincere, 'tis cheering, though so brief;
But, Juan! instant guide us to our chief:
Our greeting paid, we'll feast on our return,
And all shall hear what each may wish to learn."
Ascending slowly by the rock-hewn way,
To where his watch-tower beetles o'er the bay,
By bushy brake, and wild flowers blossoming,
And freshness breathing from each silver spring,
Whose scatter'd streams from granite basins burst,
Leap into life, and sparkling woo your thirst;

From crag to cliff they mount—Near yonder cave,
What lonely straggler looks along the wave?
In pensive posture leaning on the brand,
Not oft a resting-staff to that red hand?
"'Tis he—'tis Conrad—here, as wont, alone;
On—Juan!—on—and make our purpose known.
The bark he views—and tell him we would greet
His ear with tidings he must quickly meet:
We dare not yet approach—thou know'st his mood,
When strange or uninvited steps intrude."

VII.

Him Juan sought, and told of their intent;—
He spake not, but a sign expressed assent,
These Juan calls—they come—to their salute
He bends him slightly, but his lips are mute.
"These letters, Chief, are from the Greek—the spy,
Who still proclaims our spoil or peril nigh:
Whate'er his tidings, we can well report,
Much that"—"Peace, peace!"—he cuts their prating short.
Wondering they turn, abash'd, while each to each
Conjecture whispers in his muttering speech:
They watch his glance with many a stealing look,
To gather how that eye the tidings took;
But, this as if he guessed, with head aside,
Perchance from some emotion, doubt, or pride,
He read the scroll—"My tablets, Juan, hark—
Where is Gonsalvo?"

　　　　　　　　"In the anchor'd bark."
"There let him stay—to him this order bear—
Back to your duty—for my course prepare:
Myself this enterprise to-night will share."

"To-night, Lord Conrad?"

　　　　　　　　"Ay! at set of sun:
The breeze will freshen when the day is done.
My corslet, cloak—one hour and we are gone.
Sling on thy bugle—see that free from rust
My carbine-lock springs worthy of my trust;

Be the edge sharpen'd of my boarding-brand,
And give its guard more room to fit my hand.
This let the armourer with speed dispose;
Last time, it more fatigued my arm than foes;
Mark that the signal-gun be duly fired,
To tell us when the hour of stay's expired."

VIII.

They make obeisance, and retire in haste,
Too soon to seek again the watery waste:
Yet they repine not—so that Conrad guides;
And who dare question aught that he decides?
That man of loneliness and mystery,
Scarce seen to smile, and seldom heard to sigh;
Whose name appals the fiercest of his crew,
And tints each swarthy cheek with sallower hue;
Still sways their souls with that commanding art
That dazzles, leads, yet chills the vulgar heart.
What is that spell, that thus his lawless train
Confess and envy, yet oppose in vain?
What should it be, that thus their faith can bind?
The power of Thought—the magic of the Mind!
Link'd with success, assumed and kept with skill,
That moulds another's weakness to its will;
Wields with their hands, but, still to these unknown,
Makes even their mightiest deeds appear his own.
Such hath it been—shall be—beneath the sun
The many still must labour for the one!
'Tis Nature's doom—but let the wretch who toils,
Accuse not, hate not *him* who wears the spoils.
Oh! if he knew the weight of splendid chains,
How light the balance of his humbler pains!

IX.

Unlike the heroes of each ancient race,
Demons in act, but Gods at least in face,
In Conrad's form seems little to admire,
Though his dark eyebrow shades a glance of fire:
Robust but not Herculean—to the sight
No giant frame sets forth his common height;

Yet, in the whole, who paused to look again,
Saw more than marks the crowd of vulgar men;
They gaze and marvel how—and still confess
That thus it is, but why they cannot guess.
Sun-burnt his cheek, his forehead high and pale
The sable curls in wild profusion veil;
And oft perforce his rising lip reveals
The haughtier thought it curbs, but scarce conceals.
Though smooth his voice, and calm his general mien,
Still seems there something he would not have seen:
His features' deepening lines and varying hue
At times attracted, yet perplex'd the view,
As if within that murkiness of mind
Work'd feelings fearful, and yet undefined;
Such might it be—that none could truly tell—
Too close enquiry his stern glance would quell.
There breathe but few whose aspect might defy
The full encounter of his searching eye;
He had the skill, when Cunning's gaze would seek
To probe his heart and watch his changing cheek,
At once the observer's purpose to espy,
And on himself roll back his scrutiny,
Lest he to Conrad rather should betray
Some secret thought, than drag that chief's to day.
There was a laughing Devil in his sneer,
That raised emotions both of rage and fear;
And where his frown of hatred darkly fell,
Hope withering fled, and Mercy sigh'd farewell![2]

[2] That Conrad is a character not altogether out of nature, I shall attempt to prove by some historical coincidences which I have met with since writing "The Corsair."

"Eccelin prisonnier," dit Rolandini, "s'enfermoit dans un silence menaçant, il fixoit sur la terre son visage féroce, et ne donnoit point d'essor à sa profonde indignation   De toutes partes cependant les soldats et les peuples accouroient; ils vouloient voir cet homme, jadis si puissant, et la joie universelle éclatoit de toutes partes * * * *   Eccelin étoit d'une petite taille, mais tout l'aspect de sa personne, tous ses mouvemens, indiquoient un soldat.—Son langage étoit amer, son déportement superbe —et par son seul égard, il faisoit trembler les plus hardis."—*Sismondi*, tome iii. p. 219.

Again, "Gizericus (Genseric, king of the Vandals, the conqueror of both Carthage and Rome), staturâ mediocris, et equi casu claudicans, animo profundus, sermone rarus, luxuriæ contemptor, irâ turbidus, habendi cupidus, ad solicitandas gentes providentissimus," &c, &c.—*Jornandes de Rebus Geticis*, c 33

I beg leave to quote these gloomy realities to keep in countenance my Giaour and Corsair.

X.

Slight are the outward signs of evil thought,
Within—within—'twas there the spirit wrought!
Love shows all changes—Hate, Ambition, Guile,
Betray no further than the bitter smile;
The lip's least curl, the lightest paleness thrown
Along the govern'd aspect, speak alone
Of deeper passions; and to judge their mien,
He, who would see, must be himself unseen.
Then—with the hurried tread, the upward eye,
The clenched hand, the pause of agony,
That listens, starting, lest the step too near
Approach intrusive on that mood of fear:
Then—with each feature working from the heart,
With feelings, loosed to strengthen—not depart,
That rise, convulse, contend—that freeze, or glow,
Flush in the cheek, or damp upon the brow;
Then, Stranger! if thou canst, and tremblest not,
Behold his soul—the rest that soothes his lot!
Mark how that lone and blighted bosom sears
The scathing thought of execrated years!
Behold—but who hath seen, or e'er shall see,
Man as himself—the secret spirit free?

XI.

Yet was not Conrad thus by Nature sent
To lead the guilty—guilt's worse instrument—
His soul was changed, before his deeds had driven
Him forth to war with man and forfeit heaven.
Warp'd by the world in Disappointment's school,
In words too wise, in conduct *there* a fool;
Too firm to yield, and far too proud to stoop,
Doom'd by his very virtues for a dupe,
He cursed those virtues as the cause of ill,
And not the traitors who betray'd him still;
Nor deem'd that gifts bestow'd on better men
Had left him joy, and means to give again.
Fear'd, shunn'd, belied, ere youth had lost her force,
He hated man too much to feel remorse,

And thought the voice of wrath a sacred call,
To pay the injuries of some on all.
He knew himself a villain—but he deem'd
The rest no better than the thing he seem'd;
And scorn'd the best as hypocrites who hid ✶
Those deeds the bolder spirit plainly did.
He knew himself detested, but he knew
The hearts that loath'd him, crouch'd and dreaded too.
Lone, wild, and strange, he stood alike exempt
From all affection and from all contempt:
His name could sadden, and his acts surprise;
But they that fear'd him dared not to despise:
Man spurns the worm, but pauses ere he wake
The slumbering venom of the folded snake:
The first may turn, but not avenge the blow;
The last expires, but leaves no living foe;
Fast to the doom'd offender's form it clings,
And he may crush—not conquer—still it stings!

XII.

None are all evil—quickening round his heart,
One softer feeling would not yet depart;
Oft could he sneer at others as beguiled
By passions worthy of a fool or child;
Yet 'gainst that passion vainly still he strove,
And even in him it asks the name of Love!
Yes, it was love—unchangeable—unchanged,
Felt but for one from whom he never ranged;
Though fairest captives daily met his eye,
He shunn'd, nor sought, but coldly pass'd them by;
Though many a beauty droop'd in prison'd bower,
None ever sooth'd his most unguarded hour.
Yes—it was Love—if thoughts of tenderness,
Tried in temptation, strengthen'd by distress,
Unmoved by absence, firm in every clime,
And yet—Oh more than all!—untired by time;
Which nor defeated hope, nor baffled wile,
Could render sullen were she near to smile,
Nor rage could fire, nor sickness fret to vent
On her one murmur of his discontent;

Which still would meet with joy, with calmness part,
Lest that his look of grief should reach her heart;
Which nought removed, nor menaced to remove—
If there be love in mortals—this was love!
He was a villain—ay, reproaches shower
On him—but not the passion, nor its power,
Which only proved, all other virtues gone,
Not guilt itself could quench this loveliest one!

XIII.

He paused a moment—till his hastening men
Pass'd the first winding downward to the glen.
"Strange tidings!—many a peril have I past,
Nor know I why this next appears the last!
Yet so my heart forebodes, but must not fear,
Nor shall my followers find me falter here.
'Tis rash to meet, but surer death to wait
Till here they hunt us to undoubted fate;
And, if my plan but hold, and Fortune smile,
We'll furnish mourners for our funeral-pile.
Ay, let them slumber—peaceful be their dreams!
Morn ne'er awoke them with such brilliant beams
As kindle high to-night (but blow, thou breeze!)
To warm these slow avengers of the seas.
Now to Medora—Oh! my sinking heart,
Long may her own be lighter than thou art!
Yet was I brave—mean boast where all are brave!
Ev'n insects sting for aught they seek to save.
This common courage which with brutes we share,
That owes its deadliest efforts to despair,
Small merit claims—but 'twas my nobler hope
To teach my few with numbers still to cope;
Long have I led them—not to vainly bleed:
No medium now—we perish or succeed;
So let it be—it irks not me to die;
But thus to urge them whence they cannot fly.
My lot hath long had little of my care,
But chafes my pride thus baffled in the snare:
Is this my skill? my craft? to set at last
Hope, power, and life upon a single cast?

Oh, Fate!—accuse thy folly, not thy fate!
She may redeem thee still, nor yet too late."

xiv.

Thus with himself communion held he, till
He reach'd the summit of his tower-crown'd hill:
There at the portal paused—for wild and soft
He heard those accents never heard too oft;
Through the high lattice far yet sweet they rung,
And these the notes his bird of beauty sung:

1

"Deep in my soul that tender secret dwells,
    Lonely and lost to light for evermore,
Save when to thine my heart responsive swells,
    Then trembles into silence as before.

2.

"There, in its centre, a sepulchral lamp
    Burns the slow flame, eternal, but unseen;
Which not the darkness of despair can damp,
    Though vain its ray as it had never been.

3

"Remember me—Oh! pass not thou my grave
    Without one thought whose relics there recline:
The only pang my bosom dare not brave
    Must be to find forgetfulness in thine.

4

"My fondest, faintest, latest accents hear—
    Grief for the dead not virtue can reprove,
Then give me all I ever ask'd—a tear,
    The first—last—sole reward of so much love!"

He pass'd the portal, cross'd the corridor,
And reach'd the chamber as the strain gave o'er:
"My own Medora! sure thy song is sad—"

"In Conrad's absence would'st thou have it glad?

Without thine ear to listen to my lay,
Still must my song my thoughts, my soul betray:
Still must each accent to my bosom suit,
My heart unhush'd, although my lips were mute!
Oh! many a night on this lone couch reclined,
My dreaming fear with storms hath wing'd the wind,
And deem'd the breath that faintly fann'd thy sail
The murmuring prelude of the ruder gale;
Though soft, it seem'd the low prophetic dirge,
That mourn'd thee floating on the savage surge:
Still would I rise to rouse the beacon fire,
Lest spies less true should let the blaze expire;
And many a restless hour outwatch'd each star,
And morning came—and still thou wert afar.
Oh! how the chill blast on my bosom blew,
And day broke dreary on my troubled view,
And still I gazed and gazed—and not a prow
Was granted to my tears, my truth, my vow!
At length 'twas noon—I hail'd and blest the mast
That met my sight—it near'd—Alas! it past!
Another came—Oh God! 'twas thine at last!
Would that those days were over! wilt thou ne'er,
My Conrad! learn the joys of peace to share?
Sure thou hast more than wealth, and many a home
As bright as this invites us not to roam:
Thou know'st it is not peril that I fear,
I only tremble when thou art not here;
Then not for mine, but that far dearer life,
Which flies from love and languishes for strife—
How strange that heart, to me so tender still,
Should war with nature and its better will!" [3]

"Yea, strange indeed—that heart hath long been changed;
Worm-like 'twas trampled, adder-like avenged,
Without one hope on earth beyond thy love,
And scarce a glimpse of mercy from above.

[3] [Lord Byron has made a fine use of the gentleness and submission of the females of these regions, as contrasted with the lordly pride and martial ferocity of the men.
—JEFFREY.]

Yet the same feeling which thou dost condemn,
My very love to thee is hate to them,
So closely mingling here, that disentwined,
I cease to love thee when I love mankind:
Yet dread not this—the proof of all the past
Assures the future that my love will last;
But—Oh, Medora! nerve thy gentler heart;
This hour again—but not for long—we part."
"This hour we part!—my heart foreboded this:
Thus ever fade my fairy dreams of bliss.
This hour—it cannot be—this hour away!
Yon bark hath hardly anchor'd in the bay:
Her consort still is absent, and her crew
Have need of rest before they toil anew:
My love! thou mock'st my weakness; and wouldst steel ·
My breast before the time when it must feel;
But trifle now no more with my distress,
Such mirth hath less of play than bitterness.
Be silent, Conrad!—dearest! come and share
The feast these hands delighted to prepare;
Light toil! to cull and dress thy frugal fare!
See, I have pluck'd the fruit that promised best,
And where not sure, perplex'd, but pleased, I guess'd
At such as seem'd the fairest; thrice the hill
My steps have wound to try the coolest rill;
Yes! thy sherbet to-night will sweetly flow,
See how it sparkles in its vase of snow!
The grapes' gay juice thy bosom never cheers;
Thou more than Moslem when the cup appears:
Think not I mean to chide—for I rejoice
What others deem a penance is thy choice.
But come, the board is spread; our silver lamp
Is trimm'd, and heeds not the sirocco's damp:
Then shall my handmaids while the time along,
And join with me the dance, or wake the song;
Or my guitar, which still thou lov'st to hear,
Shall soothe or lull—or, should it vex thine ear,
We'll turn the tale, by Ariosto told,
Of fair Olympia loved and left of old. •

                              • Orlando Furioso, Canto x.

Why, thou wert worse than he who broke his vow
To that lost damsel, shouldst thou leave me now
Or even that traitor chief—I've seen thee smile,
When the clear sky show'd Ariadne's Isle,
Which I have pointed from these cliffs the while:
And thus half sportive, half in fear, I said,
Lest Time should raise that doubt to more than dread,
Thus Conrad, too, will quit me for the main:
And he deceived me—for he came again!"

"Again, again—and oft again—my love!
If there be life below, and hope above,
He will return—but now, the moments bring
The time of parting with redoubled wing:
The why, the where—what boots it now to tell?
Since all must end in that wild word—farewell!
Yet would I fain—did time allow—disclose—
Fear not—these are no formidable foes;
And here shall watch a more than wonted guard,
For sudden siege and long defence prepared:
Nor be thou lonely, though thy lord's away,
Our matrons and thy handmaids with thee stay;
And this thy comfort—that, when next we meet,
Security shall make repose more sweet.
List!—'tis the bugle!"—Juan shrilly blew—
"One kiss—one more—another—Oh! Adieu!"

She rose—she sprung—she clung to his embrace,
Till his heart heaved beneath her hidden face:
He dared not raise to his that deep-blue eye,
Which downcast droop'd in tearless agony.
Her long fair hair lay floating o'er his arms,
In all the wildness of dishevell'd charms;
Scarce beat that bosom where his image dwelt
So full—*that* feeling seem'd almost unfelt!
Hark—peals the thunder of the signal-gun!
It told 'twas sunset, and he cursed that sun.
Again—again—that form he madly press'd,
Which mutely clasp'd, imploringly caress'd!

And tottering to the couch his bride he bore,
One moment gazed, as if to gaze no more;
Felt that for him earth held but her alone,
Kiss'd her cold forehead—turn'd—is Conrad gone?

XV.

" And is he gone?"—on sudden solitude
How oft that fearful question will intrude!
" 'Twas but an instant past, and here he stood!
And now"—without the portal's porch she rush'd,
And then at length her tears in freedom gush'd;
Big, bright, and fast, unknown to her they fell;
But still her lips refused to send—" Farewell!"
For in that word—that fatal word—howe'er
We promise, hope, believe, there breathes despair.
O'er every feature of that still, pale face,
Had sorrow fix'd what time can ne'er erase:
The tender blue of that large loving eye
Grew frozen with its gaze on vacancy,
Till—Oh, how far!—it caught a glimpse of him,
And then it flow'd, and phrensied seem'd to swim
Through those long, dark, and glistening lashes dew'd
With drops of sadness oft to be renew'd.
" He's gone!"—against her heart that hand is driven,
Convulsed and quick—then gently raised to heaven:
She look'd and saw the heaving of the main;
The white sail set—she dared not look again;
But turn'd with sickening soul within the gate—
" It is no dream—and I am desolate!"

XVI.

From crag to crag descending, swiftly sped
Stern Conrad down, nor once he turn'd his head;
But shrunk whene'er the windings of his way
Forced on his eye what he would not survey,
His lone, but lovely dwelling on the steep,
That hail'd him first when homeward from the deep:
And she—the dim and melancholy star,
Whose ray of beauty reach'd him from afar,

On her he must not gaze, he must not think,
There he might rest—but on Destruction's brink:
Yet once almost he stopp'd, and nearly gave
His fate to chance, his projects to the wave:
But no—it must not be—a worthy chief
May melt, but not betray to woman's grief.
He sees his bark, he notes how fair the wind,
And sternly gathers all his might of mind:
Again he hurries on—and as he hears
The clang of tumult vibrate on his ears,
The busy sounds, the bustle of the shore,
The shout, the signal, and the dashing oar;
As marks his eye the seaboy on the mast,
The anchors rise, the sails unfurling fast,
The waving kerchiefs of the crowd that urge
That mute adieu to those who stem the surge;
And more than all, his blood-red flag aloft,
He marvell'd how his heart could seem so soft.
Fire in his glance, and wildness in his breast,
He feels of all his former self possest;
He bounds—he flies—until his footsteps reach
The verge where ends the cliff, begins the beach,
There checks his speed; but pauses less to breathe
The breezy freshness of the deep beneath,
Than there his wonted statelier step renew;
Nor rush, disturb'd by haste, to vulgar view:
For well had Conrad learn'd to curb the crowd,
By arts that veil, and oft preserve the proud;
His was the lofty port, the distant mien,
That seems to shun the sight—and awes if seen:
The solemn aspect, and the high-born eye,
That checks low mirth, but lacks not courtesy;
All these he wielded to command assent:
But where he wish'd to win, so well unbent,
That kindness cancell'd fear in those who heard,
And others' gifts show'd mean beside his word,
When echo'd to the heart as from his own
His deep yet tender melody of tone:
But such was foreign to his wonted mood,
He cared not what he soften'd, but subdued;

The evil passions of his youth had made
Him value less who loved—than what obey'd.

XVII.

Around him mustering ranged his ready guard.
Before him Juan stands—"Are all prepared?"

"They are—nay more—embark'd: the latest boat
Waits but my chief ——"
                              "My sword, and my capote."
Soon firmly girded on, and lightly slung,
His belt and cloak were o'er his shoulders flung:
"Call Pedro here!"   He comes—and Conrad bends,
With all the courtesy he deign'd his friends;
"Receive these tablets, and peruse with care,
Words of high trust and truth are graven there;
Double the guard, and when Anselmo's bark
Arrives, let him alike these orders mark:
In three days (serve the breeze) the sun shall shine
On our return—till then all peace be thine!"
This said, his brother Pirate's hand he wrung,
Then to his boat with haughty gesture sprung.
Flash'd the dipt oars, and sparkling with the stroke,
Around the waves' phosphoric[5] brightness broke;
They gain the vessel—on the deck he stands,—
Shrieks the shrill whistle, ply the busy hands—
He marks how well the ship her helm obeys,
How gallant all her crew, and deigns to praise.
His eyes of pride to young Gonsalvo turn—
Why doth he start, and inly seem to mourn?
Alas! those eyes beheld his rocky tower,
And live a moment o'er the parting hour;
She—his Medora—did she mark the prow?
Ah! never loved he half so much as now!
But much must yet be done ere dawn of day—
Again he mans himself and turns away;
Down to the cabin with Gonsalvo bends,
And there unfolds his plan, his means, and ends;

---

[5] By night, particularly in a warm latitude, every stroke of the oar, every motion of the boat or ship, is followed by a slight flash like sheet lightning from the water.

Before them burns the lamp, and spreads the chart,
And all that speaks and aids the naval art;
They to the midnight watch protract debate;
To anxious eyes what hour is ever late?
Meantime, the steady breeze serenely blew,
And fast and falcon-like the vessel flew;
Pass'd the high headlands of each clustering isle,
To gain their port—long—long ere morning smile:
And soon the night-glass through the narrow bay
Discovers where the Pacha's galleys lay.
Count they each sail, and mark how there supine
The lights in vain o'er heedless Moslem shine.
Secure, unnoted, Conrad's prow pass'd by,
And anchor'd where his ambush meant to lie;
Screen'd from espial by the jutting cape,
That rears on high its rude fantastic shape.
Then rose his band to duty—not from sleep—
Equipp'd for deeds alike on land or deep;
While lean'd their leader o'er the fretting flood,
And calmly talk'd—and yet he talk'd of blood!

CANTO THE SECOND.

———◆———

"Conosceste i dubiosi desiri?"—DANTE.

I.

In Coron's bay floats many a galley light,
Through Coron's lattices the lamps are bright,
For Seyd, the Pacha, makes a feast to-night.
A feast for promised triumph yet to come,
When he shall drag the fetter'd Rovers home;
This hath he sworn by Alla and his sword,
And faithful to his firman and his word,
His summon'd prows collect along the coast,
And great the gathering crews, and loud the boast;
Already shared the captives and the prize,
Though far the distant foe they thus despise;
'Tis but to sail—no doubt to-morrow's Sun
Will see the Pirates bound, their haven won!
Meantime the watch may slumber, if they will,
Nor only wake to war, but dreaming kill.
Though all, who can, disperse on shore and seek
To flesh their glowing valour on the Greek;
How well such deed becomes the turban'd brave—
To bare the sabre's edge before a slave!
Infest his dwelling—but forbear to slay,
Their arms are strong, yet merciful to-day,
And do not deign to smite because they may!
Unless some gay caprice suggests the blow,
To keep in practice for the coming foe.
Revel and rout the evening hours beguile,
And they who wish to wear a head must smile;
For Moslem mouths produce their choicest cheer,
And hoard their curses, till the coast is clear.

II.

High in his hall reclines the turban'd Seyd;
Around—the bearded chiefs he came to lead.
Removed the banquet, and the last pilaff—
Forbidden draughts, 'tis said, he dared to quaff,
Though to the rest the sober berry's juice[1]
The slaves bear round for rigid Moslems' use;
The long chibouque's[2] dissolving cloud supply,
While dance the Almas[3] to wild minstrelsy.
The rising morn will view the chiefs embark;
But waves are somewhat treacherous in the dark:
And revellers may more securely sleep
On silken couch than o'er the rugged deep:
Feast there who can—nor combat till they must,
And less to conquest than to Korans trust;
And yet the numbers crowded in his host
Might warrant more than even the Pacha's boast.

III.

With cautious reverence from the outer gate
Slow stalks the slave, whose office there to wait,
Bows his bent head, his hand salutes the floor,
Ere yet his tongue the trusted tidings bore:
" A captive Dervise, from the pirate's nest
Escaped, is here—himself would tell the rest."[4]
He took the sign from Seyd's assenting eye,
And led the holy man in silence nigh.
His arms were folded on his dark-green vest,
His step was feeble, and his look deprest;
Yet worn he seem'd of hardship more than years,
And pale his cheek with penance, not from fears.

---

[1] Coffee.   [2] "Chibouque," pipe.
[3] Dancing girls.
[4] It has been observed, that Conrad's entering disguised as a spy is out of nature.
Perhaps so. I find something not unlike it in history —" Anxious to explore with
his own eyes the state of the Vandals, Majorian ventured, after disguising the colour
of his hair, to visit Carthage in the character of his own ambassador, and Genseric
was afterwards mortified by the discovery, that he had entertained and dismissed the
Emperor of the Romans. Such an anecdote may be rejected as an improbable fiction;
but it is a fiction which would not have been imagined unless in the life of a hero."--
See GIBBON's Decline and Fall, vol vi. p. 180.

Vow'd to his God—his sable locks he wore,
And these his lofty cap rose proudly o'er:
Around his form his loose long robe was thrown,
And wrapt a breast bestow'd on heaven alone;
Submissive, yet with self-possession mann'd,
He calmly met the curious eyes that scann'd;
And question of his coming fain would seek,
Before the Pacha's will allow'd to speak.

IV.

"Whence com'st thou, Dervise?"

"From the outlaw's den,
A fugitive—"

"Thy capture where and when?"
"From Scalanovo's port to Scio's isle,
The Saick was bound; but Alla did not smile
Upon our course—the Moslem merchant's gains
The Rovers won; our limbs have worn their chains.
I had no death to fear, nor wealth to boast,
Beyond the wandering freedom which I lost;
At length a fisher's humble boat by night
Afforded hope, and offer'd chance of flight;
I seized the hour, and find my safety here—
With thee—most mighty Pacha! who can fear?"

"How speed the outlaws? stand they well prepared,
Their plunder'd wealth, and robber's rock, to guard?
Dream they of this our preparation, doom'd
To view with fire their scorpion nest consumed?"

"Pacha! the fetter'd captive's mourning eye,
That weeps for flight, but ill can play the spy;
I only heard the reckless waters roar,
Those waves that would not bear me from the shore;
I only mark'd the glorious sun and sky,
Too bright, too blue, for my captivity;
And felt that all which Freedom's bosom cheers
Must break my chain before it dried my tears.
This mayst thou judge, at least, from my escape,
They little deem of aught in peril's shape;

Else vainly had I pray'd or sought the chance
That leads me here—if eyed with vigilance:
The careless guard that did not see me fly,
May watch as idly when thy power is nigh.
Pacha! my limbs are faint—and nature craves
Food for my hunger, rest from tossing waves:
Permit my absence—peace be with thee! Peace
With all around!—now grant repose—release."

"Stay, Dervise! I have more to question—stay,
I do command thee—sit—dost hear?—obey!
More I must ask, and food the slaves shall bring;
Thou shalt not pine where all are banqueting:
The supper done—prepare thee to reply,
Clearly and full—I love not mystery."
'Twere vain to guess what shook the pious man,
Who look'd not lovingly on that Divan;
Nor show'd high relish for the banquet prest,
And less respect for every fellow guest.
'Twas but a moment's peevish hectic past
Along his cheek, and tranquillised as fast
He sate him down in silence, and his look
Resumed the calmness which before forsook:
The feast was usher'd in, but sumptuous fare
He shunn'd as if some poison mingled there.
For one so long condemn'd to toil and fast,
Methinks he strangely spares the rich repast.

"What ails thee, Dervise? eat—dost thou suppose
This feast a Christian's? or my friends thy foes?
Why dost thou shun the salt? that sacred pledge,
Which, once partaken, blunts the sabre's edge,
Makes ev'n contending tribes in peace unite,
And hated hosts seem brethren to the sight!"

"Salt seasons dainties—and my food is still
The humblest root, my drink the simplest rill;
And my stern vow and order's⁵ laws oppose

---

⁵ The Dervises are in colleges, and of different orders, as the monks.

To break or mingle bread with friends or foes;
It may seem strange—if there be aught to dread
That peril rests upon my single head;
But for thy sway—nay more—thy Sultan's throne,
I taste nor bread nor banquet—save alone;
Infringed our order's rule, the Prophet's rage
To Mecca's dome might bar my pilgrimage."

" Well—as thou wilt—ascetic as thou art—
One question answer; then in peace depart.
How many?—Ha! it cannot sure be day?
What star—what sun is bursting on the bay?
It shines a lake of fire!—away—away!
Ho! treachery! my guards! my scimitar!
The galleys feed the flames—and I afar!
Accursed Dervise!—these thy tidings—thou
Some villain spy—seize—cleave him—slay him now!"

Up rose the Dervise with that burst of light,
Nor less his change of form appall'd the sight:
Up rose that Dervise—not in saintly garb,
But like a warrior bounding on his barb,
Dash'd his high cap, and tore his robe away—
Shone his mail'd breast, and flash'd his sabre's ray;
His close but glittering casque, and sable plume,
More glittering eye, and black brow's sabler gloom,
Glared on the Moslems' eyes some Afrit sprite,
Whose demon death-blow left no hope for fight.
The wild confusion, and the swarthy glow
Of flames on high, and torches from below;
The shriek of terror, and the mingling yell—
For swords began to clash, and shouts to swell—
Flung o'er that spot of earth the air of hell!
Distracted, to and fro, the flying slaves
Behold but bloody shore and fiery waves;
Nought heeded they the Pacha's angry cry,
They seize that Dervise!—seize on Zatanai![6]
He saw their terror—check'd the first despair
That urged him but to stand and perish there,

[6] "Zatanai," Satan.

Since far too early and too well obey'd,
The flame was kindled ere the signal made ;
He saw their terror—from his baldric drew
His bugle—brief the blast—but shrilly blew ;
'Tis answer'd—" Well ye speed, my gallant crew !
Why did I doubt their quickness of career ?
And deem design had left me single here ? "
Sweeps his long arm—that sabre's whirling sway
Sheds fast atonement for its first delay ;
Completes his fury, what their fear begun,
And makes the many basely quail to one.
The cloven turbans o'er the chamber spread,
And scarce an arm dare rise to guard its head :
Even Seyd, convulsed, o'erwhelm'd, with rage, surprise,
Retreats before him, though he still defies.
No craven he—and yet he dreads the blow,
So much Confusion magnifies his foe !
His blazing galleys still distract his sight,
He tore his beard, and foaming fled the fight ; [7]
For now the pirates pass'd the Haram gate,
And burst within—and it were death to wait ;
Where wild Amazement shrieking—kneeling throws
The sword aside—in vain—the blood o'erflows !
The Corsairs pouring, haste to where within
Invited Conrad's bugle, and the din
Of groaning victims, and wild cries for life,
Proclaim'd how well he did the work of strife.
They shout to find him grim and lonely there,
A glutted tiger mangling in his lair !
But short their greeting, shorter his reply—
" 'Tis well—but Seyd escapes, and he must die—
Much hath been done, but more remains to do—
Their galleys blaze—why not their city too ?"

v.

Quick at the word they seized him each a torch,
And fire the dome from minaret to porch.

---

[7] A common and not very novel effect of Mussulman anger. See Prince Eugene's Memoirs, page 24. "The Seraskier received a wound in the thigh, he plucked up his beard by the roots, because he was obliged to quit the field."

A stern delight was fix'd in Conrad's eye,
But sudden sunk—for on his ear the cry
Of women struck, and like a deadly knell
Knock'd at that heart unmoved by battle's yell.
"Oh ! burst the Haram—wrong not on your lives
One female form—remember—*we* have wives.
On them such outrage Vengeance will repay ;
Man is our foe, and such 'tis ours to slay :
But still we spared—must spare the weaker prey.
Oh ! I forgot—but Heaven will not forgive
If at my word the helpless cease to live ;
Follow who will—I go—we yet have time
Our souls to lighten of at least a crime."
He climbs the crackling stair, he bursts the door,
Nor feels his feet glow scorching with the floor ;
His breath choked gasping with the volumed smoke,
But still from room to room his way he broke.
They search—they find—they save : with lusty arms
Each bears a prize of unregarded charms ;
Calm their loud fears · sustain their sinking frames
With all the care defenceless beauty claims :
So well could Conrad tame their fiercest mood,
And check the very hands with gore imbrued.
But who is she ? whom Conrad's arms convey,
From reeking pile and combat's wreck, away—
Who but the love of him he dooms to bleed ?
The Haram queen—but still the slave of Seyd !

VI.

Brief time had Conrad now to greet Gulnare,[8]
Few words to re-assure the trembling fair ;
For in that pause compassion snatch'd from war,
The foe before retiring, fast and far,
With wonder saw their footsteps unpursued,
First slowlier fled—then rallied—then withstood.
This Seyd perceives, then first perceives how few,
Compared with his, the Corsair's roving crew,

---

[8] Gulnare, a female name , it means, literally, the flower of the pomegranate.

And blushes o'er his error, as he eyes
The ruin wrought by panic and surprise.
Alla il Alla! Vengeance swells the cry—
Shame mounts to rage that must atone or die!
And flame for flame and blood for blood must tell,
The tide of triumph ebbs that flow'd too well—
When wrath returns to renovated strife,
And those who fought for conquest strike for life.
Conrad beheld the danger—he beheld
His followers faint by freshening foes repell'd :
" One effort—one—to break the circling host ! "
They form—unite—charge—waver—all is lost !
Within a narrower ring compress'd, beset,
Hopeless, not heartless, strive and struggle yet—
Ah! now they fight in firmest file no more,   ·
Hemm'd in, cut off, cleft down, and trampled o'er ;
But each strikes singly, silently, and home,
And sinks outwearied rather than o'ercome,
His last faint quittance rendering with his breath,
Till the blade glimmers in the grasp of death !

VII.

But first, ere came the rallying host to blows,
And rank to rank, and hand to hand oppose,
Gulnare and all her Haram handmaids freed,
Safe in the dome of one who held their creed,
By Conrad's mandate safely were bestow'd,
And dried those tears for life and fame that flow'd :
And when that dark-eyed lady, young Gulnare,
Recall'd those thoughts late wandering in despair,
Much did she marvel o'er the courtesy
That smooth'd his accents ; soften'd in his eye :
'Twas strange—*that* robber thus with gore bedew'd,
Seem'd gentler then than Seyd in fondest mood.
The Pacha woo'd as if he deem'd the slave
Must seem delighted with the heart he gave ;
The Corsair vow'd protection, soothed affright,
As if his homage were a woman's right.
" The wish is wrong—nay, worse for female—vain :
Yet much I long to view that chief again ;

If but to thank for, what my fear forgot,
The life—my loving lord remember'd not!"

VIII.

And him she saw, where thickest carnage spread,
But gather'd breathing from the happier dead;
Far from his band, and battling with a host
That deem right dearly won the field he lost,
Fell'd, bleeding—baffled of the death he sought,
And snatch'd to expiate all the ills he wrought;
Preserved to linger and to live in vain,
While Vengeance ponder'd o'er new plans of pain,
And stanch'd the blood she saves to shed again—
But drop for drop, for Seyd's unglutted eye
Would doom him ever dying—ne'er to die!
Can this be he? triumphant late she saw,
When his red hand's wild gesture waved, a law!
'Tis he indeed—disarm'd but undeprest,
His sole regret the life he still possest;
His wounds too slight, though taken with that will,
Which would have kiss'd the hand that then could kill.
Oh were there none, of all the many given,
To send his soul—he scarcely ask'd to heaven?
Must he alone of all retain his breath,
Who more than all had striven and struck for death?
He deeply felt—what mortal hearts must feel,
When thus reversed on faithless fortune's wheel,
For crimes committed, and the victor's threat
Of lingering tortures to repay the debt—
He deeply, darkly felt; but evil pride
That led to perpetrate, now serves to hide.
Still in his stern and self-collected mien
A conqueror's more than captive's air is seen,
Though faint with wasting toil and stiffening wound,
But few that saw—so calmly gazed around:
Though the far shouting of the distant crowd,
Their tremors o'er, rose insolently loud,
The better warriors who beheld him near,
Insulted not the foe who taught them fear;

And the grim guards that to his durance led,
In silence eyed him with a secret dread.

IX

The Leech was sent—but not in mercy—there,
To note how much the life yet left could bear;
He found enough to load with heaviest chain,
And promise feeling for the wrench of pain;
To-morrow—yea—to-morrow's evening sun
Will sinking see impalement's pangs begun,
And rising with the wonted blush of morn
Behold how well or ill those pangs are borne.
Of torments this the longest and the worst,
Which adds all other agony to thirst,
That day by day death still forbears to slake,
While famish'd vultures flit around the stake.
"Oh! water—water!"—smiling Hate denies
The victim's prayer, for if he drinks he dies.
This was his doom;—the Leech, the guard, were gone,
And left proud Conrad fetter'd and alone.

X.

'Twere vain to paint to what his feelings grew—
It even were doubtful if their victim knew.
There is a war, a chaos of the mind,
When all its elements convulsed, combined
Lie dark and jarring with perturbed force,
And gnashing with impenitent Remorse—
That juggling fiend, who never spake before,
But cries "I warn'd thee!" when the deed is o'er.
Vain voice! the spirit burning but unbent,
May writhe, rebel—the weak alone repent!
Even in that lonely hour when most it feels,
And, to itself, all, all that self reveals,—
No single passion, and no ruling thought
That leaves the rest, as once, unseen, unsought,
But the wild prospect when the soul reviews,
All rushing through their thousand avenues.
Ambition's dreams expiring, love's regret,
Endanger'd glory, life itself beset;

The joy untasted, the contempt or hate
'Gainst those who fain would triumph in our fate;
The hopeless past, the hasting future driven
Too quickly on to guess if hell or heaven;
Deeds, thoughts, and words, perhaps remember'd not
So keenly till that hour, but ne'er forgot;
Things light or lovely in their acted time,
But now to stern reflection each a crime;
The withering sense of evil unreveal'd,
Not cankering less because the more conceal'd—
All, in a word, from which all eyes must start,
That opening sepulchre—the naked heart
Bares with its buried woes, till Pride awake,
To snatch the mirror from the soul—and break.
Ay, Pride can veil, and Courage brave it all—
All—all—before—beyond—the deadliest fall.
Each hath some fear, and he who least betrays,
The only hypocrite deserving praise:
Not the loud recreant wretch who boasts and flies;
But he who looks on death—and silent dies.
So, steel'd by pondering o'er his far career,
He half-way meets him should he menace near!

XI

In the high chamber of his highest tower
Sate Conrad, fetter'd in the Pacha's power.
His palace perish'd in the flame—this fort
Contain'd at once his captive and his court.
Not much could Conrad of his sentence blame,
His foe, if vanquish'd, had but shared the same:—
Alone he sate—in solitude had scann'd
His guilty bosom, but that breast he mann'd:
One thought alone he could not—dared not meet—
"Oh, how these tidings will Medora greet?"
Then—only then—his clanking hands he raised,
And strain'd with rage the chain on which he gazed;
But soon he found, or feign'd, or dream'd relief,
And smiled in self-derision of his grief,
"And now come torture when it will—or may,
More need of rest to nerve me for the day!"

This said, with languor to his mat he crept,
And, whatsoe'er his visions, quickly slept.
'Twas hardly midnight when that fray begun,
For Conrad's plans matured, at once were done
And Havoc loathes so much the waste of time,
She scarce had left an uncommitted crime.
One hour beheld him since the tide he stemm'd—
Disguised, discover'd, conquering, ta'en, condemn'd—
A chief on land, an outlaw on the deep—
Destroying, saving, prison'd, and asleep!

XII.

He slept in calmest seeming, for his breath
Was hush'd so deep—Ah! happy if in death!
He slept—Who o'er his placid slumber bends?
His foes are gone, and here he hath no friends;
Is it some seraph sent to grant him grace?
No, 'tis an earthly form with heavenly face!
Its white arm raised a lamp—yet gently hid,
Lest the ray flash abruptly on the lid
Of that closed eye, which opens but to pain,
And once unclosed—but once may close again.
That form, with eye so dark, and cheek so fair,
And auburn waves of gemm'd and braided hair;
With shape of fairy lightness—naked foot,
That shines like snow, and falls on earth as mute—
Through guards and dunnest night how came it there?
Ah! rather ask what will not woman dare?
Whom youth and pity lead like thee, Gulnare!
She could not sleep—and while the Pacha's rest
In muttering dreams yet saw his pirate-guest,
She left his side—his signet-ring she bore,
Which oft in sport adorn'd her hand before—
And with it, scarcely question'd, won her way
Through drowsy guards that must that sign obey.
Worn out with toil, and tired with changing blows,
Their eyes had envied Conrad his repose;
And chill and nodding at the turret door,
They stretch their listless limbs, and watch no more;

Just raised their heads to hail the signet-ring,
Nor ask or what or who the sign may bring.

XIII

She gazed in wonder, "Can he calmly sleep,
While other eyes his fall or ravage weep ?
And mine in restlessness are wandering here—
What sudden spell hath made this man so dear?
True—'tis to him my life, and more, I owe,
And me and mine he spared from worse than woe:
'Tis late to think—but soft, his slumber breaks—
How heavily he sighs!—he starts—awakes!"

He raised his head, and dazzled with the light,
His eye seem'd dubious if it saw aright :
He moved his hand—the grating of his chain
Too harshly told him that he lived again
" What is that form? if not a shape of air,
Methinks, my jailor's face shows wondrous fair!"

" Pirate! thou know'st me not—but I am one,
Grateful for deeds thou hast too rarely done;
Look on me—and remember her, thy hand
Snatch'd from the flames, and thy more fearful band.
I come through darkness—and I scarce know why—
Yet not to hurt—I would not see thee die."

" If so, kind lady! thine the only eye
That would not here in that gay hope delight ·
Theirs is the chance—and let them use their right.
But still I thank their courtesy or thine,
That would confess me at so fair a shrine!"

Strange though it seem—yet with extremest grief
Is link'd a mirth—it doth not bring relief—
That playfulness of Sorrow ne'er beguiles,
And smiles in bitterness—but still it smiles;

K 2

And sometimes with the wisest and the best,
Till even the scaffold * echoes with their jest!
Yet not the joy to which it seems akin—
It may deceive all hearts, save that within.
Whate'er it was that flash'd on Conrad, now
A laughing wildness half unbent his brow:
And these his accents had a sound of mirth,
As if the last he could enjoy on earth;
Yet 'gainst his nature—for through that short life,
Few thoughts had he to spare from gloom and strife.

                                XIV.

"Corsair! thy doom is named—but I have power
To soothe the Pacha in his weaker hour.
Thee would I spare—nay more—would save thee now,
But this—time—hope—nor even thy strength allow;
But all I can, I will: at least, delay
The sentence that remits thee scarce a day.
More now were ruin—even thyself were loth
The vain attempt should bring but doom to both."

" Yes! loth indeed:—my soul is nerved to all,
Or fall'n too low to fear a further fall:
Tempt not thyself with peril—me with hope
Of flight from foes with whom I could not cope:
Unfit to vanquish shall I meanly fly,
The one of all my band that would not die?
Yet there is one to whom my memory clings,
Till to these eyes her own wild softness springs.
My sole resources in the path I trod
Were these—my bark, my sword, my love, my God!
The last I left in youth!—he leaves me now—
And Man but works his will to lay me low.
I have no thought to mock his throne with prayer

---

* In Sir Thomas More, for instance, on the scaffold, and Anne Boleyn, in the Tower,
when, grasping her neck, she remarked, that it "was too slender to trouble the
headsman much." During one part of the French Revolution, it became a fashion to
leave some " mot " as a legacy; and the quantity of facetious last words spoken during
that period would form a melancholy jest-book of a considerable size.

Wrung from the coward crouching of despair;
It is enough—I breathe, and I can bear.
My sword is shaken from the worthless hand
That might have better kept so true a brand;
My bark is sunk or captive—but my love—
For her in sooth my voice would mount above:
Oh! she is all that still to earth can bind—
And this will break a heart so more than kind,
And blight a form—till thine appear'd, Gulnare!
Mine eye ne'er ask'd if others were as fair."

"Thou lov'st another then?—but what to me
Is this—'tis nothing—nothing e'er can be:
But yet—thou lov'st—and—Oh! I envy those
Whose hearts on hearts as faithful can repose,
Who never feel the void—the wandering thought
That sighs o'er visions—such as mine hath wrought."

"Lady, methought thy love was his, for whom
This arm redeem'd thee from a fiery tomb."

"My love stern Seyd's! Oh—No—No—not my love—
Yet much this heart, that strives no more, once strove
To meet his passion—but it would not be.
I felt—I feel—love dwells with—with the free.
I am a slave, a favour'd slave at best,
To share his splendour, and seem very blest!
Oft must my soul the question undergo,
Of—'Dost thou love?' and burn to answer, 'No!'
Oh! hard it is that fondness to sustain,
And struggle not to feel averse in vain;
But harder still the heart's recoil to bear,
And hide from one—perhaps another there.
He takes the hand I give not, nor withhold—
Its pulse nor check'd nor quicken'd—calmly cold:
And when resign'd, it drops a lifeless weight
From one I never loved enough to hate.
No warmth these lips return by his imprest,
And chill'd remembrance shudders o'er the rest.

Yes—had I ever proved that passion's zeal,
The change to hatred were at least to feel:
But still he goes unmourn'd, returns unsought,
And oft when present—absent from my thought.
Or when reflection comes—and come it must—
I fear that henceforth 'twill but bring disgust;
I am his slave—but, in despite of pride,
'Twere worse than bondage to become his bride.
Oh! that this dotage of his breast would cease!
Or seek another and give mine release,
But yesterday—I could have said, to peace!
Yes, if unwonted fondness now I feign,
Remember captive! 'tis to break thy chain;
Repay the life that to thy hand I owe;
To give thee back to all endear'd below,
Who share such love as I can never know.
Farewell, morn breaks, and I must now away:
'Twill cost me dear—but dread no death to-day!"

xv.

She press'd his fetter'd fingers to her heart,
And bow'd her head, and turn'd her to depart,
And noiseless as a lovely dream is gone.
And was she here? and is he now alone?
What gem hath dropp'd and sparkles o'er his chain?
The tear most sacred, shed for others' pain,
That starts at once—bright—pure—from Pity's mine,
Already polish'd by the hand divine!
Oh! too convincing—dangerously dear—
In woman's eye the unanswerable tear!
That weapon of her weakness she can wield,
To save, subdue—at once her spear and shield:
Avoid it—Virtue ebbs and Wisdom errs,
Too fondly gazing on that grief of hers!
What lost a world, and bade a hero fly?
The timid tear in Cleopatra's eye.
Yet be the soft triumvir's fault forgiven;
By this—how many lose not earth—but heaven!
Consign their souls to man's eternal foe,
And seal their own to spare some wanton's woe!

XVI.

'Tis morn, and o'er his alter'd features play
The beams—without the hope of yesterday.
What shall he be ere night? perchance a thing
O'er which the raven flaps her funeral wing,
By his closed eye unheeded and unfelt;
While sets that sun, and dews of evening melt,
Chill, wet, and misty round each stiffen'd limb,
Refreshing earth—reviving all but him!

CANTO THE THIRD.

I.

SLOW sinks, more lovely ere his race be run,[1]
Along Morea's hills the setting sun;
Not, as in Northern climes, obscurely bright,
But one unclouded blaze of living light!
O'er the hush'd deep the yellow beam he throws,
Gilds the green wave, that trembles as it glows.
On old Ægina's rock, and Idra's isle,
The god of gladness sheds his parting smile;
O'er his own regions lingering, loves to shine,
Though there his altars are no moré divine.
Descending fast the mountain shadows kiss
Thy glorious gulf, unconquered Salamis!
Their azure arches through the long expanse
More deeply purpled met his mellowing glance,
And tenderest tints, along their summits driven,
Mark his gay course, and own the hues of heaven;
Till, darkly shaded from the land and deep,
Behind his Delphian cliff he sinks to sleep.

On such an eve, his palest beam he cast,
When—Athens! here thy Wisest look'd his last.

---

[1] The opening lines, as far as section ii., have, perhaps, little business here, and were annexed to an unpublished (though printed) poem, ["The Curse of Minerva,"]; but they were written on the spot, in the Spring of 1811, and—I scarce know why—the reader must excuse their appearance here—if he can.

How watch'd thy better sons his farewell ray,
That closed their murder'd sage's[2] latest day !
Not yet—not yet—Sol pauses on the hill—
The precious hour of parting lingers still ;
But sad his light to agonising eyes,
And dark the mountain's once delightful dyes
Gloom o'er the lovely land he seem'd to pour,
The land, where Phœbus never frown'd before ;
But ere he sunk below Cithæron's head,
The cup of woe was quaff'd—the spirit fled ;
The soul of him who scorn'd to fear or fly—
Who lived and died, as none can live or die !

But lo ! from high Hymettus to the plain,
The queen of night asserts her silent reign.[3]
No murky vapour, herald of the storm,
Hides her fair face, nor girds her glowing form ;
With cornice glimmering as the moon-beams play,
There the white column greets her grateful ray,
And bright around with quivering beams beset,
Her emblem sparkles o'er the minaret :
The groves of olive scatter'd dark and wide
Where meek Cephisus pours his scanty tide,
The cypress saddening by the sacred mosque,
The gleaming turret of the gay kiosk,[4]
And, dun and sombre 'mid the holy calm,
Near Theseus' fane yon solitary palm,
All tinged with varied hues arrest the eye—
And dull were his that pass'd them heedless by.

Again the Ægean, heard no more afar.
Lulls his chafed breast from elemental war ;
Again his waves in milder tints unfold
Their long array of sapphire and of gold,

[2] Socrates drank the hemlock a short time before sunset (the hour of execution),
notwithstanding the entreaties of his disciples to wait till the sun went down.
[3] The twilight in Greece is much shorter than in our own country the days in
winter are longer, but in summer of shorter duration
[4] The Kiosk is a Turkish summer house · the palm is without the present walls of
Athens, not far from the temple of Theseus, between which and the tree, the wall
intervenes —·Cephisus' stream is indeed scanty, and Ilissus has no stream at all.

Mix'd with the shades of many a distant isle,
That frown—where gentler ocean seems to smile.[*]

II.

Not now my theme—why turn my thoughts to thee?
Oh! who can look along thy native sea,
Nor dwell upon thy name, whate'er the tale,
So much its magic must o'er all prevail?
Who that beheld that Sun upon thee set,
Fair Athens! could thine evening face forget?
Not he—whose heart nor time nor distance frees,
Spell-bound within the clustering Cyclades!
Nor seems this homage foreign to its strain,
His Corsair's isle was once thine own domain—
Would that with freedom it were thine again!

III.

The Sun hath sunk—and, darker than the night,
Sinks with its beam upon the beacon height
Medora's heart—the third day's come and gone—
With it he comes not—sends not—faithless one!
The wind was fair though light; and storms were none.
Last eve Anselmo's bark return'd, and yet
His only tidings that they had not met!
Though wild, as now, far different were the tale
Had Conrad waited for that single sail.

The night-breeze freshens—she that day had pass'd
In watching all that Hope proclaim'd a mast;
Sadly she sate on high—Impatience bore
At last her footsteps to the midnight shore,
And there she wander'd, heedless of the spray
That dash'd her garments oft, and warn'd away:

[*] [Of the brilliant skies and variegated landscapes of Greece every one has formed to himself a general notion, from having contemplated them through the hazy atmosphere of some prose narration, but, in Lord Byron's poetry, every image is distinct and glowing, as if it were illuminated by its native sunshine, and in the figures which people the landscape we behold, not only the general form and costume, but the countenance, and the attitude, and the play of features and of gesture accompanying, and indicating, the sudden impulses of momentary feelings.—GEORGE ELLIS]

She saw not, felt not this—nor dared depart,
Nor deem'd it cold—her chill was at her heart;
Till grew such certainty from that suspense—
His very Sight had shock'd from life or sense!

It came at last—a sad and shatter'd boat,
Whose inmates first beheld whom first they sought;
Some bleeding—all most wretched—these the few—
Scarce knew they how escaped—*this* all they knew.
In silence, darkling, each appear'd to wait
His fellow's mournful guess at Conrad's fate :
Something they would have said; but seem'd to fear
To trust their accents to Medora's ear.
She saw at once, yet sunk not—trembled not—
Beneath that grief, that loneliness of lot,
Within that meek fair form, were feelings high,
That deem'd not till they found their energy.
While yet was Hope they soften'd, flutter'd, wept—
All lost—that softness died not—but it slept;
And o'er its slumber rose that Strength which said,
" With nothing left to love, there's nought to dread."
'Tis more than nature's; like the burning might
Delirium gathers from the fever's height.

" Silent you stand—nor would I hear you tell
What—speak not—breathe not—for I know it well—
Yet would I ask—almost my lip denies
The—quick your answer—tell me where he lies."

" Lady ! we know not—scarce with life we fled;
But here is one denies that he is dead :
He saw him bound; and bleeding—but alive."

She heard no further—'twas in vain to strive—
So throbb'd each vein—each thought—till then withstood.
Her own dark soul—these words at once subdued :
She totters—falls—and senseless had the wave
Perchance but snatch'd her from another grave;
But that with hands though rude, yet weeping eyes,
They yield such aid as Pity's haste supplies :

Dash o'er her deathlike cheek the ocean dew,
Raise, fan, sustain—till life returns anew;
Awake her handmaids, with the matrons leave
That fainting form o'er which they gaze and grieve;
Then seek Anselmo's cavern, to report
The tale too tedious—when the triumph short.

IV.

In that wild council words wax'd warm and strange,
With thoughts of ransom, rescue, and revenge;
All, save repose or flight: still lingering there
Breathed Conrad's spirit, and forbade despair;
Whate'er his fate—the breasts he form'd and led
Will save him living, or appease him dead.
Woe to his foes! there yet survive a few,
Whose deeds are daring, as their hearts are true.

V.

Within the Haram's secret chamber sate
Stern Seyd, still pondering o'er his Captive's fate;
His thoughts on love and hate alternate dwell,
Now with Gulnare, and now in Conrad's cell;
Here at his feet the lovely slave reclined
Surveys his brow—would soothe his gloom of mind:
While many an anxious glance her large dark eye
Sends in its idle search for sympathy,
His only bends in seeming o'er his beads,⁕
But inly views his victim as he bleeds.

"Pacha! the day is thine; and on thy crest
Sits Triumph—Conrad taken—fall'n the rest!
His doom is fix'd—he dies; and well his fate
Was earn'd—yet much too worthless for thy hate:
Methinks, a short release, for ransom told
With all his treasure, not unwisely sold;
Report speaks largely of his pirate-hoard—
Would that of this my Pacha were the lord!

⁕ The comboloio, or Mahometan rosary; the beads are in number ninety-nine.

While baffled, weaken'd by this fatal fray—
Watch'd—follow'd—he were then an easier prey;
But once cut off—the remnant of his band
Embark their wealth, and seek a safer strand."

"Gulnare!—if for each drop of blood a gem
Were offer'd rich as Stamboul's diadem;
If for each hair of his a massy mine
Of virgin ore should supplicating shine;
If all our Arab tales divulge or dream
Of wealth were here—that gold should not redeem!
It had not now redeem'd a single hour;
But that I know him fetter'd, in my power,
And, thirsting for revenge, I ponder still
On pangs that longest rack, and latest kill."

"Nay, Seyd!   I seek not to restrain thy rage,
Too justly moved for mercy to assuage;
My thoughts were only to secure for thee
His riches, thus released, he were not free:
Disabled, shorn of half his might and band,
His capture could but wait thy first command."

"His capture *could!*—and shall I then resign
One day to him—the wretch already mine?
Release my foe!—at whose remonstrance ?—thine!
Fair suitor!—to thy virtuous gratitude,
That thus repays this Giaour's relenting mood,
Which thee and thine alone of all could spare,
No doubt—regardless if the prize were fair,
My thanks and praise alike are due—now hear!
I have a counsel for thy gentler ear:
I do mistrust thee, woman! and each word
Of thine stamps truth on all Suspicion heard.
Borne in his arms through fire from yon Serai—
Say, wert thou lingering there with him to fly?
Thou need'st not answer—thy confession speaks,
Already reddening on thy guilty cheeks:
Then, lovely dame, bethink thee! and beware:
'Tis not *his* life alone may claim such care!

Another word and—nay—I need no more.
Accursed was the moment when he bore
Thee from the flames, which better far—but no—
I then had mourn'd thee with a lover's woe—
Now 'tis thy lord that warns—deceitful thing !
Know'st thou that I can clip thy wanton wing ?
In words alone I am not wont to chafe :
Look to thyself, nor deem thy falsehood safe !"

He rose—and slowly, sternly thence withdrew,
Rage in his eye, and threats in his adieu :
Ah ! little reck'd that chief of womanhood—
Which frowns ne'er quell'd, nor menaces subdued ;
And little deem'd he what thy heart, Gulnare !
When soft could feel, and when incensed could dare.
His doubts appear'd to wrong—nor yet she knew
How deep the root from whence compassion grew—
She was a slave—from such may captives claim
A fellow-feeling, differing but in name ;
Still half unconscious—heedless of his wrath,
Again she ventured on the dangerous path,
Again his rage repell'd—until arose
That strife of thought, the source of woman's woes !

VI.

Meanwhile long, anxious, weary, still the same
Roll'd day and night : his soul could terror tame—
This fearful interval of doubt and dread,
When every hour might doom him worse than dead,
When every step that echo'd by the gate,
Might entering lead where axe and stake await ;
When every voice that grated on his ear
Might be the last that he could ever hear ;
Could terror tame—that spirit stern and high
Had proved unwilling as unfit to die ;
'Twas worn—perhaps decay'd—yet silent bore
That conflict, deadlier far than all before :
The heat of fight, the hurry of the gale,
Leave scarce one thought inert enough to quail :

But bound and fix'd in fetter'd solitude,
To pine, the prey of every changing mood;
To gaze on thine own heart; and meditate
Irrevocable faults, and coming fate—
Too late the last to shun—the first to mend—
To count the hours that struggle to thine end,
With not a friend to animate and tell
To other ears that death became thee well;
Around thee foes to forge the ready lie,
And blot life's latest scene with calumny;
Before thee tortures, which the soul can dare,
Yet doubts how well the shrinking flesh may bear;
But deeply feels a single cry would shame,
To valour's praise thy last and dearest claim;
The life thou leav'st below, denied above
By kind monopolists of heavenly love;
And more than doubtful paradise—thy heaven
Of earthly hope—thy loved one from thee riven.
Such were the thoughts that outlaw must sustain,
And govern pangs surpassing mortal pain:
And those sustain'd he—boots it well or ill?
Since not to sink beneath, is something still!

VII.

The first day pass'd—he saw not her—Gulnare—
The second, third—and still she came not there;
But what her words avouch'd, her charms had done,
Or else he had not seen another sun.
The fourth day roll'd along, and with the night
Came storm and darkness in their mingling might.
Oh! how he listen'd to the rushing deep,
That ne'er till now so broke upon his sleep;
And his wild spirit wilder wishes sent,
Roused by the roar of his own element!
Oft had he ridden on that winged wave,
And loved its roughness for the speed it gave;
And now its dashing echo'd on his ear,
A long known voice—alas! too vainly near!
Loud sung the wind above; and, doubly loud,
Shook o'er his turret cell the thunder-cloud;

And flash'd the lightning by the latticed bar,
To him more genial than the midnight star:
Close to the glimmering grate he dragg'd his chain,
And hoped *that* peril might not prove in vain.
He rais'd his iron hand to Heaven, and pray'd
One pitying flash to mar the form it made:
His steel and impious prayer attract alike—
The storm roll'd onward, and disdain'd to strike;
Its peal wax'd fainter—ceased—he felt alone,
As if some faithless friend had spurn'd his groan!

VIII.

The midnight pass'd, and to the massy door
A light step came—it paused—it moved once more;
Slow turns the grating bolt and sullen key:
'Tis as his heart foreboded—that fair she!
Whate'er her sins, to him a guardian saint,
And beauteous still as hermit's hope can paint;
Yet changed since last within that cell she came,
More pale her cheek, more tremulous her frame:
On him she cast her dark and hurried eye,
Which spoke before her accents—"Thou must die!
Yes, thou must die—there is but one resource,
The last—the worst—if torture were not worse."

"Lady! I look to none; my lips proclaim
What last proclaim'd they—Conrad still the same:
Why should'st thou seek an outlaw's life to spare,
And change the sentence I deserve to bear?
Well have I earn'd—nor here alone—the meed
Of Seyd's revenge, by many a lawless deed."

"Why should I seek? because—Oh! did'st thou not
Redeem my life from worse than slavery's lot?
Why should I seek?—hath misery made thee blind
To the fond workings of a woman's mind?
And must I say?—albeit my heart rebel
With all that woman feels, but should not tell—
Because, despite thy crimes, that heart is moved:
It fear'd thee, thank'd thee, pitied, madden'd, loved.

Reply not, tell not now thy tale again,
Thou lov'st another, and I love in vain :
Though fond as mine her bosom, form more fair,
I rush through peril which she would not dare.
If that thy heart to hers were truly dear,
Were I thine own thou wert not lonely here :
An outlaw's spouse and leave her lord to roam !
What hath such gentle dame to do with home ?
But speak not now—o'er thine and o'er my head
Hangs the keen sabre by a single thread ;
If thou hast courage still, and would'st be free,
Receive this poniard—rise and follow me ! "

" Ay in my chains ! my steps will gently tread,
With these adornments, o'er each slumbering head !
Thou hast forgot—is this a garb for flight ?
Or is that instrument more fit for fight ? "

" Misdoubting Corsair ! I have gained the guard,
Ripe for revolt, and greedy for reward.
A single word of mine removes that chain :
Without some aid how here could I remain ?
Well, since we met, hath sped my busy time,
If in aught evil, for thy sake the crime :
The crime—'tis none to punish those of Seyd.
That hated tyrant, Conrad—he must bleed !
I see thee shudder, but my soul is changed—
Wrong'd, spurn'd, reviled, and it shall be avenged—
Accused of what till now my heart disdain'd—
Too faithful, though to bitter bondage chain'd.
Yes, smile !—but he had little cause to sneer,
I was not treacherous then, nor thou too dear :
But he has said it—and the jealous well,—
Those tyrants, teasing, tempting to rebel,—
Deserve the fate their fretting lips foretell.
I never loved—he bought me—somewhat high—
Since with me came a heart he could not buy.
I was a slave unmurmuring ; he hath said,
But for his rescue I with thee had fled.
'Twas false thou know'st—but let such augurs rue,

Their words are omens insult renders true.
Nor was thy respite granted to my prayer ;
This fleeting grace was only to prepare
New torments for thy life, and my despair.
Mine too he threatens ; but his dotage still
Would fain reserve me for his lordly will :
When wearier of these fleeting charms and me,
There yawns the sack, and yonder rolls the sea !
What, am I then a toy for dotard's play,
To wear but till the gilding frets away ?
I saw thee—loved thee—owe thee all—would save,
If but to show how grateful is a slave.
But had he not thus menaced fame and life,—
And well he keeps his oaths pronounced in strife—
I still had saved thee, but the Pacha spared.
Now I am all thine own, for all prepared :
Thou lov'st me not, nor know'st—or but the worst.
Alas ! *this* love—*that* hatred—are the first—
Oh ! could'st thou prove my truth, thou would'st not start,
Nor fear the fire that lights an Eastern heart ;
'Tis now the beacon of thy safety—now
It points within the port a Mainote prow :
But in one chamber, where our path must lead,
There sleeps—he must not wake—the oppressor Seyd !"

" Gulnare—Gulnare—I never felt till now
My abject fortune, wither'd fame so low :
Seyd is mine enemy ; had swept my band
From earth with ruthless but with open hand,
And therefore came I, in my bark of war,
To smite the smiter with the scimitar ;
Such is my weapon—not the secret knife ;
Who spares a woman's seeks not slumber's life.
Thine saved I gladly, Lady—not for this ;
Let me not deem that mercy shown amiss.
Now fare thee well—more peace be with thy breast !
Night wears apace, my last of earthly rest !"

" Rest ! rest ! by sunrise must thy sinews shake,
And thy limbs writhe around the ready stake,

I heard the order—saw—I will not see—
If thou wilt perish, I will fall with thee.
My life, my love, my hatred—all below
Are on this cast—Corsair! 'tis but a blow!
Without it flight were idle—how evade
His sure pursuit?—my wrongs too unrepaid,
My youth disgraced, the long, long wasted years,
One blow shall cancel with our future fears;
But since the dagger suits thee less than brand,
I'll try the firmness of a female hand.
The guards are gain'd—one moment all were o'er
Corsair! we meet in safety or no more;
If errs my feeble hand, the morning cloud
Will hover o'er thy scaffold, and my shroud."

IX

She turn'd, and vanish'd ere he could reply,
But his glance follow'd far with eager eye;
And gathering, as he could, the links that bound
His form, to curl their length, and curb their sound,
Since bar and bolt no more his steps preclude,
He, fast as fetter'd limbs allow, pursued.
'Twas dark and winding, and he knew not where
That passage led; nor lamp nor guard was there:
He sees a dusky glimmering—shall he seek
Or shun that ray so indistinct and weak?
Chance guides his steps—a freshness seems to bear
Full on his brow as if from morning air;
He reach'd an open gallery—on his eye
Gleam'd the last star of night, the clearing sky:
Yet scarcely heeded these—another light
From a lone chamber struck upon his sight.
Towards it he moved; a scarcely closing door
Reveal'd the ray within, but nothing more.
With hasty step a figure outward past,
Then paused, and turn'd—and paused—'tis She at last!
No poniard in that hand, nor sign of ill—
"Thanks to that softening heart—she could not kill!"
Again he look'd, the wildness of her eye
Starts from the day abrupt and fearfully.

She stopp'd—threw back her dark far-floating hair,
That nearly veil'd her face and bosom fair,
As if she late had bent her leaning head
Above some object of her doubt or dread.
They meet—upon her brow—unknown, forgot—
Her hurrying hand had left—'twas but a spot—
Its hue was all he saw, and scarce withstood—
Oh! slight but certain pledge of crime—'tis blood!

x.

He had seen battle—he had brooded lone
O'er promised pangs to sentenced guilt foreshown;
He had been tempted, chasten'd, and the chain
Yet on his arms might ever there remain:
But ne'er from strife, captivity, remorse—
From all his feelings in their inmost force—
So thrill'd, so shudder'd every creeping vein,
As now they froze before that purple stain.
That spot of blood, that light but guilty streak,
Had banish'd all the beauty from her cheek!
Blood he had view'd, could view unmoved—but then
It flow'd in combat, or was shed by men!

xi.

"'Tis done—he nearly waked—but it is done.
Corsair! he perish'd—thou art dearly won.
All words would now be vain—away—away!
Our bark is tossing—'tis already day.
The few gain'd over, now are wholly mine,
And these thy yet surviving band shall join:
Anon my voice shall vindicate my hand,
When once our sail forsakes this hated strand."

xii.

She clapp'd her hands, and through the gallery pour,
Equipp'd for flight, her vassals—Greek and Moor;
Silent but quick they stoop, his chains unbind;
Once more his limbs are free as mountain wind!
But on his heavy heart such sadness sate,
As if they there transferr'd that iron weight.

No words are utter'd—at her sign, a door
Reveals the secret passage to the shore;
The city lies behind—they speed, they reach
The glad waves dancing on the yellow beach;
And Conrad following, at her beck, obey'd,
Nor cared he now if rescued or betray'd;
Resistance were as useless as if Seyd
Yet lived to view the doom his ire decreed.

XIII.

Embark'd, the sail unfurl'd, the light breeze blew—
How much had Conrad's memory to review!
Sunk he in contemplation, till the cape
Where last he anchor'd rear'd its giant shape.
Ah! since that fatal night, though brief the time,
Had swept an age of terror, grief, and crime.
As its far shadow frown'd above the mast,
He veil'd his face, and sorrow'd as he pass'd;
He thought of all—Gonsalvo and his band,
His fleeting triumph and his failing hand;
He thought on her afar, his lonely bride:
He turn'd and saw—Gulnare, the homicide!

XIV.

She watch'd his features till she could not bear
Their freezing aspect and averted air;
And that strange fierceness foreign to her eye
Fell quench'd in tears, too late to shed or dry.
She knelt beside him and his hand she press'd,
"Thou may'st forgive though Allah's self detest;
But for that deed of darkness what wert thou?
Reproach me but not yet—Oh! spare me *now!*
I am not what I seem—this fearful night
My brain bewilder'd—do not madden quite!
If I had never loved, though less my guilt,
Thou hadst not lived to—hate me—if thou wilt."

XV.

She wrongs his thoughts, they more himself upbraid
Than her, though undesign'd, the wretch he made;

But speechless all, deep, dark, and unexprest,
They bleed within that silent cell—his breast.
Still onward, fair the breeze, nor rough the surge,
The blue waves sport around the stern they urge,
Far on the horizon's verge appears a speck,
A spot—a mast—a sail—an armed deck !
Their little bark her men of watch descry,
And ampler canvass woos the wind from high;
She bears her down majestically near,
Speed on her prow, and terror in her tier;
A flash is seen—the ball beyond her bow
Booms harmless, hissing to the deep below.
Up rose keen Conrad from his silent trance,
A long, long absent gladness in his glance;
"'Tis mine —my blood-red flag! again—again—
I am not all deserted on the main !"
They own the signal, answer to the hail,
Hoist out the boat at once, and slacken sail.
"'Tis Conrad! Conrad!" shouting from the deck,
Command nor duty could their transport check !
With light alacrity and gaze of pride,
They view him mount once more his vessel's side;
A smile relaxing in each rugged face,
Their arms can scarce forbear a rough embrace.
He, half forgetting danger and defeat,
Returns their greeting as a chief may greet,
Wrings with a cordial grasp Anselmo's hand,
And feels he yet can conquer and command !

XVI

These greetings o'er, the feelings that o'erflow,
Yet grieve to win him back without a blow,
They sail'd prepared for vengeance—had they known
A woman's hand secured that deed her own,
She were their queen—less scrupulous are they
Than haughty Conrad how they win their way.
With many an asking smile, and wondering stare,
They whisper round, and gaze upon Gulnare;
And her, at once above—beneath her sex,
Whom blood appall'd not, their regards perplex.

To Conrad turns her faint imploring eye,
She drops her veil, and stands in silence by;
Her arms are meekly folded on that breast,
Which—Conrad safe—to fate resign'd the rest.
Though worse than frenzy could that bosom fill,
Extreme in love or hate, in good or ill,
The worst of crimes had left her woman still!

XVII.

This Conrad mark'd, and felt—ah! could he less?—
Hate of that deed, but grief for her distress;
What she has done no tears can wash away,
And Heaven must punish on its angry day:
But—it was done: he knew, whate'er her guilt,
For him that poniard smote, that blood was spilt;
And he was free! and she for him had given
Her all on earth, and more than all in heaven!
And now he turn'd him to that dark-eyed slave
Whose brow was bow'd beneath the glance he gave,
Who now seem'd changed and humbled, faint and meek,
But varying oft the colour of her cheek
To deeper shades of paleness—all its red
That fearful spot which stain'd it from the dead!
He took that hand—it trembled—now too late—
So soft in love, so wildly nerved in hate;
He clasp'd that hand—it trembled—and his own
Had lost its firmness, and his voice its tone.
"Gulnare!"—but she replied not—"dear Gulnare!"
She raised her eye—her only answer there—
At once she sought and sunk in his embrace:
If he had driven her from that resting-place,
His had been more or less than mortal heart,
But—good or ill—it bade her not depart.
Perchance, but for the bodings of his breast,
His latest virtue then had join'd the rest.
Yet even Medora might forgive the kiss
That ask'd from form so fair no more than this,
The first, the last that Frailty stole from Faith—
To lips where Love had lavish'd all his breath,

To lips—whose broken sighs such fragrance fling,
As he had fann'd them freshly with his wing!

XVIII.

They gain by twilight's hour their lonely isle.
To them the very rocks appear to smile;
The haven hums with many a cheering sound,
The beacons blaze their wonted stations round,
The boats are darting o'er the curly bay,
And sportive dolphins bend them through the spray;
Even the hoarse sea-bird's shrill, discordant shriek,
Greets like the welcome of his tuneless beak!
Beneath each lamp that through its lattice gleams,
Their fancy paints the friends that trim the beams.
Oh! what can sanctify the joys of home,
Like Hope's gay glance from Ocean's troubled foam?

XIX.

The lights are high on beacon and from bower,
And 'midst them Conrad seeks Medora's tower:
He looks in vain—'tis strange—and all remark,
Amid so many, hers alone is dark.
'Tis strange—of yore its welcome never fail'd,
Nor now, perchance, extinguish'd, only veil'd.
With the first boat descends he for the shore,
And looks impatient on the lingering oar.
Oh! for a wing beyond the falcon's flight,
To bear him like an arrow to that height!
With the first pause the resting rowers gave,
He waits not, looks not—leaps into the wave,
Strives through the surge, bestrides the beach, and high
Ascends the path familiar to his eye.
He reach'd his turret door—he paused—no sound
Broke from within; and all was night around.
He knock'd, and loudly—footstep nor reply
Announced that any heard or deem'd him nigh;
He knock'd, but faintly—for his trembling hand
Refused to aid his heavy heart's demand.
The portal opens—'tis a well known face,
But not the form he panted to embrace.

Its lips are silent—twice his own essay'd,
And fail'd to frame the question they delay'd;
He snatch'd the lamp—its light will answer all—
It quits his grasp, expiring in the fall.
He would not wait for that reviving ray—
As soon could he have linger'd there for day;
But, glimmering through the dusky corridor,
Another chequers o'er the shadow'd floor;
His steps the chamber gain—his eyes behold
All that his heart believed not—yet foretold!

xx

He turn'd not—spoke not—sunk not—fix'd his look,
And set the anxious frame that lately shook:
He gazed—how long we gaze despite of pain,
And know, but dare not own, we gaze in vain!
In life itself she was so still and fair,
That death with gentler aspect wither'd there;
And the cold flowers⁷ her colder hand contain'd,
In that last grasp as tenderly were strain'd
As if she scarcely felt, but feign'd a sleep,
And made it almost mockery yet to weep:
The long dark lashes fringed her lids of snow,
And veil'd—thought shrinks from all that lurk'd below—
Oh! o'er the eye Death most exerts his might,
And hurls the spirit from her throne of light,
Sinks those blue orbs in that long last eclipse,
But spares, as yet, the charm around her lips—
Yet, yet they seem as they forebore to smile,
And wish'd repose,—but only for a while;
But the white shroud, and each extended tress,
Long, fair—but spread in utter lifelessness,
Which, late the sport of every summer wind,
Escaped the baffled wreath that strove to bind;
These—and the pale pure cheek, became the bier—
But she is nothing—wherefore is he here?

---

⁷ In the Levant it is the custom to strew flowers on the bodies of the dead, and in
the hands of young persons to place a nosegay.

XXI.

He ask'd no question—all were answer'd now
By the first glance on that still, marble brow.
It was enough—she died—what reck'd it how?
The love of youth, the hope of better years,
The source of softest wishes, tenderest fears,
The only living thing he could not hate,
Was reft at once—and he deserved his fate,
But did not feel it less;—the good explore,
For peace, those realms where guilt can never soar:
The proud, the wayward—who have fix'd below
Their joy, and find this earth enough for woe,
Lose in that one their all—perchance a mite—
But who in patience parts with all delight?
Full many a stoic eye and aspect stern
Mask hearts where grief hath little left to learn;
And many a withering thought lies hid, not lost,
In smiles that least befit who wear them most.

XXII.

By those, that deepest feel, is ill exprest
The indistinctness of the suffering breast;
Where thousand thoughts begin to end in one,
Which seeks from all the refuge found in none;
No words suffice the secret soul to show,
For Truth denies all eloquence to Woe.
On Conrad's stricken soul exhaustion prest,
And stupor almost lull'd it into rest;
So feeble now—his mother's softness crept
To those wild eyes, which like an infant's wept:
It was the very weakness of his brain,
Which thus confess'd without relieving pain.
None saw his trickling tears—perchance, if seen,
That useless flood of grief had never been:
Nor long they flow'd—he dried them to depart,
In helpless—hopeless—brokenness of heart.
The sun goes forth, but Conrad's day is dim:
And the night cometh—ne'er to pass from him.
There is no darkness like the cloud of mind,
On grief's vain eye—the blindest of the blind!

Which may not—dare not see—but turns aside
To blackest shade—nor will endure a guide !

XXIII.

His heart was form'd for softness—warp'd to wrong,
Betray'd too early, and beguiled too long ;
Each feeling pure—as falls the dropping dew
Within the grot, like that had harden'd too ;
Less clear, perchance, its earthly trials pass'd,
But sunk, and chill'd, and petrified at last.
Yet tempests wear, and lightning cleaves the rock ;
If such his heart, so shatter'd it the shock.
There grew one flower beneath its rugged brow,
Though dark the shade—it shelter'd—saved till now.
The thunder came—that bolt hath blasted both,
The Granite's firmness, and the Lily's growth :
The gentle plant hath left no leaf to tell
Its tale, but shrunk and wither'd where it fell ;
And of its cold protector, blacken round
But shiver'd fragments on the barren ground !

XXIV.

'Tis morn—to venture on his lonely hour
Few dare ; though now Anselmo sought his tower.
He was not there, nor seen along the shore ;
Ere night, alarm'd, their isle is traversed o'er :
Another morn—another bids them seek,
And shout his name till echo waxeth weak ;
Mount, grotto, cavern, valley search'd in vain,
They find on shore a sea-boat's broken chain :
Their hope revives—they follow o'er the main.
'Tis idle all—moons roll on moons away,
And Conrad comes not, came not since that day :
Nor trace nor tidings of his doom declare
Where lives his grief, or perish'd his despair !
Long mourn'd his band whom none could mourn beside ;
And fair the monument they gave his bride :
For him they raise not the recording stone—
His death yet dubious, deeds too widely known ;

He left a Corsair's name to other times,
Link'd with one virtue, and a thousand crimes.[5]

[5] That the point of honour which is represented in one instance of Conrad's character
has not been carried beyond the bounds of probability, may perhaps be in some degree
confirmed by the following anecdote of a brother buccaneer in the year 1814 ·—"Our
readers have all seen the account of the enterprise against the pirates of Barrataria;
but few, we believe, were informed of the situation, history, or nature of that establishment.   For the information of such as were unacquainted with it, we have pro-
cured from a friend the following interesting narrative of the main facts, of which he
has personal knowledge, and which cannot fail to interest some of our readers.—
Barrataria is a bay, or a narrow arm of the Gulf of Mexico; it runs through a rich
but very flat country, until it reaches within a mile of the Mississippi river, fifteen
miles below the city of New Orleans.   The bay has branches almost innumerable, in
which persons can be concealed from the severest scrutiny.   It communicates with
three lakes which lie on the south-west side, and these, with the lake of the same
name, and which lies contiguous to the sea, where there is an island formed by the
two arms of this lake and the sea   The east and west points of this island were
fortified, in the year 1811, by a band of pirates, under the command of one Monsieur
La Fitte.   A large majority of these outlaws are of that class of the population of the
state of Louisiana who fled from the island of St Domingo during the troubles there,
and took refuge in the island of Cuba, and when the last war between France and
Spain commenced, they were compelled to leave that island with the short notice of a
few days.   Without ceremony they entered the United States, the most of them the
state of Louisiana, with all the negroes they had possessed in Cuba.   They were
notified by the Governor of that State of the clause in the constitution which forbade
the importation of slaves, but, at the same time, received the assurance of the
Governor that he would obtain, if possible, the approbation of the General Government for their retaining this property.—The island of Barrataria is situated about
lat 29 deg 15 min., lon 92 30., and is as remarkable for its health as for the
superior scale and shell fish with which its waters abound.   The chief of this horde,
like Charles de Moor, had. mixed with his many vices, some virtues   In the year
1813, this party had, from its turpitude and boldness, claimed the attention of the
Governor of Louisiana; and to break up the establishment he thought proper to strike
at the head   He therefore, offered a reward of 500 dollars for the head of Monsieur
La Fitte, who was well known to the inhabitants of the city of New Orleans, from his
immediate connection, and his once having been a fencing-master in that city of great
reputation, which art he learnt in Buonaparte's army, where he was a captain.   The
reward which was offered by the Governor for the head of La Fitte was answered by
the offer of a reward from the latter of 15,000 for the head of the Governor   The
Governor ordered out a company to march from the city to La Fitte's island, and to
burn and destroy all the property, and to bring to the city of New Orleans all his
banditti   This company, under the command of a man who had been the intimate
associate of this bold Captain, approached very near to the fortified island, before he
saw a man, or heard a sound, until he heard a whistle, not unlike a boatswain's call.
Then it was he found himself surrounded by armed men who had emerged from the
secret avenues which led into Bayou.   Here it was that the modern Charles de Moor
developed his few noble traits, for to this man, who had come to destroy his life and
all that was dear to him, he not only spared his life, but offered him that which would
have made the honest soldier easy for the remainder of his days, which was indignantly
refused   He then, with the approbation of his captor, returned to the city.   This
circumstance, and some concomitant events, proved that this band of pirates was not
to be taken by land   Our naval force having always been small in that quarter,
exertions for the destruction of this illicit establishment could not be expected from
them until augmented, for an officer of the navy, with most of the gun-boats on that
station, had to retreat from an overwhelming force of La Fitte's   So soon as the
augmentation of the navy authorised an attack, one was made, the overthrow of this

banditti has been the result . and now this almost invulnerable point and key to New Orleans is clear .of an enemy, it is to be hoped the government will hold it by a strong military force."—*American Newspaper.*

In Noble's continuation of "Granger's Biographical History," there is a singular passage in his account of Archbishop Blackbourne , and as in some measure connected with the profession of the hero of the foregoing poem, I cannot resist the temptation of extracting it —"There is something mysterious in the history and character of Dr Blackbourne. The former is but imperfectly known , and report has even asserted he was a buccaneer ; and that one of his brethren in that profession having asked, on his arrival in England, what had become of his old chum, Blackbourne, was answered, he is Archbishop of York We are informed, that Blackbourne was installed sub-dean of Exeter in 1694, which office he resigned in 1702 ; but after his successor Lewis Barnet's death, in 1704, he regained it In the following year he became dean , and in 1714 held with it the archdeanery of Cornwall. He was consecrated Bishop of Exeter, February 24, 1716 , and translated to York, November 28, 1724, as a reward, according to court scandal, for uniting George I. to the Duchess of Munster This, however, appears to have been an unfounded calumny. As archbishop he behaved with great prudence, and was equally respectable as the guardian of the revenues of the see Rumour whispered he retained the vices of his youth, and that a passion for the fair sex formed an item in the list of his weaknesses , but so far from being convicted by seventy witnesses, he does not appear to have been directly criminated by one In short, I look upon these aspersions as the effects of mere malice How is it possible a buccaneer should have been so good a scholar as Blackbourne certainly was ? He who had so perfect a knowledge of the classics (particularly of the Greek tragedians), as to be able to read them with the same ease as he could Shakspeare, must have taken great pains to acquire the learned languages , and have had both leisure and good masters. But he was undoubtedly educated at Christ-church College, Oxford. He is allowed to have been a pleasant man , this, however. was turned against him, by its being said, ' he gained more hearts than souls ' "

"The only voice that could soothe the passions of the savage (Alphonso III.) was that of an amiable and virtuous wife, the sole object of his love , the voice of Donna Isabella, the daughter of the Duke of Savoy, and the grand-daughter of Philip II. King of Spain.—Her dying words sunk deep into his memory , his fierce spirit melted into tears , and, after the last embrace, Alphonso retired into his chamber to bewail his irreparable loss, and to meditate on the vanity of human life."—*Gibbon's Miscellaneous Works,* vol. iii , p. 473.

LARA.

INTRODUCTION TO LARA.

In the Dedication to "The Corsair" (Jan. 2, 1814), Lord Byron announced that he should publish nothing further for several years For a time the resolution increased in strength, and in the April following he came to the most extraordinary decision that ever entered the mind of a successful author, which was not only to write no more in future, but to recall every line he had already penned He sent Mr Murray a draft for the sum which had been paid for the copyrights, and an appeal to his good nature from the publisher, alone prevented the execution of the scheme. While Europe rang with his fame, the hisses of envy, hatred, and malice made themselves heard amid the loud applause. His friends, who acknowledged that no one wrote so well, feared he would write too much , and he himself doubted the solid worth of what he wrote so fast Under the united influence of these impressions he resolved to lay by, and meant perhaps, in the interval, to gather himself up for a mighty spring, when the appetite of the public was increased by abstinence But he might have determined not to breathe with an equal chance of keeping his vow Before the end of May "Lara" was begun, and was carried on chiefly while the author undressed after balls and masquerades It was published, anonymously, in August, in the same volume with the "Jacqueline" of Rogers, a conjunction too unnatural to last beyond the hour An acquaintance of Lord Byron, who was reading the book in the Brighton coach, was asked by a passenger the name of the author, and on replying that they were two, "Ay, Ay," rejoined the querist,—"a joint concern, I suppose,—*summot* like Sternhold and Hopkins." The "vile comparison" delighted Lord Byron, always pleased with any ludicrous absurdity which struck at literary fame It is evident that the tale is the sequel of "The Corsair"—that Lara is Conrad ; Kaled, Gulnare, and that Medora was snatched from Sir Ezzelin and fled with her lover to the Pirate's Island A few months after the appearance of the poem Lord Byron pronounced that it was "his most unpopular effervescence, being too little narrative, and too metaphysical to please the majority of readers" The continuation is certainly tame in comparison with "The Corsair" The character of Lara—in which Lord Byron drew again from his personal history—is rather tediously minute ; and, with much fine verse, there is not the former living language, and hurrying action, to bear us onward with breathless haste George Ellis objected that the mysterious vision, which appears to Lara in his antique hall, was an excrescence on the poem, and it is now obvious that the connection was not with the story, but with the author's recollections of his own old haunted Gothic Abbey. The skull, too, placed beside Lara's book was part of the cherished furniture of Newstead ; and, at one period of Lord Byron's history, the woman, disguised like a page, was also there, to complete the picture. The conclusion of the second canto, commencing from the sixteenth section, is full of spirit and pathos, and many of the elegant and elaborate descriptions only disappoint from the inevitable contrast with the more brilliant "Corsair" Lord Byron fancied he had varied the couplet of "Lara" from that of its predecessor, but, except that the latter is more antithetical, we have not been able to detect the difference Seven hundred pounds was the price of the copyright.

LARA.

CANTO THE FIRST.

I.

THE Serfs[1] are glad through Lara's wide domain,
And Slavery half forgets her feudal chain;
He, their unhoped, but unforgotten lord,
The long self-exiled chieftain, is restored:
There be bright faces in the busy hall,
Bowls on the board, and banners on the wall;
Far checkering o'er the pictured window, plays
The unwonted faggot's hospitable blaze;
And gay retainers gather round the hearth,
With tongues all loudness, and with eyes all mirth.

II.

The chief of Lara is return'd again:
And why had Lara cross'd the bounding main?
Left by his sire, too young such loss to know,
Lord of himself,—that heritage of woe,
That fearful empire which the human breast
But holds to rob the heart within of rest!—

[1] The reader is apprised, that the name of Lara being Spanish, and no circumstance of local and natural description fixing the scene or hero of the poem to any country or age, the word "Serf," which could not be correctly applied to the lower classes in Spain, who were never vassals of the soil, has nevertheless been employed to designate the followers of our fictitious chieftain —[Lord Byron elsewhere intimates, that he meant Lara for a chief of the Morea.]

With none to check, and few to point in time
The thousand paths that slope the way to crime;
Then, when he most required commandment, then
Had Lara's daring boyhood govern'd men.
It skills not, boots not step by step to trace
His youth through all the mazes of its race;
Short was the course his restlessness had run,
But long enough to leave him half undone.

III.

And Lara left in youth his father-land;
But from the hour he waved his parting hand
Each trace wax'd fainter of his course, till all
Had nearly ceased his memory to recall.
His sire was dust, his vassals could declare,
'Twas all they knew, that Lara was not there;
Nor sent, nor came he, till conjecture grew
Cold in the many, anxious in the few.
His hall scarce echoes with his wonted name,
His portrait darkens in its fading frame,
Another chief consoled his destined bride,
The young forgot him, and the old had died;
" Yet doth he live ! " exclaims the impatient heir,
And sighs for sables which he must not wear.
A hundred scutcheons deck with gloomy grace
The Laras' last and longest dwelling-place;
But one is absent from the mouldering file,
That now were welcome in that Gothic pile.

IV.

He comes at last in sudden loneliness,
And whence they know not, why they need not guess;
They more might marvel, when the greeting's o'er
Not that he came, but came not long before:
No train is his beyond a single page,
Of foreign aspect, and of tender age.
Years had roll'd on, and fast they speed away
To those that wander as to those that stay;
But lack of tidings from another clime
Had lent a flagging wing to weary Time.

They see, they recognise, yet almost deem
The present dubious, or the past a dream.

He lives, nor yet is past his manhood's prime,
Though sear'd by toil, and something touch'd by time;
His faults, whate'er they were, if scarce forgot,
Might be untaught him by his varied lot;
Nor good nor ill of late were known, his name
Might yet uphold his patrimonial fame:
His soul in youth was haughty, but his sins
No more than pleasure from the stripling wins;
And such, if not yet harden'd in their course,
Might be redeem'd, nor ask a long remorse.

v.

And they indeed were changed—'tis quickly seen,
Whate'er he be, 'twas not what he had been:
That brow in furrow'd lines had fix'd at last,
And spake of passions, but of passion past:
The pride, but not the fire, of early days,
Coldness of mien, and carelessness of praise;
A high demeanour, and a glance that took
Their thoughts from others by a single look;
And that sarcastic levity of tongue,
The stinging of a heart the world hath stung,
That darts in seeming playfulness around,
And makes those feel that will not own the wound;
All these seem'd his, and something more beneath
Than glance could well reveal, or accent breathe.
Ambition, glory, love, the common aim,
That some can conquer, and that all would claim,
Within his breast appear'd no more to strive,
Yet seem'd as lately they had been alive;
And some deep feeling it were vain to trace
At moments lighten'd o'er his livid face.

vi.

Not much he loved long question of the past,
Nor told of wondrous wilds, and deserts vast,

In those far lands where he had wander'd lone,
And—as himself would have it seem—unknown:
Yet these in vain his eye could scarcely scan,
Nor glean experience from his fellow man;
But what he had beheld he shunn'd to show,
As hardly worth a stranger's care to know;
If still more prying such enquiry grew,
His brow fell darker, and his words more few.

VII.

Not unrejoiced to see him once again,
Warm was his welcome to the haunts of men;
Born of high lineage, link'd in high command,
He mingled with the magnates of his land;
Join'd the carousals of the great and gay,
And saw them smile or sigh their hours away;
But still he only saw, and did not share,
The common pleasure or the general care;
He did not follow what they all pursued
With hope still baffled still to be renew'd;
Nor shadowy honour, nor substantial gain,
Nor beauty's preference, and the rival's pain:
Around him some mysterious circle thrown
Repell'd approach, and show'd him still alone;
Upon his eye sat something of reproof,
That kept at least frivolity aloof;
And things more timid that beheld him near
In silence gazed, or whisper'd mutual fear;
And they the wiser, friendlier few confess'd
They deem'd him better than his air express'd.

VIII

'Twas strange—in youth all action and all life,
Burning for pleasure, not averse from strife;
Woman, the field, the ocean, all that gave
Promise of gladness, peril of a grave,
In turn he tried—he ransack'd all below,
And found his recompense in joy or woe,
No tame, trite medium; for his feelings sought
In that intenseness an escape from thought:

The tempest of his heart in scorn had gazed
On that the feebler elements hath raised;
The rapture of his heart had look'd on high,
And ask'd if greater dwelt beyond the sky:
Chain'd to excess, the slave of each extreme,
How woke he from the wildness of that dream!
Alas! he told not—but he did awake
To curse the wither'd heart that would not break.

IX

Books, for his volume heretofore was Man,
With eye more curious he appear'd to scan,
And oft in sudden mood, for many a day,
From all communion he would start away:
And then, his rarely call'd attendants said,
Through night's long hours would sound his hurried tread
O'er the dark gallery, where his fathers frown'd
In rude but antique portraiture around:
They heard, but whisper'd—"*that* must not be known—
The sound of words less earthly than his own.
Yes, they who chose might smile, but some had seen
They scarce knew what, but more than should have been.
Why gazed he so upon the ghastly head
Which hands profane had gather'd from the dead,
That still beside his open'd volume lay,
As if to startle all save him away?
Why slept he not when others were at rest?
Why heard no music, and received no guest?
All was not well, they deem'd—but where the wrong?
Some knew perchance—but 'twere a tale too long;
And such besides were too discreetly wise,
To more than hint their knowledge in surmise,
But if they would—they could"—around the board
Thus Lara's vassals prattled of their lord.

X.

It was the night—and Lara's glassy stream
The stars are studding, each with imaged beam;
So calm, the waters scarcely seem to stray,
And yet they glide like happiness away;

Reflecting far and fairy-like from high
The immortal lights that live along the sky:
Its banks are fringed with many a goodly tree,
And flowers the fairest that may feast the bee ;
Such in her chaplet infant Dian wove,
And Innocence would offer to her love.
These deck the shore; the waves their channel make
In windings bright and mazy like the snake.
All was so still, so soft in earth and air,
You scarce would start to meet a spirit there ;
Secure that nought of evil could delight
To walk in such a scene, on such a night !
It was a moment only for the good :
So Lara deem'd, nor longer there he stood,
But turn'd in silence to his castle-gate ;
Such scene his soul no more could contemplate :
Such scene reminded him of other days,
Of skies more cloudless, moons of purer blaze,
Of nights more soft and frequent, hearts that now—
No—no—the storm may beat upon his brow,
Unfelt, unsparing—but a night like this,
A night of beauty, mock'd such breast as his.

XI.

He turn'd within his solitary hall,
And his high shadow shot along the wall :
There were the painted forms of other times,
'Twas all they left of virtues or of crimes,
Save vague tradition; and the gloomy vaults
That hid their dust, their foibles, and their faults ;
And half a column of the pompous page,
That speeds the specious tale from age to age ;
Where history's pen its praise or blame supplies,
And lies like truth, and still most truly lies.
He wandering mused, and as the moonbeam shone
Through the dim lattice, o'er the floor of stone,
And the high fretted roof, and saints, that there
O'er Gothic windows knelt in pictured prayer,
Reflected in fantastic figures grew,
Like life, but not like mortal life, to view ;

His bristling locks of sable, brow of gloom,
And the wide waving of his shaken plume,
Glanced like a spectre's attributes, and gave
His aspect all that terror gives the grave.

XII.

'Twas midnight—all was slumber; the lone light
Dimm'd in the lamp, as loth to break the night.
Hark! there be murmurs heard in Lara's hall—
A sound, a voice, a shriek, a fearful call!
A long, loud shriek—and silence—did they hear
That frantic echo burst the sleeping ear?
They heard and rose, and, tremulously brave,
Rush where the sound invoked their aid to save;
They come with half-lit tapers in their hands,
And snatch'd in startled haste unbelted brands.

XIII.

Cold as the marble where his length was laid,
Pale as the beam that o'er his features play'd,
Was Lara stretch'd; his half-drawn sabre near,
Dropp'd it should seem in more than nature's fear;
Yet he was firm, or had been firm till now,
And still defiance knit his gather'd brow,
Though mix'd with terror, senseless as he lay,
There lived upon his lip the wish to slay;
Some half form'd threat in utterance there had died,
Some imprecation of despairing pride;
His eye was almost seal'd, but not forsook,
Even in its trance, the gladiator's look,
That oft awake his aspect could disclose,
And now was fix'd in horrible repose.
They raise him—bear him;—hush! he breathes, he speaks,
The swarthy blush recolours in his cheeks,
His lip resumes its red, his eye, though dim,
Rolls wide and wild, each slowly quivering limb
Recalls its function, but his words are strung
In terms that seem not of his native tongue;
Distinct but strange, enough they understand
To deem them accents of another land;

And such they were, and meant to meet an ear
That hears him not—alas! that cannot hear!

XIV.

His page approach'd, and he alone appear'd
To know the import of the words they heard;
And, by the changes of his cheek and brow,
They were not such as Lara should avow,
Nor he interpret,—yet with less surprise
Than those around their chieftain's state he eyes,
But Lara's prostrate form he bent beside,
And in that tongue which seem'd his own replied,
And Lara heeds those tones that gently seem
To soothe away the horrors of his dream—
If dream it were, that thus could overthrow
A breast that needed not ideal woe.

XV.

Whate'er his frenzy dream'd or eye beheld,—
If yet remember'd ne'er to be reveal'd,—
Rests at his heart: the custom'd morning came,
And breathed new vigour in his shaken frame;
And solace sought he none from priest nor leech,
And soon the same in movement and in speech,
As heretofore he fill'd the passing hours,
Nor less he smiles, nor more his forehead lowers,
Than these were wont; and if the coming night
Appear'd less welcome now to Lara's sight,
He to his marvelling vassals show'd it not,
Whose shuddering proved *their* fear was less forgot.
In trembling pairs (alone they dared not) crawl
The astonish'd slaves, and shun the fated hall;
The waving banner, and the clapping door,
The rustling tapestry, and the echoing floor;
The long dim shadows of surrounding trees,
The flapping bat, the night song of the breeze;
Aught they behold or hear their thought appals,
As evening saddens o'er the dark grey walls.

XVI.

Vain thought! that hour of ne'er unravell'd gloom
Came not again, or Lara could assume
A seeming of forgetfulness, that made
His vassals more amazed nor less afraid.
Had memory vanish'd then with sense restored?
Since word, nor look, nor gesture of their lord
Betray'd a feeling that recall'd to these
That fever'd moment of his mind's disease.
Was it a dream? was his the voice that spoke
Those strange wild accents; his the cry that broke
Their slumber? his the oppress'd, o'erlabour'd heart
That ceased to beat, the look that made them start?
Could he who thus had suffer'd so forget,
When such as saw that suffering shudder yet?
Or did that silence prove his memory fix'd
Too deep for words, indelible, unmix'd
In that corroding secrecy which gnaws
The heart to show the effect, but not the cause?
Not so in him; his breast had buried both,
Nor common gazers could discern the growth
Of thoughts that mortal lips must leave half told;
They choke the feeble words that would unfold.

XVII.

In him inexplicably mix'd appear'd
Much to be loved and hated, sought and fear'd;
Opinion varying o'er his hidden lot,
In praise or railing ne'er his name forgot:
His silence form'd a theme for others' prate—
They guess'd, they gazed, they fain would know his fate.
What had he been? what was he, thus unknown,
Who walk'd their world, his lineage only known?
A hater of his kind? yet some would say,
With them he could seem gay amidst the gay;
But own'd that smile, if oft observed and near,
Waned in its mirth, and wither'd to a sneer;
That smile might reach his lip, but pass'd not by,
Nor e'er could trace its laughter to his eye:

Yet there was softness too in his regard,
At times, a heart as not by nature hard,
But once perceived, his spirit seem'd to chide
Such weakness, as unworthy of its pride,
And steel'd itself, as scorning to redeem
One doubt from others' half withheld esteem;
In self-inflicted penance of a breast
Which tenderness might once have wrung from rest;
In vigilance of grief that would compel
The soul to hate for having loved too well.

XVIII.

There was in him a vital scorn of all:
As if the worst had fall'n which could befall,
He stood a stranger in this breathing world,
An erring spirit from another hurl'd;
A thing of dark imaginings, that shaped
By choice the perils he by chance escaped;
But 'scaped in vain, for in their memory yet
His mind would half exult and half regret:
With more capacity for love than earth
Bestows on most of mortal mould and birth,
His early dreams of good outstripp'd the truth,
And troubled manhood follow'd baffled youth;
With thought of years in phantom chase mispent,
And wasted powers for better purpose lent;
And fiery passions that had pour'd their wrath
In hurried desolation o'er his path,
And left the better feelings all at strife
In wild reflection o'er his stormy life;
But haughty still, and loth himself to blame,
He call'd on Nature's self to share the shame,
And charged all faults upon the fleshly form
She gave to clog the soul, and feast the worm;
Till he at last confounded good and ill,
And half mistook for fate the acts of will:
Too high for common selfishness, he could
At times resign his own for others' good,
But not in pity, not because he ought,
But in some strange perversity of thought,

That sway'd him onward with a secret pride
To do what few or none would do beside;
And this same impulse would, in tempting time,
Mislead his spirit equally to crime;
So much he soar'd beyond, or sunk beneath,
The men with whom he felt condemn'd to breathe,
And long'd by good or ill to separate
Himself from all who shared his mortal state;
His mind abhorring this had fix'd her throne
Far from the world, in regions of her own:
Thus coldly passing all that pass'd below,
His blood in temperate seeming now would flow:
Ah! happier if it ne'er with guilt had glow'd,
But ever in that icy smoothness flow'd!
'Tis true, with other men their path he walk'd,
And like the rest in seeming did and talk'd,
Nor outraged Reason's rules by flaw nor start,
His madness was not of the head, but heart;
And rarely wander'd in his speech, or drew
His thoughts so forth as to offend the view.

XIX.

With all that chilling mystery of mien,
And seeming gladness to remain unseen,
He had (if 'twere not nature's boon) an art
Of fixing memory on another's heart:
It was not love perchance, nor hate, nor aught
That words can image to express the thought;
But they who saw him did not see in vain,
And once beheld, would ask of him again:
And those to whom he spake remember'd well,
And on the words, however light, would dwell:
None knew, nor how, nor why, but he entwined
Himself perforce around the hearer's mind;
There he was stamp'd, in liking, or in hate,
If greeted once; however brief the date
That friendship, pity, or aversion knew,
Still there within the inmost thought he grew.
You could not penetrate his soul, but found,
Despite your wonder, to your own he wound;

His presence haunted still; and from the breast
He forced an all unwilling interest:
Vain was the struggle in that mental net,
His spirit seem'd to dare you to forget!

XX.

There is a festival, where knights and dames,
And aught that wealth or lofty lineage claims,
Appear—a high-born and a welcome guest
To Otho's hall came Lara with the rest.
The long carousal shakes the illumined hall,
Well speeds alike the banquet and the ball,
And the gay dance of bounding Beauty's train
Links grace and harmony in happiest chain:
Blest are the early hearts and gentle hands
That mingle there in well according bands,
It is a sight the careful brow might smooth,
And make Age smile, and dream itself to youth,
And Youth forget such hour was past on earth,
So springs the exulting bosom to that mirth!

XXI.

And Lara gazed on these, sedately glad,
His brow belied him if his soul was sad;
And his glance follow'd fast each fluttering fair,
Whose steps of lightness woke no echo there:
He lean'd against the lofty pillar nigh,
With folded arms and long attentive eye,
Nor mark'd a glance so sternly fix'd on his—
Ill brook'd high Lara scrutiny like this:
At length he caught it, 'tis a face unknown,
But seems as searching his, and his alone;
Prying and dark, a stranger's by his mien,
Who still till now had gazed on him unseen:
At length encountering meets the mutual gaze
Of keen enquiry, and of mute amaze;
On Lara's glance emotion gathering grew,
As if distrusting that the stranger threw;
Along the stranger's aspect, fix'd and stern,
Flash'd more than thence the vulgar eye could learn.

" 'Tis he !" the stranger cried, and those that heard
Re-echoed fast and far the whisper'd word.
" 'Tis he !"—" 'Tis who ?" they question far and near,
Till louder accents rung on Lara's ear ;
So widely spread, few bosoms well could brook
The general marvel, or that single look :
But Lara stirr'd not, changed not, the surprise
That sprung at first to his arrested eyes
Seem'd now subsided, neither sunk nor raised
Glanced his eye round, though still the stranger gazed ;
And drawing nigh, exclaim'd, with haughty sneer,
" 'Tis he!—how came he thence ?—what doth he here ?"

It were too much for Lara to pass by
Such questions, so repeated fierce and high ;
With look collected, but with accent cold,
More mildly firm than petulantly bold,
He turn'd, and met the inquisitorial tone—
" My name is Lara—when thine own is known,
Doubt not my fitting answer to requite
The unlook'd for courtesy of such a knight.
'Tis Lara !—further wouldst thou mark or ask ?
I shun no question, and I wear no mask."
" Thou shunn'st no question ! Ponder—is there none
Thy heart must answer, though thine ear would shun ?
And deem'st thou me unknown too ? Gaze again !
At least thy memory was not given in vain.
Oh ! never canst thou cancel half her debt,
Eternity forbids thee to forget."
With slow and searching glance upon his face
Grew Lara's eyes, but nothing there could trace
They knew, or chose to know—with dubious look
He deign'd no answer, but his head he shook,
And half contemptuous turn'd to pass away ;
But the stern stranger motion'd him to stay.
" A word !—I charge thee stay, and answer here
To one, who, wert thou noble, were thy peer,
But as thou wast and art—nay, frown not, lord,

If false, 'tis easy to disprove the word—
But as thou wast and art, on thee looks down,
Distrusts thy smiles, but shakes not at thy frown.
Art thou not he? whose deeds——"
　　　　　　　　　　　　"Whate'er I be,
Words wild as these, accusers like to thee,
I list no further; those with whom they weigh
May hear the rest, nor venture to gainsay
The wondrous tale no doubt thy tongue can tell,
Which thus begins so courteously and well.
Let Otho cherish here his polish'd guest,
To him my thanks and thoughts shall be express'd."
And here their wondering host hath interposed—
"Whate'er there be between you undisclosed,
This is no time nor fitting place to mar
The mirthful meeting with a wordy war.
If thou, Sir Ezzelin, hast aught to show
Which it befits Count Lara's ear to know,
To-morrow, here, or elsewhere, as may best
Beseem your mutual judgment, speak the rest;
I pledge myself for thee, as not unknown,
Though, like Count Lara, now return'd alone
From other lands, almost a stranger grown;
And if from Lara's blood and gentle birth
I augur right of courage and of worth,
He will not that untainted line belie,
Nor aught that knighthood may accord, deny."

"To-morrow be it," Ezzelin replied,
"And here our several worth and truth be tried;
I gage my life, my falchion to attest
My words, so may I mingle with the blest!"
What answers Lara? to its centre shrunk
His soul, in deep abstraction sudden sunk;
The words of many, and the eyes of all
That there were gather'd, seem'd on him to fall;
But his were silent, his appear'd to stray
In far forgetfulness away—away—
Alas! that heedlessness of all around
Bespoke remembrance only too profound.

XXIV.

"To-morrow!—ay, to-morrow!" further word
Than those repeated none from Lara heard;
Upon his brow no outward passion spoke;
From his large eye no flashing anger broke;
Yet there was something fix'd in that low tone,
Which show'd resolve, determined, though unknown.
He seized his cloak—his head he slightly bow'd,
And passing Ezzelin, he left the crowd;
And as he pass'd him, smiling met the frown
With which that chieftain's brow would bear him down:
It was nor smile of mirth, nor struggling pride
That curbs to scorn the wrath it cannot hide;
But that of one in his own heart secure
Of all that he would do, or could endure.
Could this mean peace? the calmness of the good?
Or guilt grown old in desperate hardihood?
Alas! too like in confidence are each,
For man to trust to mortal look or speech;
From deeds, and deeds alone, may he discern
Truths which it wrings the unpractised heart to learn.

XXV.

And Lara call'd his page, and went his way—
Well could that stripling word or sign obey:
His only follower from those climes afar,
Where the soul glows beneath a brighter star;
For Lara left the shore from whence he sprung,
In duty patient, and sedate though young,
Silent as him he served, his faith appears
Above his station, and beyond his years.
Though not unknown the tongue of Lara's land,
In such from him he rarely heard command,
But fleet his step, and clear his tones would come,
When Lara's lip breathed forth the words of home:
Those accents, as his native mountains dear,
Awake their absent echoes in his ear,
Friends', kindred's, parents', wonted voice recall,
Now lost, abjured, for one—his friend, his all:

For him earth now disclosed no other guide;
What marvel then he rarely left his side?

XXVI.

Light was his form, and darkly delicate
That brow whereon his native sun had sate,
But had not marr'd, though in his beams he grew,
The cheek where oft the unbidden blush shone through;
Yet not such blush as mounts when health would show
All the heart's hue in that delighted glow;
But 'twas a hectic tint of secret care
That for a burning moment fever'd there;
And the wild sparkle of his eye seem'd caught
From high, and lighten'd with electric thought,
Though its black orb those long low lashes fringe
Had temper'd with a melancholy tinge;
Yet less of sorrow than of pride was there,
Or, if 'twere grief, a grief that none should share:
And pleased not him the sports that please his age,
The tricks of youth, the frolics of the page;
For hours on Lara he would fix his glance,
As all-forgotten in that watchful trance;
And from his chief withdrawn, he wander'd lone,
Brief were his answers, and his questions none;
His walk the wood, his sport some foreign book;
His resting-place the bank that curbs the brook:
He seem'd, like him he served, to live apart
From all that lures the eye, and fills the heart;
To know no brotherhood, and take from earth
No gift beyond that bitter boon—our birth.

XXVII.

If aught he loved, 'twas Lara; but was shown
His faith in reverence and in deeds alone;
In mute attention; and his care, which guess'd
Each wish, fulfill'd it ere the tongue express'd.
Still there was haughtiness in all he did,
A spirit deep that brook'd not to be chid;
His zeal, though more than that of servile hands,
In act alone obeys, his air commands;

As if 'twas Lara's less than *his* desire
That thus he served, but surely not for hire.
Slight were the tasks enjoin'd him by his lord,
To hold the stirrup, or to bear the sword;
To tune his lute, or, if he will'd it more,
On tomes of other times and tongues to pore;
But ne'er to mingle with the menial train,
To whom he show'd nor deference nor disdain,
But that well-worn reserve which proved he knew
No sympathy with that familiar crew:
His soul, whate'er his station or his stem,
Could bow to Lara, not descend to them.
Of higher birth he seem'd, and better days,
Nor mark of vulgar toil that hand betrays,
So femininely white it might bespeak
Another sex, when match'd with that smooth cheek,
But for his garb, and something in his gaze,
More wild and high than woman's eye betrays;
A latent fierceness that far more became
His fiery climate than his tender frame:
True, in his words it broke not from his breast,
But from his aspect might be more than guess'd.
Kaled his name, though rumour said he bore
Another ere he left his mountain-shore;
For sometimes he would hear, however nigh,
That name repeated loud without reply,
As unfamiliar, or, if roused again,
Start to the sound, as but remember'd then;
Unless 'twas Lara's wonted voice that spake,
For then, ear, eyes, and heart would all awake.

XXVIII.

He had look'd down upon the festive hall,
And mark'd that sudden strife so mark'd of all:
And when the crowd around and near him told
Their wonder at the calmness of the bold,
Their marvel how the high-born Lara bore
Such insult from a stranger, doubly sore,
The colour of young Kaled went and came,
The lip of ashes, and the cheek of flame;

And o'er his brow the dampening heart-drops threw
The sickening iciness of that cold dew,
That rises as the busy bosom sinks
With heavy thoughts from which reflection shrinks.
Yes—there be things which we must dream and dare,
And execute ere thought be half aware :
Whate'er might Kaled's be, it was enow
To seal his lip, but agonise his brow.
He gazed on Ezzelin till Lara cast
That sidelong smile upon the knight he past;
When Kaled saw that smile his visage fell,
As if on something recognised right well :
His memory read in such a meaning more
Than Lara's aspect unto others wore:
Forward he sprung—a moment, both were gone,
And all within that hall seem'd left alone;
Each had so fix'd his eye on Lara's mien,
All had so mix'd their feelings with that scene,
That when his long dark shadow through the porch
No more relieves the glare of yon high torch,
Each pulse beats quicker, and all bosoms seem
To bound as doubting from too black a dream,
Such as we know is false, yet dread in sooth,
Because the worst is ever nearest truth.
And they are gone—but Ezzelin is there,
With thoughtful visage and imperious air;
But long remain'd not; ere an hour expired
He waved his hand to Otho, and retired.

XXIX.

The crowd are gone, the revellers at rest;
The courteous host, and all-approving guest,
Again to that accustom'd couch must creep
Where joy subsides, and sorrow sighs to sleep,
And man, o'erlabour'd with his being's strife,
Shrinks to that sweet forgetfulness of life :
There lie love's feverish hope, and cunning's guile,
Hate's working brain, and lull'd ambition's wile;
O'er each vain eye oblivion's pinions wave,
And quench'd existence crouches in a grave.

What better name may slumber's bed become?
Night's sepulchre, the universal home,
Where weakness, strength, vice, virtue, sunk supine,
Alike in naked helplessness recline;
Glad for a while to heave unconscious breath,
Yet wake to wrestle with the dread of death,
And shun, though day but dawn on ills increased,
That sleep, the loveliest, since it dreams the least.

CANTO THE SECOND.

I.

NIGHT wanes—the vapours round the mountains curl'd
Melt into morn, and Light awakes the world,
Man has another day to swell the past,
And lead him near to little, but his last;
But mighty Nature bounds as from her birth,
The sun is in the heavens, and life on earth;
Flowers in the valley, splendour in the beam,
Health on the gale, and freshness in the stream.
Immortal man! behold her glories shine,
And cry, exulting inly, "They are thine!"
Gaze on, while yet thy gladden'd eye may see:
A morrow comes when they are not for thee:
And grieve what may above thy senseless bier,
Nor earth nor sky will yield a single tear;
Nor cloud shall gather more, nor leaf shall fall,
Nor gale breathe forth one sigh for thee, for all;[1]
But creeping things shall revel in their spoil,
And fit thy clay to fertilise the soil.

II.

'Tis morn—'tis noon—assembled in the hall,
The gather'd chieftains come to Otho's call;
'Tis now the promised hour, that must proclaim
The life or death of Lara's future fame;
When Ezzelin his charge may here unfold,
And whatsoe'er the tale, it must be told.

---

[1] [Mr. Alexander Dyce points out the resemblance between these lines and a passage in one of Pope's letters to Steele: "The morning after my exit the sun will rise as bright as ever, the flowers smell as sweet, the plants spring as green."]

His faith was pledged, and Lara's promise given,
To meet it in the eye of man and heaven.
Why comes he not?   Such truths to be divulged,
Methinks the accuser's rest is long indulged.

III.

The hour is past, and Lara too is there,
With self-confiding, coldly patient air;
Why comes not Ezzelin?   The hour is past,
And murmurs rise, and Otho's brow's o'ercast.
" I know my friend ! his faith I cannot fear,
If yet he be on earth, expect him here;
The roof that held him in the valley stands
Between my own and noble Lara's lands;
My halls from such a guest had honour gain'd,
Nor had Sir Ezzelin his host disdain'd,
But that some previous proof forbade his stay,
And urged him to prepare against to-day;
The word I pledged for his I pledge again,
Or will myself redeem his knighthood's stain."

He ceased—and Lara answer'd, " I am here
To lend at thy demand a listening ear
To tales of evil from a stranger's tongue,
Whose words already might my heart have wrung,
But that I deem'd him scarcely less than mad,
Or, at the worst, a foe ignobly bad.
I know him not—but me it seems he knew
In lands where—but I must not trifle too :
Produce this babbler—or redeem the pledge;
Here in thy hold, and with thy falchion's edge."

Proud Otho on the instant, reddening, threw
His glove on earth, and forth his sabre flew.
" 'The last alternative befits me best,
And thus I answer for mine absent guest."

With cheek unchanging from its sallow gloom,
However near his own or other's tomb;

With hand, whose almost careless coolness spoke
Its grasp well-used to deal the sabre-stroke;
With eye, though calm, determined not to spare,
Did Lara too his willing weapon bare.
In vain the circling chieftains round them closed,
For Otho's frenzy would not be opposed;
And from his lip those words of insult fell—
His sword is good who can maintain them well.

IV.

Short was the conflict; furious, blindly rash,
Vain Otho gave his bosom to the gash:
He bled, and fell; but not with deadly wound,
Stretch'd by a dextrous sleight along the ground.
"Demand thy life!"   He answer'd not: and then
From that red floor he ne'er had risen again,
For Lara's brow upon the moment grew
Almost to blackness in its demon hue;[2]
And fiercer shook his angry falchion now
Than when his foe's was levell'd at his brow;
Then all was stern collectedness and art,
Now rose the unleaven'd hatred of his heart;
So little sparing to the foe he fell'd,
That when the approaching crowd his arm withheld,
He almost turn'd the thirsty point on those
Who thus for mercy dared to interpose;
But to a moment's thought that purpose bent;
Yet look'd he on him still with eye intent,
As if he loathed the ineffectual strife
That left a foe, howe'er o'erthrown, with life;
As if to search how far the wound he gave
Had sent its victim onward to his grave.

V.

They raised the bleeding Otho, and the Leech
Forbade all present question, sign, and speech;

---

[2] [This incident, says Mr Alexander Dyce, is undoubtedly derived from the
Mysteries of Udolpho "The Count then fell back into the arms of his servants,
while Montoni held his sword over him and bade him ask his life . . his complexion
changed almost to blackness as he looked upon his fallen adversary."]

The others met within a neighbouring hall,
And he, incensed, and heedless of them all,
The cause and conqueror in this sudden fray,
In haughty silence slowly strode away;
He back'd his steed, his homeward path he took,
Nor cast on Otho's towers a single look.

VI.

But where was he? that meteor of a night,
Who menaced but to disappear with light.
Where was this Ezzelin? who came and went,
To leave no other trace of his intent.
He left the dome of Otho long ere morn,
In darkness, yet so well the path was worn
He could not miss it: near his dwelling lay;
But there he was not, and with coming day
Came fast inquiry, which unfolded nought,
Except the absence of the chief it sought.
A chamber tenantless, a steed at rest,
His host alarm'd, his murmuring squires distress'd:
Their search extends along, around the path,
In dread to meet the marks of prowlers' wrath:
But none are there, and not a brake hath borne
Nor gout of blood, nor shred of mantle torn;
Nor fall nor struggle hath defaced the grass,
Which still retains a mark where murder was;
Nor dabbling fingers left to tell the tale,
The bitter print of each convulsive nail,
When agonised hands that cease to guard,
Wound in that pang the smoothness of the sward.
Some such had been, if here a life was reft,
But these were not; and doubting hope is left;
And strange suspicion, whispering Lara's name,
Now daily mutters o'er his blacken'd fame,
Then sudden silent when his form appear'd,
Awaits the absence of the thing it fear'd
Again its wonted wondering to renew,
And dye conjecture with a darker hue.

VII.

Days roll along, and Otho's wounds are heal'd,
But not his pride; and hate no more conceal'd:
He was a man of power, and Lara's foe,
The friend of all who sought to work him woe,
And from his country's justice now demands
Account of Ezzelin at Lara's hands.
Who else than Lara could have cause to fear
His presence? who had made him disappear,
If not the man on whom his menaced charge
Had sate too deeply were he left at large?
The general rumour ignorantly loud,
The mystery dearest to the curious crowd;
The seeming friendlessness of him who strove
To win no confidence, and wake no love;
The sweeping fierceness which his soul betray'd,
The skill with which he wielded his keen blade;
Where had his arm unwarlike caught that art?
Where had that fierceness grown upon his heart?
For it was not the blind capricious rage
A word can kindle and a word assuage;
But the deep working of a soul unmix'd
With aught of pity where its wrath had fix'd;
Such as long power and overgorged success
Concentrates into all that's merciless:
These, link'd with that desire which ever sways
Mankind, the rather to condemn than praise,
'Gainst Lara gathering raised at length a storm,
Such as himself might fear, and foes would form,
And he must answer for the absent head
Of one that haunts him still, alive or dead.

VIII.

Within that land was many a malcontent,
Who cursed the tyranny to which he bent;
That soil full many a wringing despot saw,
Who work'd his wantonness in form of law;
Long war without and frequent broil within
Had made a path for blood and giant sin,
That waited but a signal to begin

New havoc, such as civil discord blends,
Which knows no neuter, owns but foes or friends;
Fix'd in his feudal fortress each was lord,
In word and deed obey'd, in soul abhorr'd.
Thus Lara had inherited his lands,
And with them pining hearts and sluggish hands;
But that long absence from his native clime
Had left him stainless of oppression's crime,
And now, diverted by his milder sway,
All dread by slow degrees had worn away.
The menials felt their usual awe alone,
But more for him than them that fear was grown;
They deem'd him now unhappy, though at first
Their evil judgment augur'd of the worst,
And each long restless night, and silent mood,
Was traced to sickness, fed by solitude:
And though his lonely habits threw of late
Gloom o'er his chamber, cheerful was his gate;
For thence the wretched ne'er unsoothed withdrew,
For them, at least, his soul compassion knew.
Cold to the great, contemptuous to the high,
The humble pass'd not his unheeding eye;
Much he would speak not, but beneath his roof
They found asylum oft, and ne'er reproof.
And they who watch'd might mark that, day by day,
Some new retainers gather'd to his sway,
But most of late, since Ezzelin was lost,
He play'd the courteous lord and bounteous host:
Perchance his strife with Otho made him dread
Some snare prepared for his obnoxious head;
Whate'er his view, his favour more obtains
With these, the people, than his fellow thanes.
If this were policy, so far 'twas sound,
The million judged but of him as they found;
From him by sterner chiefs to exile driven
They but required a shelter, and 'twas given.
By him no peasant mourn'd his rifled cot,
And scarce the Serf could murmur o'er his lot;
With him old avarice found its hoard secure,
With him contempt forbore to mock the poor;

Youth present cheer and promised recompense
Detain'd, till all too late to part from thence:
To hate he offer'd, with the coming change,
The deep reversion of delay'd revenge;
To love, long baffled by the unequal match,
The well-won charms success was sure to snatch.
All now was ripe, he waits but to proclaim
That slavery nothing which was still a name.
The moment came, the hour when Otho thought
Secure at last the vengeance which he sought:
His summons found the destined criminal
Begirt by thousands in his swarming hall,
Fresh from their feudal fetters newly riven,
Defying earth, and confident of heaven.
That morning he had freed the soil-bound slaves,
Who dig no land for tyrants but their graves!
Such is their cry—some watchword for the fight
Must vindicate the wrong, and warp the right;
Religion—freedom—vengeance—what you will,
A word's enough to raise mankind to kill;
Some factious phrase by cunning caught and spread,
That guilt may reign, and wolves and worms be fed!

IX.

Throughout that clime the feudal chiefs had gain'd
Such sway, their infant monarch hardly reign'd;
Now was the hour for faction's rebel growth,
The Serfs contemn'd the one, and hated both:
They waited but a leader, and they found
One to their cause inseparably bound;
By circumstance compell'd to plunge again,
In self-defence, amidst the strife of men.
Cut off by some mysterious fate from those
Whom birth and nature meant not for his foes,
Had Lara from that night, to him accurst,
Prepared to meet, but not alone, the worst:
Some reason urged, whate'er it was, to shun
Enquiry into deeds at distance done;
By mingling with his own the cause of all,
E'en if he fail'd, he still delay'd his fall.

The sullen calm that long his bosom kept,
The storm that once had spent itself and slept,
Roused by events that seem'd foredoom'd to urge
His gloomy fortunes to their utmost verge,
Burst forth, and made him all he once had been,
And is again; he only changed the scene.
Light care had he for life, and less for fame,
But not less fitted for the desperate game:
He deem'd himself mark'd out for others' hate,
And mock'd at ruin so they shared his fate.
What cared he for the freedom of the crowd?
He raised the humble but to bend the proud.
He had hoped quiet in his sullen lair,
But man and destiny beset him there:
Inured to hunters, he was found at bay;
And they must kill, they cannot snare the prey.
Stern, unambitious, silent, he had been
Henceforth a calm spectator of life's scene;
But dragg'd again upon the arena, stood
A leader not unequal to the feud;
In voice, mien, gesture, savage nature spoke,
And from his eye the gladiator broke.

X.

What boots the oft-repeated tale of strife,
The feast of vultures, and the waste of life?
The varying fortune of each separate field,
The fierce that vanquish, and the faint that yield?
The smoking ruin, and the crumbled wall?
In this the struggle was the same with all;
Save that distemper'd passions lent their force
In bitterness that banish'd all remorse.
None sued, for Mercy knew her cry was vain,
The captive died upon the battle-plain .
In either cause, one rage alone possess'd
The empire of the alternate victor's breast;
And they that smote for freedom or for sway,
Deem'd few were slain, while more remain'd to slay.
It was too late to check the wasting brand,
And Desolation reap'd the famish'd land;

The torch was lighted, and the flame was spread,
And Carnage smiled upon her daily dead.

XI.

Fresh with the nerve the new-born impulse strung,
The first success to Lara's numbers clung :
But that vain victory hath ruin'd all;
They form no longer to their leader's call :
In blind confusion on the foe they press,
And think to snatch is to secure success.
The lust of booty, and the thirst of hate,
Lure on the broken brigands to their fate :
In vain he doth whate'er a chief may do,
To check the headlong fury of that crew ;
In vain their stubborn ardour he would tame,
The hand that kindles cannot quench the flame ;
The wary foe alone hath turn'd their mood,
And shown their rashness to that erring brood :
The feign'd retreat, the nightly ambuscade,
The daily harass, and the fight delay'd,
The long privation of the hoped supply,
The tentless rest beneath the humid sky,
The stubborn wall that mocks the leaguer's art,
And palls the patience of his baffled art,
Of these they had not deem'd : the battle-day
They could encounter as a veteran may ;
But more preferr'd the fury of the strife,
And present death, to hourly suffering life :
And famine wrings, and fever sweeps away
His numbers melting fast from their array ;
Intemperate triumph fades to discontent,
And Lara's soul alone seems still unbent :
But few remain to aid his voice and hand,
And thousands dwindled to a scanty band :
Desperate, though few, the last and best remain'd
To mourn the discipline they late disdain'd.
One hope survives, the frontier is not far,
And thence they may escape from native war ;
And bear within them to the neighbouring state
An exile's sorrows, or an outlaw's hate :

Hard is the task their father-land to quit,
But harder still to perish or submit.

· XII.

It is resolved—they march—consenting Night
Guides with her star their dim and torchless flight;
Already they perceive its tranquil beam
Sleep on the surface of the barrier stream;
Already they descry—Is yon the bank?
Away! 'tis lined with many a hostile rank.
Return or fly!—What glitters in the rear?
'Tis Otho's banner—the pursuer's spear!
Are those the shepherds' fires upon the height?
Alas! they blaze too widely for the flight:
Cut off from hope, and compass'd in the toil,
Less blood perchance hath bought a richer spoil!

XIII.

A moment's pause—'tis but to breathe their band,
Or shall they onward press, or here withstand?
It matters little—if they charge the foes
Who by their border-stream their march oppose,
Some few, perchance, may break and pass the line,
However link'd to baffle such design.
"The charge be ours! to wait for their assault
Were fate well worthy of a coward's halt."
Forth flies each sabre, rein'd is every steed,
And the next word shall scarce outstrip the deed:
In the next tone of Lara's gathering breath
How many shall but hear the voice of death!

XIV.

His blade is bared,—in him there is an air
As deep, but far too tranquil for despair;
A something of indifference more than then
Becomes the bravest, if they feel for men.
He turn'd his eye on Kaled, ever near,
And still too faithful to betray one fear;
Perchance 'twas but the moon's dim twilight threw
Along his aspect an unwonted hue

Of mournful paleness, whose deep tint express'd
The truth, and not the terror of his breast.
This Lara mark'd, and laid his hand on his:
It trembled not in such an hour as this;
His lip was silent, scarcely beat his heart,
His eye alone proclaim'd, "We will not part!
Thy band may perish, or thy friends may flee,
Farewell to life, but not adieu to thee!"

The word hath pass'd his lips, and onward driven,
Pours the link'd band through ranks asunder riven:
Well has each steed obey'd the armed heel,
And flash the scimitars, and rings the steel;
Outnumber'd, not outbraved, they still oppose
Despair to daring, and a front to foes;
And blood is mingled with the dashing stream,
Which runs all redly till the morning beam.

XV.

Commanding, aiding, animating all,
Where foe appear'd to press, or friend to fall,
Cheers Lara's voice, and waves or strikes his steel,
Inspiring hope himself had ceased to feel.
None fled, for well they knew that flight were vain;
But those that waver turn to smite again,
While yet they find the firmest of the foe
Recoil before their leader's look and blow:
Now girt with numbers, now almost alone,
He foils their ranks, or re-unites his own;
Himself he spared not—once they seem'd to fly—
Now was the time, he waved his hand on high,
And shook—Why sudden droops that plumed crest?
The shaft is sped—the arrow's in his breast!
That fatal gesture left the unguarded side,
And Death has stricken down yon arm of pride.
The word of triumph fainted from his tongue;
That hand, so raised, how droopingly it hung!
But yet the sword instinctively retains,
Though from its fellow shrink the falling reins;

These Kaled snatches : dizzy with the blow,
And senseless bending o'er his saddle-bow,
Perceives not Lara that his anxious page
Beguiles his charger from the combat's rage :
Meantime his followers charge, and charge again ;
Too mix'd the slayers now to heed the slain !

XVI.

Day glimmers on the dying and the dead,
The cloven cuirass, and the helmless head :
The war-horse masterless is on the earth,
And that last gasp hath burst his bloody girth ;
And near, yet quivering with what life remain'd,
The heel that urged him and the hand that rein'd ;
And some too near that rolling torrent lie,
Whose waters mock the lip of those that die ;
That panting thirst which scorches in the breath
Of those that die the soldier's fiery death,
In vain impels the burning mouth to crave
One drop—the last—to cool it for the grave ;
With feeble and convulsive effort swept,
Their limbs along the crimson'd turf have crept ;
The faint remains of life such struggles waste,
But yet they reach the stream, and bend to taste :
They feel its freshness, and almost partake—
Why pause ?   No further thirst have they to slake—
It is unquench'd, and yet they feel it not ;
It was an agony—but now forgot !

XVII.

Beneath a lime, remoter from the scene,
Where but for him that strife had never been,
A breathing but devoted warrior lay :
'Twas Lara bleeding fast from life away.
His follower once, and now his only guide,
Kneels Kaled watchful o'er his welling side,
And with his scarf would stanch the tides that rush,
With each convulsion, in a blacker gush ;
And then, as his faint breathing waxes low,
In feebler, not less fatal tricklings flow :

He scarce can speak, but motions him 'tis vain,
And merely adds another throb to pain.
He clasps the hand that pang which would assuage,
And sadly smiles his thanks to that dark page,
Who nothing fears, nor feels, nor heeds, nor sees,
Save that damp brow which rests upon his knees ;
Save that pale aspect, where the eye, though dim,
Held all the light that shone on earth for him. '

XVIII.

The foe arrives, who long had search'd the field,
Their triumph nought till Lara too should yield :
They would remove him, but they see 'twere vain,
And he regards them with a calm disdain,
That rose to reconcile him with his fate,
And that escape to death from living hate :
And Otho comes, and leaping from his steed,
Looks on the bleeding foe that made him bleed,
And questions of his state ; he answers not,
Scarce glances on him as on one forgot,
And turns to Kaled .—each remaining word
They understood not, if distinctly heard ;
His dying tones are in that other tongue,
To which some strange remembrance wildly clung.
They spake of other scenes, but what—is known
To Kaled, whom their meaning reach'd alone ;
And he replied, though faintly, to their sound,
While gazed the rest in dumb amazement round :
They seem'd even then—that twain—unto the last
To half forget the present in the past ;
To share between themselves some separate fate,
Whose darkness none beside should penetrate.

XIX.

Their words though faint were many—from the tone
Their import those who heard could judge alone ;
From this, you might have deem'd young Kaled's death
More near than Lara's by his voice and breath,
So sad, so deep, and hesitating broke
The accents his scarce-moving pale lips spoke ;

But Lara's voice, though low, at first was clear
And calm, till murmuring death gasp'd hoarsely near;
But from his visage little could we guess,
So unrepentant, dark, and passionless,
Save that when struggling nearer to his last,
Upon that page his eye was kindly cast;
And once, as Kaled's answering accents ceased,
Rose Lara's hand, and pointed to the East:
Whether (as then the breaking sun from high
Roll'd back the clouds) the morrow caught his eye,
Or that 'twas chance, or some remember'd scene,
That raised his arm to point where such had been,
Scarce Kaled seem'd to know, but turn'd away,
As if his heart abhorr'd that coming day,
And shrunk his glance before that morning light,
To look on Lara's brow—where all grew night.
Yet sense seem'd left, though better were its loss;
For when one near display'd the absolving cross,
And proffer'd to his touch the holy bead,
Of which his parting soul might own the need,
He look'd upon it with an eye profane,
And smiled—Heaven pardon! if 'twere with disdain:
And Kaled, though he spoke not, nor withdrew
From Lara's face his fix'd despairing view,
With brow repulsive, and with gesture swift,
Flung back the hand which held the sacred gift,
As if such but disturb'd the expiring man,
Nor seem'd to know his life but *then* began,
That life of Immortality, secure
To none, save them whose faith in Christ is sure.

xx.

But gasping heaved the breath that Lara drew,
And dull the film along his dim eye grew;
His limbs stretch'd fluttering, and his head droop'd o'er
The weak yet still untiring knee that bore;
He press'd the hand he held upon his heart—
It beats no more, but Kaled will not part
With the cold grasp, but feels, and feels in vain,
For that faint throb which answers not again.

"It beats!"—Away, thou dreamer! he is gone—
It once was Lara which thou look'st upon.'

XXI

He gazed, as if not yet had pass'd away
The haughty spirit of that humbled clay;
And those around have roused him from his trance,
But cannot tear from thence his fixed glance;
And when, in raising him from where he bore
Within his arms the form that felt no more,
He saw the head his breast would still sustain,
Roll down like earth to earth upon the plain;
He did not dash himself thereby, nor tear
The glossy tendrils of his raven hair,
But strove to stand and gaze, but reel'd and fell,
Scarce breathing more than that he loved so well.
Than that *he* loved! Oh! never yet beneath
The breast of man such trusty love may breathe!
That trying moment hath at once reveal'd
The secret long and yet but half conceal'd;
In baring to revive that lifeless breast,
Its grief seem'd ended, but the sex confess'd;
And life return'd, and Kaled felt no shame—
What now to her was Womanhood or Fame?

XXII.

And Lara sleeps not where his fathers sleep,
But where he died his grave was dug as deep;
Nor is his mortal slumber less profound,
Though priest nor bless'd nor marble deck'd the mound,
And he was mourn'd by one whose quiet grief,
Less loud, outlasts a people's for their chief.
Vain was all question ask'd her of the past,
And vain e'en menace—silent to the last;

' [The death of Lara, is by far the finest passage in the poem, and is fully equal
to any thing else which the author ever wrote. The physical horror of the event,
though described with a terrible force and fidelity, is both relieved and enhanced by
the beautiful pictures of mental energy and affection with which it is combined —
JEFFREY]

She told nor whence, nor why she left behind
Her all for one who seem'd but little kind.
Why did she love him? Curious fool!—be still—
Is human love the growth of human will?
To her he might be gentleness; the stern
Have deeper thoughts than your dull eyes discern,
And when they love, your smilers guess not how
Beats the strong heart, though less the lips avow.
They were not common links, that form'd the chain
That bound to Lara Kaled's heart and brain;
But that wild tale she brook'd not to unfold,
And seal'd is now each lip that could have told.

XXIII.

They laid him in the earth, and on his breast,
Besides the wound that sent his soul to rest,
They found the scatter'd dints of many a scar,
Which were not planted there in recent war;
Where'er had pass'd his summer years of life,
It seems they vanish'd in a land of strife;
But all unknown his glory or his guilt,
These only told that somewhere blood was spilt,
And Ezzelin, who might have spoke the past,
Return'd no more—that night appear'd his last.

XXIV.

Upon that night (a peasant's is the tale)
A Serf that cross'd the intervening vale,[4]

[4] The event in this section was suggested by the description of the death or rather burial of the Duke of Gandia. The most interesting and particular account of it is given by Burchard, and is in substance as follows :—" On the eighth day of June, the Cardinal of Valenza and the Duke of Gandia, sons of the Pope, supped with their mother, Vanozza, near the church of S. *Pietro ad vincula :* several other persons being present at the entertainment. A late hour approaching, and the cardinal having reminded his brother that it was time to return to the apostolic palace, they mounted their horses or mules, with only a few attendants, and proceeded together as far as the palace of Cardinal Ascanio Sforza, when the duke informed the cardinal that, before he returned home, he had to pay a visit of pleasure. Dismissing therefore all his attendants, excepting his *staffiero*, or footman, and a person in a mask, who had paid him a visit whilst at supper, and who, during the space of a month or thereabouts, previous to this time, had called upon him almost daily at the apostolic palace, he took this person behind him on his mule, and proceeded to the street of the Jews, where he quitted his servant, directing him to remain there until a certain hour; when, if he

o 2

When Cynthia's light almost gave way to morn,
And nearly· veil'd in mist her waning horn ;
A Serf, that rose betimes to thread the wood,
And hew the bough that bought his children's food,
Pass'd by the river that divides the plain
Of Otho's lands and Lara's broad domain :

did not return, he might repair to the palace. The duke then seated the person in
the mask behind him, and rode I know not whither , but in that night he was
assassinated, and thrown into the river The servant, after having been dismissed,
was also assaulted and mortally wounded , and although he was attended with great
care, yet such was his situation, that he could give no intelligible account of what had
befallen his master In the morning, the duke not having returned to the palace, his
servants began to be alarmed , and one of them informed the pontiff of the evening
excursion of his sons, and that the duke had not yet made his appearance. This gave
the pope no small anxiety , but he conjectured that the duke had been attracted by
some courtesan to pass the night with her, and, not choosing to quit the house in open
day, had waited till the following evening to return home. When, howevei, the
evening arrived, and he found himself disappointed in his expectations, he became
deeply afflicted, and began to make inquiries from different persons, whom he ordered
to attend him for that purpose Amongst these was a man named Giorgio Schiavoni,
who, having discharged some timber from a bark in the river, had remained on board
the vessel to watch it ; and being interrogated whether he had seen any one thrown
into the river on the night preceding, he replied, that he saw two men on foot, who
came down the street, and looked diligently about to observe whether any person was
passing That seeing no one, they returned, and a short time afterwards two others
came, and looked around in the same manner as the former no person still appearing,
they gave a sign to their companions, when a man came, mounted on a white horse,
having behind him a dead body, the head and arms of which hung on one side. and
the feet on the other side of the horse , the two persons on foot supporting the body,
to prevent its falling They thus proceeded towards that part where the filth of the
city is usually discharged into the river, and turning the horse, with his tail towards
the water, the two persons took the dead body by the arms and feet, and with all their
strength flung it into the river. The person on horseback then asked if they had
thrown it in , to which they replied, *Signor, si* (yes, Sir). He then looked towards
the rivei, and seeing a mantle floating on the stream, he enquired what it was that
appeared black, to which they answered, it was a mantle ; and one of them threw
stones upon it, in consequence of which it sunk. The attendants of the pontiff then
enquired from Giorgio, why he had not revealed this to the governor of the city ; to
which he replied, that he had seen in his time a hundred dead bodies thrown into the
river at the same place, without any inquiry being made respecting them ; and that
he had not, therefore, considered it as a matter of any importance. The fishermen
and seamen were then collected, and ordered to search the river, where, on the
following evening, they found the body of the duke, with his habit entire, and thirty
ducats in his purse He was pierced with nine wounds, one of which was in his
throat, the others in his head, body, and limbs No sooner was the pontiff informed
of the death of his son, and that he had been thrown, like filth, into the river, than,
giving way to his grief, he shut himself up in a chamber, and wept bitterly. The
Cardinal of Segovia, and other attendants on the pope, went to the door, and after
many hours spent in persuasions and exhortations, prevailed upon him to admit them.
From the evening of Wednesday till the following Saturday the pope took no food ; nor
did he sleep from Thursday morning till the same hour on the ensuing day At length,
however, giving way to the entreaties of his attendants, he began to restrain his
sorrow, and to consider the injury which his own health might sustain by the further
indulgence of his grief "—Roscoe's *Leo Tenth*, vol 1 p 265.

i

He heard a tramp—a horse and horseman broke
From out the wood—before him was a cloak
Wrapt round some burthen at his saddle-bow,
Bent was his head, and hidden was his brow.
Roused by the sudden sight at such a time,
And some foreboding that it might be crime,
Himself unheeded watch'd the stranger's course,
Who reach'd the river, bounded from his horse,
And lifting thence the burthen which he bore,
Heaved up the bank, and dash'd it from the shore,
Then paused, and look'd, and turn'd, and seem'd to watch,
And still another hurried glance would snatch,
And follow with his step the stream that flow'd,
As if even yet too much its surface show'd;
At once he started, stoop'd, around him strown
The winter floods had scatter'd heaps of stone;
Of these the heaviest thence he gather'd there,
And slung them with a more than common care.
Meantime the Serf had crept to where unseen
Himself might safely mark what this might mean;
He caught a glimpse, as of a floating breast,
And something glitter'd starlike on the vest;
But ere he well could mark the buoyant trunk,
A massy fragment smote it, and it sunk:
It rose again, but indistinct to view,
And left the waters of a purple hue,
Then deeply disappear'd: the horseman gazed
Till ebb'd the latest eddy it had raised;
Then turning, vaulted on his pawing steed,
And instant spurr'd him into panting speed.
His face was mask'd—the features of the dead,
If dead it were, escaped the observer's dread;
But if in sooth a star its bosom bore,
Such is the badge that knighthood ever wore,
And such 'tis known Sir Ezzelin had worn
Upon the night that led to such a morn.
If thus he perish'd, Heaven receive his soul!
His undiscover'd limbs to ocean roll;
And charity upon the hope would dwell
It was not Lara's hand by which he fell.

XXV.

And Kaled—Lara—Ezzelin, are gone,
Alike without their monumental stone!
The first, all efforts vainly strove to wean
From lingering where her chieftain's blood had been:
Grief had so tamed a spirit once too proud,
Her tears were few, her wailing never loud;
But furious would you tear her from the spot
Where yet she scarce believed that he was not,
Her eye shot forth with all the living fire
That haunts the tigress in her whelpless ire;
But left to waste her weary moments there,
She talk'd all idly unto shapes of air,
Such as the busy brain of Sorrow paints,
And woos to listen to her fond complaints:
And she would sit beneath the very tree
Where lay his drooping head upon her knee;
And in that posture where she saw him fall,
His words, his looks, his dying grasp recall;
And she had shorn, but saved her raven hair,
And oft would snatch it from her bosom there,
And fold, and press it gently to the ground,
As if she stanch'd anew some phantom's wound.
Herself would question, and for him reply;
Then rising, start, and beckon him to fly
From some imagined spectre in pursuit;
Then seat her down upon some linden's root,
And hide her visage with her meagre hand,
Or trace strange characters along the sand—
This could not last—she lies by him she loved;
Her tale untold—her truth too dearly proved.

THE SIEGE OF CORINTH.

TO

JOHN HOBHOUSE, ESQ.,

𝕿𝖍𝖎𝖘 𝕻𝖔𝖊𝖒 𝖎𝖘 𝕴𝖓𝖘𝖈𝖗𝖎𝖇𝖊𝖉,

BY HIS

FRIEND.

January 22nd, 1816.

ADVERTISEMENT.

"THE grand army of the Turks (in 1715), under the Prime Vizier, to open to themselves a way into the heart of the Morea, and to form the siege of Napoli di Romania, the most considerable place in all that country,* thought it best in the first place to attack Corinth, upon which they made several storms. The garrison being weakened, and the governor seeing it was impossible to hold out against so mighty a force, thought it fit to beat a parley : but while they were treating about the articles, one of the magazines in the Turkish camp, wherein they had six hundred barrels of powder, blew up by accident, whereby six or seven hundred men were killed ; which so enraged the infidels, that they would not grant any capitulation, but stormed the place with so much fury, that they took it, and put most of the garrison, with Signior Minotti, the governor, to the sword. The rest, with Antonio Bembo, proveditor extraordinary, were made prisoners of war."—*History of the Turks,* vol. iii. p. 151.

---

* Napoli di Romania is not now the most considerable place in the Morea, but Tripolitza, where the Pacha resides, and maintains his government. Napoli is near Argos   I visited all three in 1810-11 ; and, in the course of journeying through the country from my first arrival in 1809, I crossed the Isthmus eight times in my way from Attica to the Morea, over the mountains , or in the other direction, when passing from the Gulf of Athens to that of Lepanto   Both the routes are picturesque and beautiful, though very different   that by sea has more sameness, but the voyage being always within sight of land, and often very near it, presents many attractive views of the islands Salamis, Ægina, Poro, &c., and the coast of the Continent

INTRODUCTION TO THE SIEGE OF CORINTH.

THE "Siege of Corinth" and "Parisina" appeared—nearly simultaneously—the first in January, the second in February, 1816, and a thousand guineas were paid for the copyright of the two. Lord Byron considered neither of them to have much pretension, which may be the reason he kept them back, though chiefly written before other pieces which were earlier published. The motive he assigned for continuing to linger over the scenes of his travels was that they were growing confused in his mind, and from partiality to the places, he was anxious to fix the colours before they faded away. His fondness for these recollections is expressed in the concluding passage of the prefatory lines to the "Siege of Corinth," which were only printed after his death. It was objected to the tale that parts of it were composed, through negligence, in a very irregular metre. What was thought to be carelessness, was, however, design , nor can it be denied that, besides the charm of variety, an increased effect is imparted to shifting emotions by a change in the melody. In the "Siege of Corinth" the artifice has been carried to excess. Several of the transitions are discordant, and while the metre is sometimes too jingling for passionate verse, the language has often less energy and polish than is usual with Byron. Mr. Gifford revised the tale, at the request of the author, and drew his pen through a popular, but by no means faultless passage, in the sixteenth section. His advice in other respects seems sound, and by removing blemishes would have heightened the beauty of the poem. This, after all deductions, is great. The slight, but skilfully constructed tale, is, as usual, one of hapless love, and, as usual, there is a blight upon the soul of the hero ; but the tone is not altogether the same with that of its predecessors. Instead of tumultuous deeds and passions, the larger portion is pervaded by an oppressive gloom or a tender melancholy. Alp, a traitor to his creed and country, is leagued with the Turks, to wrest Corinth from the Venetians, and hopes on the morrow to win the fortress, and more precious still, his once promised bride. The awful stillness of the night, the restlessness of the conscience-stricken hero, the sickening spectacle of the dogs devouring the dead, are a fitting introduction to the vision of Francesca, who comes to reproach her lover with his crime, and urge him to repentance. From the pathos, the solemnity and the mystery of this beautiful scene, we pass to the animated description of the siege. Nothing can be more finely imagined than the passage in which Alp, confronting Francesca's father, learns that she died before their last night's colloquy, or than the verification of her prophecy in his instant death,

"Ere his very thought could pray,"

while staggering under the intelligence which reveals to him that she was a visitant from the other world.   The execution here is hardly equal to the thought, and it is the want, in places, of a little more pains in the workmanship which has alone prevented the "Siege of Corinth" from ranking with the best of Byron's tales   The interest ceases with the death of Alp, and there the piece should have been contrived to end.

THE SIEGE OF CORINTH.

In the year since Jesus died for men,
Eighteen hundred years and ten,
We were a gallant company,
Riding o'er land, and sailing o'er sea.
Oh! but we went merrily!
We forded the river, and clomb the high hill,
Never our steeds for a day stood still,
Whether we lay in the cave or the shed,
Our sleep fell soft on the hardest bed;
Whether we couch'd in our rough capote,
On the rougher plank of our gliding boat,
Or stretch'd on the beach, or our saddles spread
As a pillow beneath the resting head,
Fresh we woke upon the morrow:
   All our thoughts and words had scope,
   We had health, and we had hope,
Toil and travel, but no sorrow.
We were of all tongues and creeds;—
Some were those who counted beads,
Some of mosque, and some of church,
   And some, or I mis-say, of neither;
Yet through the wide world might ye search,
   Nor find a motler crew nor blither.

But some are dead, and some are gone,
And some are scatter'd and alone,

And some are rebels on the hills[1]
  That look along Epirus' valleys,
  Where freedom still at moments rallies,
And pays in blood oppression's ills;
  And some are in a far countree,
And some all restlessly at home;
  But never more, oh! never, we
Shall meet to revel and to roam.

But those hardy days flew cheerily!
And when they now fall drearily,
My thoughts, like swallows, skim the main,
And bear my spirit back again
Over the earth, and through the air,
A wild bird and a wanderer.
'Tis this that ever wakes my strain,
And oft, too oft, implores again
The few who may endure my lay,
To follow me so far away.
Stranger—wilt thou follow now,
And sit with me on Acro-Corinth's brow?

I.

Many a vanish'd year and age,
And tempest's breath, and battle's rage,
Have swept o'er Corinth; yet she stands,
A fortress form'd to Freedom's hands.[2]
The whirlwind's wrath, the earthquake's shock,
Have left untouch'd her hoary rock,
The keystone of a land, which still,
Though fall'n, looks proudly on that hill,
The landmark to the double tide
That purpling rolls on either side,
As if their waters chafed to meet,
Yet pause and crouch beneath her feet.

[1] The last tidings recently heard of Dervish (one of the Arnauts who followed me) state him to be in revolt upon the mountains, at the head of some of the bands common in that country in times of trouble
[2] ["A marvel from her Moslem bands "—MS]

But could the blood before her shed
Since first Timoleon's brother bled,[3]
Or baffled Persia's despot fled,
Arise from out the earth which drank
The stream of slaughter as it sank,
That sanguine ocean would o'erflow
Her isthmus idly spread below:
Or could the bones of all the slain,
Who perish'd there, be piled again,
That rival pyramid would rise
More mountain-like, through those clear skies
Than yon tower-capp'd Acropolis,
Which seems the very clouds to kiss.

II.

On dun Cithæron's ridge appears
The gleam of twice ten thousand spears;
And downward to the Isthmian plain,
From shore to shore of either main,
The tent is pitch'd, the crescent shines
Along the Moslem's leaguering lines;
And the dusk Spahi's bands [4] advance
Beneath each bearded pacha's glance;
And far and wide as eye can reach
The turban'd cohorts throng the beach;
And there the Arab's camel kneels,
And there his steed the Tartar wheels;
The Turcoman hath left his herd,[5]
The sabre round his loins to gird;
And there the volleying thunders pour,
Till waves grow smoother to the roar.
The trench is dug, the cannon's breath
Wings the far hissing globe of death;

[3] [Timoleon, who had saved the life of his brother Timophanes in battle, afterwards killed him for aiming at the supreme power in Corinth, preferring his duty to his country to the obligations of relationship. Dr. Warton says, that Pope once intended to write an epic poem on the story, and that Akenside had the same design.]

[4] [Turkish holders of military fiefs, which oblige them to join the army, mounted at their own expense.]

[5] The life of the Turcomans is wandering and patriarchal: they dwell in tents.

Fast whirl the fragments from the wall,
Which crumbles with the ponderous ball;
And from that wall the foe replies,
O'er dusty plain and smoky skies,
With fires that answer fast and well
The summons of the infidel.

III.

But near and nearest to the wall
Of those who wish and work its fall,
With deeper skill in war's black art,
Than Othman's sons, and high of heart
As any chief that ever stood
Triumphant in the fields of blood;
From post to post, and deed to deed,
Fast spurring on his reeking steed,
Where sallying ranks the trench assail,
And make the foremost Moslem quail,
Or where the battery, guarded well,
Remains as yet impregnable,
Alighting cheerly to inspire
The soldier slackening in his fire;
The first and freshest of the host
Which Stamboul's sultan there can boast,
To guide the follower o'er the field,
To point the tube, the lance to wield,
Or whirl around the bickering blade;—
Was Alp, the Adrian renegade!

IV.

From Venice—once a race of worth
His gentle sires—he drew his birth;
But late an exile from her shore,
Against his countrymen he bore
The arms they taught to bear; and now
The turban girt his shaven brow.
Through many a change had Corinth pass'd
With Greece to Venice' rule at last;
And here, before her walls, with those
To Greece and Venice equal foes,

He stood a foe, with all the zeal
Which young and fiery converts feel,
Within whose heated bosom throngs
The memory of a thousand wrongs.
To him had Venice ceased to be
Her ancient civic boast—"the Free;"
And in the palace of St. Mark
Unnamed accusers in the dark
Within the "Lion's mouth" had placed
A charge against him uneffaced:
He fled in time, and saved his life,
To waste his future years in strife,
That taught his land how great her loss
In him who triumph'd o'er the Cross,
'Gainst which he rear'd the Crescent high,
And battled to avenge or die.

Coumourgi[e]—he whose closing scene
Adorn'd the triumph of Eugene,
When on Carlowitz' bloody plain,
The last and mightiest of the slain,
He sank, regretting not to die,
But cursed the Christian's victory—
Coumourgi—can his glory cease,
That latest conqueror of Greece,
Till Christian hands to Greece restore
The freedom Venice gave of yore?
A hundred years have roll'd away
Since he refix'd the Moslem's sway;
And now he led the Mussulman,
And gave the guidance of the van

[e] Ali Coumourgi, the favourite of three sultans, and Grand Vizier to Achmet III, after recovering Peloponnesus from the Venetians in one campaign, was mortally wounded in the next, against the Germans, at the battle of Peterwaradin (in the plain of Carlowitz), in Hungary, endeavouring to rally his guards. He died of his wounds next day. His last order was the decapitation of General Breuner, and some other German prisoners, and his last words, "Oh, that I could thus serve all the Christian dogs!" a speech and act not unlike one of Caligula. He was a young man of great ambition and unbounded presumption: on being told that Prince Eugene, then opposed to him, "was a great general," he said, "I shall become a greater, and at his expense."

To Alp, who well repaid the trust
By cities levell'd with the dust;
And proved, by many a deed of death,
How firm his heart in novel faith.

vi.

The walls grew weak; and fast and hot
Against them pour'd the ceaseless shot,
With unabating fury sent
From battery to battlement;
And thunder-like the pealing din
Rose from each heated culverin;
And here and there some crackling dome
Was fired before the exploding bomb;
And as the fabric sank beneath
The shatt'ring shell's volcanic breath,
In red and wreathing columns flash'd
The flame, as loud the ruin crash'd,
Or into countless meteors driven,
Its earth-stars melted into heaven;
Whose clouds that day grew doubly dun,
Impervious to the hidden sun,
With volumed smoke that slowly grew
To one wide sky of sulphurous hue.

vii

But not for vengeance, long delay'd,
Alone, did Alp, the renegade,
The Moslem warriors sternly teach
His skill to pierce the promised breach:
Within these walls a maid was pent
His hope would win, without consent
Of that inexorable sire,
Whose heart refused him in its ire,
When Alp, beneath his Christian name,
Her virgin hand aspired to claim.
In happier mood, and earlier time,
While unimpeach'd for traitorous crime,
Gayest in gondola or hall,
He glitter'd through the Carnival;

And tuned the softest serenade
That e'er on Adria's waters play'd
At midnight to Italian maid.

VIII.

And many deem'd her heart was won,
For sought by numbers, given to none,
Had young Francesca's hand remain'd
Still by the church's bonds unchain'd:
And when the Adriatic bore
Lanciotto to the Paynim shore,
Her wonted smiles were seen to fail,
And pensive wax'd the maid and pale;
More constant at confessional,
More rare at masque and festival;
Or seen at such, with downcast eyes,
Which conquer'd hearts they ceased to prize·
With listless look she seems to gaze:
With humbler care her form arrays;
Her voice less lively in the song;
Her step, though light, less fleet among
The pairs, on whom the Morning's glance
Breaks, yet unsated with the dance.

IX

Sent by the state to guard the land,
(Which, wrested from the Moslem's hand,
While Sobieski tamed his pride
By Buda's wall and Danube's side,
The chiefs of Venice wrung away
From Patra to Eubœa's bay,)
Minotti held in Corinth's towers
The Doge's delegated powers,
While yet the pitying eye of Peace
Smiled o'er her long forgotten Greece:
And ere that faithless truce was broke
Which freed her from the unchristian yoke,
With him his gentle daughter came;
Nor there, since Menelaus' dame

Forsook her lord and land, to prove
What woes await on lawless love,
Had fairer form adorn'd the shore
Than she, the matchless stranger, bore.

x.

The wall is rent, the ruins yawn;
And, with to-morrow's earliest dawn,
O'er the disjointed mass shall vault
The foremost of the fierce assault.
The bands are rank'd; the chosen van
Of Tartar and of Mussulman,
The full of hope, misnamed "forlorn,"
Who hold the thought of death in scorn,
And win their way with falchion's force,
Or pave the path with many a corse,
O'er which the following brave may rise,
Their stepping-stone—the last who dies!

xi.

'Tis midnight: on the mountains brown
The cold, round moon shines deeply down;
Blue roll the waters, blue the sky
Spreads like an ocean hung on high,
Bespangled with those isles of light,
So wildly, spiritually bright;
Who ever gazed upon them shining
And turn'd to earth without repining,
Nor wish'd for wings to flee away,
And mix with their eternal ray?
The waves on either shore lay there
Calm, clear, and azure as the air;
And scarce their foam the pebbles shook,
But murmur'd meekly as the brook.
The winds were pillow'd on the waves;
The banners droop'd along their staves,
And, as they fell around them furling,
Above them shone the crescent curling;
And that deep silence was unbroke,
Save where the watch his signal spoke,

Save where the steed neigh'd oft and shrill,
And echo answer'd from the hill,
And the wide hum of that wild host
Rustled like leaves from coast to coast,
As rose the Muezzin's voice in air
In midnight call to wonted prayer;
It rose, that chanted mournful strain,
Like some lone spirit's o'er the plain:
'Twas musical, but sadly sweet,
Such as when winds and harp-strings meet,
And take a long unmeasured tone,
To mortal minstrelsy unknown.[7]
It seem'd to those within the wall
A cry prophetic of their fall:
It struck even the besieger's ear
With something ominous and drear,
An undefined and sudden thrill,
Which makes the heart a moment still,
Then beat with quicker pulse, ashamed
Of that strange sense its silence framed;
Such as a sudden passing-bell
Wakes, though but for a stranger's knell.[8]

XII.

The tent of Alp was on the shore;
The sound was hush'd, the prayer was o'er;
The watch was set, the night-round made,
All mandates issued and obey'd:
'Tis but another anxious night,
His pains the morrow may requite
With all revenge and love can pay,
In guerdon for their long delay.
Few hours remain, and he hath need
Of rest, to nerve for many a deed
Of slaughter; but within his soul
The thoughts like troubled waters roll.

[7] ["And make a melancholy moan,
To mortal voice and ear unknown "—MS.]

[8] [" Which rings a deep, internal knell,
A visionary passing-bell,"—MS.]

He stood alone among the host;
Not his the loud fanatic boast
To plant the crescent o'er the cross,
Or risk a life with little loss,
Secure in paradise to be
By Houris loved immortally:
Nor his, what burning patriots feel,
The stern exaltedness of zeal,
Profuse of blood, untired in toil,
When battling on the parent soil.
He stood alone—a renegade
Against the country he betray'd;
He stood alone amidst his band,
Without a trusted heart or hand:
They follow'd him, for he was brave,
And great the spoil he got and gave;
They crouch'd to him, for he had skill
To warp and wield the vulgar will:
But still his Christian origin
With them was little less than sin.
They envied even the faithless fame
He earn'd beneath a Moslem name;
Since he, their mightiest chief, had been
In youth a bitter Nazarene.
They did not know how pride can stoop,
When baffled feelings withering droop;
They did not know how hate can burn
In hearts once changed from soft to stern;
Nor all the false and fatal zeal
The convert of revenge can feel.
He ruled them—man may rule the worst,
By ever daring to be first:
So lions o'er the jackals sway;
The jackal points, he fells the prey,[9]
Then on the vulgar yelling press,
To gorge the relics of success.

[9] [" As lions o'er the jackal sway
       By springing dauntless on the prey;
       They follow on. and yelling press
       To gorge the fragments of success "—MS]

XIII.

His head grows fever'd, and his pulse
The quick successive throbs convulse;
In vain from side to side he throws
His form, in courtship of repose;[1]
Or if he dozed, a sound, a start
Awoke him with a sunken heart.
The turban on his hot brow press'd,
The mail weigh'd lead-like on his breast,
Though oft and long beneath its weight
Upon his eyes had slumber sate,
Without or couch or canopy,
Except a rougher field and sky
Than now might yield a warrior's bed,
Than now along the heaven was spread
He could not rest, he could not stay
Within his tent to wait for day,
But walk'd him forth along the sand,
Where thousand sleepers strew'd the strand.
What pillow'd them? and why should he
More wakeful than the humblest be,
Since more their peril, worse their toil?
And yet they fearless dream of spoil,
While he alone, where thousands pass'd
A night of sleep, perchance their last,
In sickly vigil wander'd on,
And envied all he gazed upon.

XIV

He felt his soul become more light
Beneath the freshness of the night.
Cool was the silent sky, though calm,
And bathed his brow with airy balm:
Behind, the camp—before him lay,
In many a winding creek and bay,
Lepanto's gulf, and, on the brow
Of Delphi's hill, unshaken snow,

[1] ["He vainly turn'd from side to side,
And each reposing posture tried."—MS.]

High and eternal, such as shone
Through thousand summers brightly gone,
Along the gulf, the mount, the clime;
It will not melt, like man, to time:
Tyrant and slave are swept away,
Less form'd to wear before the ray;
But that white veil, the lightest, frailest,
Which on the mighty mount thou hailest,
While tower and tree are torn and rent,
Shines o'er its craggy battlement;
In form a peak, in height a cloud,
In texture like a hovering shroud,
Thus high by parting Freedom spread,
As from her fond abode she fled,
And linger'd on the spot, where long
Her prophet spirit spake in song.
Oh ! still her step at moments falters
O'er wither'd fields, and ruin'd altars,
And fain would wake, in souls too broken,
By pointing to each glorious token:
But vain her voice, till better days
Dawn in those yet remember'd rays,
Which shone upon the Persian flying,
And saw the Spartan smile in dying.

xv.

Not mindless of these mighty times
Was Alp, despite his flight and crimes;
And through this night, as on he wander'd,
And o'er the past and present ponder'd,
And thought upon the glorious dead
Who there in better cause had bled,
He felt how faint and feebly dim
The fame that could accrue to him,
Who cheer'd the band, and waved the sword,
A traitor in a turban'd horde;
And led them to the lawless siege,
Whose best success were sacrilege.
Not so had those his fancy number'd,
The chiefs whose dust around him slumber'd;

Their phalanx marshall'd on the plain,
Whose bulwarks were not then in vain.
They fell devoted, but undying;
The very gale their names seem'd sighing;
The waters murmur'd of their name;
The woods were peopled with their fame;
The silent pillar, lone and grey,
Claim'd kindred with their sacred clay;
Their spirits wrapp'd the dusky mountain,
Their memory sparkled o'er the fountain;
The meanest rill, the mightiest river
Roll'd mingling with their fame for ever.
Despite of every yoke she bears,
That land is glory's still and theirs![2]
'Tis still a watch-word to the earth:
When man would do a deed of worth
He points to Greece, and turns to tread,
So sanction'd, on the tyrant's head:
He looks to her, and rushes on
Where life is lost, or freedom won.[3]

XVI.

Still by the shore Alp mutely mused,
And woo'd the freshness Night diffused.
There shrinks no ebb in that tideless sea,[4]
Which changeless rolls eternally;
So that wildest of waves, in their angriest mood,
Scarce break on the bounds of the land for a rood;
And the powerless moon beholds them flow,
Heedless if she come or go:
Calm or high, in main or bay,
On their course she hath no sway.
The rock unworn its base doth bare,
And looks o'er the surf, but it comes not there;

---

[2] [Here follows, in the MS —

"Immortal—boundless—undecay'd—
Their souls the very soil pervade."]

[3]   ["Where Freedom loveliest may be won."—MS.]

[4] The reader need hardly be reminded that there are no perceptible tides in the Mediterranean

And the fringe of the foam may be seen below,
On the line that it left long ages ago :
A smooth short space of yellow sand
Between it and the greener land.

He wander'd on along the beach,
Till within the range of a carbine's reach
Of the leaguer'd wall ; but they saw him not,
Or how could he 'scape from the hostile shot ? *
Did traitors lurk in the Christians' hold ?
Were their hands grown stiff, or their hearts wax'd cold ?
I know not, in sooth ; but from yonder wall
There flash'd no fire, and there hiss'd no ball,
Though he stood beneath the bastion's frown,
That flank'd the seaward gate of the town ;
Though he heard the sound, and could almost tell
The sullen words of the sentinel,
As his measured step on the stone below
Clank'd, as he paced it to and fro ;
And he saw the lean dogs beneath the wall
Hold o'er the dead their carnival,*
Gorging and growling o'er carcass and limb ;
They were too busy to bark at him !
From a Tartar's skull they had stripp'd the flesh,
As ye peel the fig when its fruit is fresh ;
And their white tusks crunch'd o'er the whiter skull,'
As it slipp'd through their jaws, when their edge grew dull,
As they lazily mumbled the bones of the dead,
When they scarce could rise from the spot where they fed ;
So well had they broken a lingering fast
With those who had fallen for that night's repast.
And Alp knew, by the turbans that roll'd on the sand,
The foremost of these were the best of his band :

*   [" Or would not waste on a single head
        The ball on numbers better sped."—MS.]

c [Omit the rest of this section.—GIFFORD]
7 This spectacle I have seen, such as described, beneath the wall of the Seraglio at Constantinople, in the little cavities worn by the Bosphorus in the rock, a narrow terrace of which projects between the wall and the water I think the fact is also mentioned in Hobhouse's Travels The bodies were probably those of some refractory Janizaries.

Crimson and green were the shawls of their wear,
And each scalp had a single long tuft of hair,[8]
All the rest was shaven and bare.
The scalps were in the wild dog's maw,
The hair was tangled round his jaw:
But close by the shore, on the edge of the gulf,
There sat a vulture flapping a wolf,
Who had stolen from the hills, but kept away,
Scared by the dogs, from the human prey;
But he seized on his share of a steed that lay,
Pick'd by the birds, on the sands of the bay.

XVII

Alp turn'd him from the sickening sight:
Never had shaken his nerves in fight;
But he better could brook to behold the dying,
Deep in the tide of their warm blood lying,[9]
Scorch'd with the death-thirst, and writhing in vain,
Than the perishing dead who are past all pain.[1]
There is something of pride in the perilous hour,
Whate'er be the shape in which death may lower;
For Fame is there to say who bleeds,
And Honour's eye on daring deeds!
But when all is past, it is humbling to tread
O'er the weltering field of the tombless dead,[2]
And see worms of the earth, and fowls of the air,
Beasts of the forest, all gathering there;
All regarding man as their prey,
All rejoicing in his decay.[3]

[8] This tuft, or long lock, is left from a superstition that Mahomet will draw them into Paradise by it.

[9]   [Than the mangled corpse in its own blood lying.—GIFFORD]

[1] [Strike out—

    "Scorch'd with the death-thirst, and writhing in vain,
    Than the perishing dead who are past all pain."

What is a " perishing dead ?"—GIFFORD]

[2]   [O'er the weltering *limbs* of the tombless dead.—GIFFORD.]

[3]   [" All that liveth on man will prey,
    All rejoice in his decay,
    All that can kindle dismay and disgust
    Follow his frame from the bier to the dust."—MS]

XVIII.

There is a temple in ruin stands,
Fashion'd by long forgotten hands;
Two or three columns, and many a stone,
Marble and granite, with grass o'ergrown !
Out upon Time ! it will leave no more
Of the things to come than the things before !'
Out upon Time ! who for ever will leave
But enough of the past for the future to grieve
O'er that which hath been, and o'er that which must be:
What we have seen, our sons shall see ;
Remnants of things that have pass'd away,
Fragments of stone, rear'd by creatures of clay !'

XIX.

He sate him down at a pillar's base,'
And pass'd his hand athwart his face ;
Like one in dreary musing mood,
Declining was his attitude ;
His head was drooping on his breast,
Fever'd, throbbing, and oppress'd ;
And o'er his brow, so downward bent,
Oft his beating fingers went,
Hurriedly, as you may see
Your own run over the ivory key,
Ere the measured tone is taken
By the chords you would awaken.

' [Omit this couplet.—GIFFORD.]
' [After this follows in the MS —

                " Monuments that the coming age
                Leaves to the spoil of the season's rage—
                Till Ruin makes the relics scarce,
                Then Learning acts her solemn farce,
                And, roaming through the marble waste,
                Prates of beauty, art, and taste.

                        XIX.
                " That Temple was more in the midst c. the plain ;
                What of that shrine did yet remain
                Lay to his left ———".]

' [From this all is beautiful to—

        " He saw not, he knew not ; but nothing is there."—GIFFORD.]

There he sate all heavily,
As he heard the night-wind sigh.
Was it the wind through some hollow stone,
Sent that soft and tender moan?[7]
He lifted his head, and he look'd on the sea,
But it was unrippled as glass may be;
He look'd on the long grass—it waved not a blade;
How was that gentle sound convey'd?
He look'd to the banners—each flag lay still,
So did the leaves on Cithæron's hill,
And he felt not a breath come over his cheek;
What did that sudden sound bespeak?
He turn'd to the left—is he sure of sight?
There sate a lady, youthful and bright!

xx.

He started up with more of fear
Than if an armed foe were near.
"God of my fathers! what is here?
Who art thou? and wherefore sent
So near a hostile armament?"
His trembling hands refused to sign
The cross he deem'd no more divine:
He had resumed it in that hour,
But conscience wrung away the power.

[7] I must here acknowledge a close, though unintentional, resemblance in these twelve lines to a passage in an unpublished poem of Mr Coleridge, called "Christabel" It was not till after these lines were written that I heard that wild and singularly original and beautiful poem recited, and the MS of that production I never saw till very recently, by the kindness of Mr. Coleridge himself, who, I hope, is convinced that I have not been a wilful plagiarist The original idea undoubtedly pertains to Mr Coleridge, whose poem has been composed above fourteen years Let me conclude by a hope that he will not longer delay the publication of a production, of which I can only add my mite of approbation to the applause of far more competent judges.—[The lines in "Christabel" are these:—

> "The night is chill, the forest bare,
> Is it the wind that moaneth bleak?
> There is not wind enough in the air
> To move away the ringlet curl
> From the lovely lady's cheek—
> There is not wind enough to twirl
> The one red leaf, the last of its clan,
> That dances as often as dance it can,
> Hanging so light, and hanging so high,
> On the topmost twig that looks up at the sky."]

He gazed, he saw : he knew the face
Of beauty, and the form of grace ;
It was Francesca by his side,
The maid who might have been his bride!

The rose was yet upon her cheek,
But mellow'd with a tenderer streak :
Where was the play of her soft lips fled?
Gone was the smile that enliven'd their red.
The ocean's calm within their view,
Beside her eye had less of blue ;
But like that cold wave it stood still,
And its glance,[8] though clear, was chill.
Around her form a thin robe twining,
Nought conceal'd her bosom shining ;
Through the parting of her hair,
Floating darkly downward there,
Her rounded arm show'd white and bare :
And ere yet she made reply,
Once she raised her hand on high ;
It was so wan, and transparent of hue,
You might have seen the moon shine through.

XXI.

" I come from my rest to him I love best,
That I may be happy, and he may be bless'd.
I have pass'd the guards, the gate, the wall ;
Sought thee in safety through foes and all.
'Tis said the lion will turn and flee
From a maid in the pride of her purity ;
And the Power on high, that can shield the good
Thus from the tyrant of the wood,
Hath extended its mercy to guard me as well
From the hands of the leaguering infidel.
I come—and if I come in vain,
Never, oh never, we meet again !
Thou hast done a fearful deed
In falling away from thy fathers' creed :

---

[8] [And its *thrilling* glance, &c.—GIFFORD.

But dash that turban to earth, and sign
The sign of the cross, and for ever be mine;
Wring the black drop from thy heart,
And to-morrow unites us no more to part."

" And where should our bridal couch be spread?
In the midst of the dying and the dead?
For to-morrow we give to the slaughter and flame
The sons and the shrines of the Christian name.
None, save thou and thine, I've sworn,
Shall be left upon the morn:
But thee will I bear to a lovely spot,
Where our hands shall be join'd, and our sorrow forgot.
There thou yet shalt be my bride,
When once again I've quell'd the pride
Of Venice; and her hated race
Have felt the arm they would debase
Scourge, with a whip of scorpions, those
Whom vice and envy made my foes."

Upon his hand she laid her own—
Light was the touch, but it thrill'd to the bone,
And shot a chillness to his heart,
Which fix'd him beyond the power to start.
Though slight was that grasp so mortal cold,
He could not loose him from its hold;
But never did clasp of one so dear
Strike on the pulse with such feeling of fear,
As those thin fingers, long and white,
Froze through his blood by their touch that night.
The feverish glow of his brow was gone,
And his heart sank so still that it felt like stone,
As he look'd on the face, and beheld its hue,
So deeply changed from what he knew:
Fair but faint—without the ray
Of mind, that made each feature play
Like sparkling waves on a sunny day;
And her motionless lips lay still as death,
And her words came forth without her breath

And there rose not a heave o'er her bosom's swell,
And there seem'd not a pulse in her veins to dwell.
Though her eye shone out, yet the lids were fix'd,
And the glance that it gave was wild and unmix'd
With aught of change, as the eyes may seem
Of the restless who walk in a troubled dream;
Like the figures on arras, that gloomily glare,
Stirr'd by the breath of the wintry air,[9]
So seen by the dying lamp's fitful light,
Lifeless, but life-like, and awful to sight;
As they seem, through the dimness, about to come down
From the shadowy wall where their images frown;
Fearfully flitting to and fro,
As the gusts on the tapestry come and go.

" If not for love of me be given
Thus much, then, for the love of heaven,—
Again I say—that turban tear
From off thy faithless brow, and swear
Thine injured country's sons to spare,
Or thou art lost; and never shalt see—
Not earth—that's past—but heaven or me.
If this thou dost accord, albeit
A heavy doom 'tis thine to meet,
That doom shall half absolve thy sin,
And mercy's gate may receive thee within:
But pause one moment more, and take
The curse of Him thou didst forsake;
And look once more to heaven, and see
Its love for ever shut from thee.
There is a light cloud by the moon—[1]
'Tis passing, and will pass full soon—

---

9   [MS —"Like a picture, that magic had charm'd from its frame,
            Lifeless but life-like, and ever the same "

In the summer 'of 1803, when in his sixteenth year, Lord Byron, though offered a
bed at Annesley, used at first to return every night to Newstead , alleging that he
was afraid of the family pictures of the Chaworths, which he fancied "had taken a
grudge to him on account of the duel." Moore thinks this passage may have been
suggested by the recollection]
¹ I have been told that the idea expressed in this and the five following lines has
been admired by those whose approbation is valuable I am glad of it; but it is not
original--at least not mine , it may be found much better expressed in pages 182 3-4

If, by the time its vapoury sail
Hath ceased her shaded orb to veil,
Thy heart within thee is not changed,
Then God and man are both avenged;
Dark will thy doom be, darker still
Thine immortality of ill."

Alp look'd to heaven, and saw on high
The sign she spake of.in the sky;
But his heart was swollen, and turn'd aside,
By deep interminable pride.
This first false passion of his breast
Roll'd like a torrent o'er the rest.
He sue for mercy! *He* dismay'd
By wild words of a timid maid!
He, wrong'd by Venice, vow to save
Her sons, devoted to the grave!
No—though that cloud were thunder's worst,
And charged to crush him—let it burst!

He look'd upon it earnestly,
Without an accent of reply;
He watch'd it passing; it is flown:
Full on his eye the clear moon shone,
And thus he spake—" Whate'er my fate,
I am no changeling—'tis too late:
The reed in storms may bow and quiver,
Then rise again; the tree must shiver.
What Venice made me, I must be,
Her foe in all, save love to thee:
But thou art safe: oh, fly with me!"

of the English version of "Vathek" (I forget the precise page of the French), a work
to which I have before referred, and never recur to, or read, without a renewal of
gratification —[The following is the passage —" 'Deluded prince!' said the Genius,
addressing the Caliph, 'this moment is the last of grace allowed thee give back
Nouronahar to her father, who still retains a few sparks of life destroy thy tower,
with all its abominations drive Carathis from thy councils . be just to thy subjects
respect the ministers of the prophet compensate for thy impieties by an exemplary
life, and, instead of squandering thy days in voluptuous indulgence, lament thy
crimes on the sepulchres of thy ancestors. Thou beholdest the clouds that obscure the
sun at the instant he recovers his splendour, if thy heart be not changed, the time of
mercy assigned thee will be past for ever '"]

He turn'd, but she is gone!
Nothing is there but the column stone.
Hath she sunk in the earth, or melted in air?
He saw not—he knew not—but nothing is there.

XXII.

The night is past, and shines the sun
As if that morn were a jocund one.[2]
Lightly and brightly breaks away
The Morning from her mantle grey,
And the Noon will look on a sultry day.[3]
Hark to the trump, and the drum,
And the mournful sound of the barbarous horn,
And the flap of the banners, that flit as they're borne,
And the neigh of the steed, and the multitude's hum,
And the clash, and the shout, "They come! they come!"
The horsetails[4] are pluck'd from the ground, and the sword
From its sheath; and they form, and but wait for the word.
Tartar, and Spahi, and Turcoman,
Strike your tents, and throng to the van;
Mount ye, spur ye, skirr the plain,
That the fugitive may flee in vain,
When he breaks from the town; and none escape,
Aged or young, in the Christian shape;
While your fellows on foot, in a fiery mass,
Bloodstain the breach through which they pass.[5]
The steeds are all bridled, and snort to the rein;
Curved is each neck, and flowing each mane;
White is the foam of their champ on the bit;
The spears are uplifted; the matches are lit;
The cannon are pointed, and ready to roar,
And crush the wall they have crumbled before:[6]

---

[2] [Leave out this couplet.—GIFFORD]
[3] [Strike out—" And the Noon will look on a sultry day."—GIFFORD.]
[4] The horsetails, fixed upon a lance, a pacha's standard.
[5] [Omit—

    "While your fellows on foot, in a fiery mass,
      Bloodstain the breach through which they pass "—GIFFORD.]

[6]   [And crush the wall they have *shaken* before.—GIFFORD.]

Forms in his phalanx each janizar;
Alp at their head; his right arm is bare,
So is the blade of his scimitar;
The khan and the pachas are all at their post;
The vizier himself at the head of the host.
When the culverin's signal is fired, then on;
Leave not in Corinth a living one—
A priest at her altars, a chief in her halls,
A hearth in her mansions, a stone on her walls.
God and the prophet—Alla Hu!
Up to the skies with that wild halloo!
"There the breach lies for passage, the ladder to scale;
And your hands on your sabres, and how should ye fail?
He who first downs with the red cross may crave'
His heart's dearest wish; let him ask it, and have!"
Thus utter'd Coumourgi, the dauntless vizier;
The reply was the brandish of sabre and spear,
And the shout of fierce thousands in joyous ire :—
Silence—hark to the signal—fire!

XXIII.

As the wolves, that headlong go
On the stately buffalo,
Though with fiery eyes, and angry roar,
And hoofs that stamp, and horns that gore,
He tramples on earth, or tosses on high
The foremost, who rush on his strength but to die :
Thus against the wall they went,
Thus the first were backward bent;[8]
Many a bosom, sheathed in brass,
Strew'd the earth like broken glass,
Shiver'd by the shot, that tore
The ground whereon they moved no more :
Even as they fell, in files they lay,
Like the mower's grass at the close of day,

---

7   ["He who first *downs* with the red cross may crave," &c.
What vulgarism is this !—
          He who *lowers*,—or *plucks down*, &c.—GIFFORD.]

8   [Thus against the wall they *bent*,
          Thus the first were backward *sent*.—GIFFORD.]

When his work is done on the levell'd plain;
Such was the fall of the foremost slain.[*]

XXIV.

As the spring-tides, with heavy plash,
From the cliffs invading dash
Huge fragments, sapp'd by the ceascless flow,
Till white and thundering down they go,
Like the avalanche's snow
On the Alpine vales below;
Thus at length, outbreathed and worn,
Corinth's sons were downward borne
By the long and oft renew'd
Charge of the Moslem multitude.
In firmness they stood, and in masses they fell,
Heap'd by the host of the infidel,
Hand to hand, and foot to foot:
Nothing there, save death, was mute;
Stroke, and thrust, and flash, and cry
For quarter, or for victory,
Mingle there with the volleying thunder,
Which makes the distant cities wonder
How the sounding battle goes,
If with them, or for their foes;
If they must mourn, or may rejoice
In that annihilating voice,
Which pierces the deep hills through and through
With an echo dread and new:
You might have heard it, on that day,
O'er Salamis and Megara;
(We have heard the hearers say,)
Even unto Piræus' bay.

XXV.

From the point of encountering blades to the hilt,
Sabres and swords with blood were gilt;
But the rampart is won, and the spoil begun,
And all but the after carnage done.

[*] [Such was the fall of the foremost train.—GIFFORD.]

Shriller shrieks now mingling come
From within the plunder'd dome:
Hark to the haste of flying feet,
That splash in the blood of the slippery street;
But here and there, where 'vantage ground
Against the foe may still be found,
Desperate groups, of twelve or ten,
Make a pause, and turn again—
With banded backs against the wall,
Fiercely stand, or fighting fall.

There stood an old man[1]—his hairs were white,
But his veteran arm was full of might:
So gallantly bore he the brunt of the fray,
The dead before him, on that day,
In a semicircle lay;
Still he combated unwounded,
Though retreating, unsurrounded.
Many a scar of former fight
Lurk'd[2] beneath his corslet bright;
But of every wound his body bore,
Each and all had been ta'en before:
Though aged, he was so iron of limb,
Few of our youth could cope with him,
And the foes, whom he singly kept at bay,
Outnumber'd his thin hairs[3] of silver grey.
From right to left his sabre swept:
Many an Othman mother wept
Sons that were unborn, when dipp'd[4]
His weapon first in Moslem gore,
Ere his years could count a score.
Of all he might have been the sire[5]
Who fell that day beneath his ire:
For, sonless left long years ago,
His wrath made many a childless foe;

[1]   [There stood a man, &c.—GIFFORD]
[2] ["*Lurk'd*," a bad word—say " *Was hid*."—GIFFORD.]
[3]   [Outnumber'd his hairs, &c.—GIFFORD.]
[4]   [Sons that were unborn, when *he* dipp'd —GIFFORD]
[5] [Bravo !—this is better than King Priam's fifty sons —GIFFORD]

And since the day, when in the strait[8]
His only boy had met his fate,
His parent's iron hand did doom
More than a human hecatomb.[7]
If shades by carnage be appeased,
Patroclus' spirit less was pleased
Than his, Minotti's son, who died
Where Asia's bounds and ours divide.
Buried he lay, where thousands before
For thousands of years were inhumed on the shore;
What of them is left, to tell
Where they lie, and how they fell?
Not a stone on their turf, nor a bone in their graves;
But they live in the verse that immortally saves.

XXVI.

Hark to the Allah shout![8] a band
Of the Mussulman bravest and best is at hand;
Their leader's nervous arm is bare,
Swifter to smite, and never to spare—
Unclothed to the shoulder it waves them on;
Thus in the fight is he ever known:
Others a gaudier garb may show,
To tempt the spoil of the greedy foe;
Many a hand's on a richer hilt,
But none on a steel more ruddily gilt;
Many a loftier turban may wear,—
Alp is but known by the white arm bare;
Look through the thick of the fight, 'tis there!
There is not a standard on that shore
So well advanced the ranks before;
There is not a banner in Moslem war
Will lure the Delhis half so far;
It glances like a falling star!

---

[6] In the naval battle at the mouth of the Dardanelles, between the Venetians and Turks

[7] [There can be no such thing; but the whole of this is poor, and spun out — GIFFORD]

[8]   [Hark to the Alla Hu ! &c.—GIFFORD.]

Where'er that mighty arm is seen,
The bravest be, or late have been;[*]
There the craven cries for quarter
Vainly to the vengeful Tartar;
Or the hero, silent lying,
Scorns to yield a groan in dying;
Mustering his last feeble blow
'Gainst the nearest levell'd foe,
Though faint beneath the mutual wound,
Grappling on the gory ground.

XXVII.

Still the old man stood erect,
And Alp's career a moment check'd.
"Yield thee, Minotti; quarter take,
For thine own, thy daughter's sake."

"Never, renegado, never!
Though the life of thy gift would last for ever."[1]

"Francesca!—Oh, my promised bride![2]
Must she too perish by thy pride!"

"She is safe."—"Where? where?"—"In heaven;
From whence thy traitor soul is driven—
Far from thee, and undefiled."
Grimly then Minotti smiled,
As he saw Alp staggering bow
Before his words, as with a blow.

"Oh God! when died she?"—"Yesternight—
Nor weep I for her spirit's flight:
None of my pure race shall be
Slaves to Mahomet and thee—
Come on!"—That challenge is in vain—
Alp's already with the slain!

[*] [Omit the remainder of the section —GIFFORD]
[1] [In the original MS —
"Though the life of thy giving would last for ever."]
[2] ["Where's Francesca?—my promised bride!"—MS.]

While Minotti's words were wreaking
More revenge in bitter speaking
Than his falchion's point had found,
Had the time allow'd to wound,
From within the neighbouring porch
Of a long defended church,
Where the last and desperate few
Would the failing fight renew,
The sharp shot dash'd Alp to the ground ;
Ere an eye could view the wound
That crash'd through the brain of the infidel,
Round he spun, and down he fell;
A flash like fire within his eyes
Blazed, as he bent no more to rise,
And then eternal darkness sunk
Through all the palpitating trunk ;[3]
Nought of life left, save a quivering
Where his limbs were slightly shivering :
They turn'd him on his back; his breast
And brow were stain'd with gore and dust,
And through his lips the life-blood oozed,
From its deep veins lately loosed ;
But in his pulse there was no throb,
Nor on his lips one dying sob ;
Sigh, nor word, nor struggling breath
Heralded his way to death :
Ere his very thought could pray,
Unanel'd he pass'd away,
Without a hope from mercy's aid,—
To the last a Renegade.

XXVIII.

Fearfully the yell arose
Of his followers, and his foes ;
These in joy, in fury those :[4]

---

[3] [Here follows in MS —

> "Twice and once he roll'd a space,
> Then lead-like lay upon his face "]

[4]   ["These in rage, in triumph those."—MS.

Then again in conflict mixing,
Clashing swords, and spears transfixing,
Interchanged the blow and thrust,
Hurling warriors in the dust.
Street by street, and foot by foot,
Still Minotti dares dispute
The latest portion of the land
Left beneath his high command;
With him, aiding heart and hand,
The remnant of his gallant band.
Still the church is tenable,
　　Whence issued late the fated ball
　　That half avenged the city's fall,
When Alp, her fierce assailant, fell:
Thither bending sternly back,
They leave before a bloody track;
And, with their faces to the foe,
Dealing wounds with every blow,[b]
The chief, and his retreating train,
Join to those within the fane;
There they yet may breathe awhile,
Shelter'd by the massy pile.

XXIX.

Brief breathing-time! the turban'd host,
With added ranks and raging boast,
Press onwards with such strength and heat,
Their numbers balk their own retreat;
For narrow the way that led to the spot
Where still the Christians yielded not;
And the foremost, if fearful, may vainly try
Through the massy column to turn and fly;
They perforce must do or die.
They die; but ere their eyes could close,
Avengers o'er their bodies rose;
Fresh and furious, fast they fill
The ranks unthinn'd, though slaughter'd still;

[b] [Dealing *death* with every blow.—GIFFORD.]

And faint the weary Christians wax
Before the still renew'd attacks:
And now the Othmans gain the gate;
Still resists its iron weight,
And still, all deadly aim'd and hot,
From every crevice comes the shot;
From every shatter'd window pour
The volleys of the sulphurous shower:
But the portal wavering grows and weak—
The iron yields, the hinges creak—
It bends—it falls—and all is o'er;
Lost Corinth may resist no more!

xxx.

Darkly, sternly, and all alone,
Minotti stood o'er the altar stone:
Madonna's face upon him shone,
Painted in heavenly hues above,
With eyes of light and looks of love;
And placed upon that holy shrine
To fix our thoughts on things divine,
When pictured there, we kneeling see
Her, and the boy-God on her knee,
Smiling sweetly on each prayer
To heaven, as if to waft it there.
Still she smiled; even now she smiles,
Though slaughter streams along her aisles:
Minotti lifted his aged eye,
And made the sign of a cross with a sigh,
Then seized a torch which blazed thereby;
And still he stood, while with steel and flame,
Inward and onward the Mussulman came.

xxxi.

The vaults beneath the mosaic stone
Contain'd the dead of ages gone;
Their names were on the graven floor,
But now illegible with gore;
The carved crests, and curious hues
The varied marble's veins diffuse,

Were smear'd, and slippery—stain'd, and strown
With broken swords, and helms o'erthrown:
There were dead above, and the dead below
Lay cold in many a coffin'd row;
You might see them piled in sable state,
By a pale light through a gloomy grate;
But War had enter'd their dark caves,
And stored along the vaulted graves
Her sulphurous treasures, thickly spread
In masses by the fleshless dead:
Here, throughout the siege, had been
The Christians' chiefest magazine;
To these a late form'd train now led,
Minotti's last and stern resource
Against the foe's o'erwhelming force.

XXXII.

The foe came on, and few remain
To strive, and those must strive in vain:
For lack of further lives, to slake
The thirst of vengeance now awake,
With barbarous blows they gash the dead,
And lop the already lifeless head,
And fell the statues from their niche,
And spoil the shrines of offerings rich,
And from each other's rude hands wrest
The silver vessels saints had bless'd.
To the high altar on they go;
Oh, but it made a glorious show!*
On its table still behold
The cup of consecrated gold;
Massy and deep, a glittering prize,
Brightly it sparkles to plunderers' eyes:
That morn it held the holy wine,
Converted by Christ to his blood so divine,
Which his worshippers drank at the break of day,
To shrive their souls ere they join'd in the fray.
Still a few drops within it lay;

* ["Oh, but it made a glorious show!!!" Out —GIFFORD.]

And round the sacred table glow
Twelve lofty lamps, in splendid row,
From the purest metal cast;
A spoil—the richest, and the last.

XXXIII.

So near they came, the nearest stretch'd
To grasp the spoil he almost reach'd
    When old Minotti's hand
Touch'd with the torch the train—
        'Tis fired!
Spire, vaults, the shrine, the spoil, the slain,
    The turban'd victors, the Christian band,
All that of living or dead remain,
Hurl'd on high with the shiver'd fane,
        In one wild roar expired!
The shatter'd town—the walls thrown down—
The waves a moment backward bent—
The hills that shake, although unrent,
    As if an earthquake pass'd—
The thousand shapeless things all driven
In cloud and flame athwart the heaven,
    By that tremendous blast—
Proclaim'd the desperate conflict o'er
On that too long afflicted shore:[1]
Up to the sky like rockets go
All that mingled there below:
Many a tall and goodly man,
Scorch'd and shrivell'd to a span,
When he fell to earth again
Like a cinder strew'd the plain:
Down the ashes shower like rain;
Some fell in the gulf, which received the sprinkles
With a thousand circling wrinkles;
Some fell on the shore, but, far away,
Scatter'd o'er the isthmus lay;

[1] [Strike out from "Up to the sky," &c. to "All blacken'd there and reeking lay." Despicable stuff —GIFFORD.]

Christian or Moslem, which be they?
Let their mothers see and say!
When in cradled rest they lay,
And each nursing mother smiled
On the sweet sleep of her child,
Little deem'd she such a day
Would rend those tender limbs away.
Not the matrons that them bore
Could discern their offspring more;
That one moment left no trace
More of human form or face
Save a scatter'd scalp or bone:
And down came blazing rafters, strown
Around, and many a falling stone,
Deeply dinted in the clay,
All blacken'd there and reeking lay.
All the living things that heard
The deadly earth-shock disappear'd:
The wild birds flew; the wild dogs fled,
And howling left the unburied dead;[8]
The camels from their keepers broke;
The distant steer forsook the yoke—
The nearer steed plunged o'er the plain,
And burst his girth, and tore his rein;
The bull-frog's note, from out the marsh,
Deep-mouth'd arose, and doubly harsh;
The wolves yell'd on the cavern'd hill
Where echo roll'd in thunder still;
The jackal's troop, in gather'd cry,[9]
Bay'd from afar complainingly,
With a mix'd and mournful sound,
Like crying babe, and beaten hound:[1]
With sudden wing, and ruffled breast,
The eagle left his rocky nest,
And mounted nearer to the sun,

[8] [Omit the next six lines.—GIFFORD]
[9] I believe I have taken a poetical licence to transplant the jackal from Asia. In Greece I never saw nor heard these animals, but among the ruins of Ephesus I have heard them by hundreds They haunt ruins, and follow armies
[1] [Leave out this couplet —GIFFORD]

The clouds beneath him seem'd so dun ;
Their smoke assail'd his startled beak,
And made him higher soar and shriek—
Thus was Corinth lost and won ! [2]

[2] [The "Siege of Corinth," though written, perhaps, with too visible an effort, and not very well harmonised in all its parts, cannot but be regarded as a magnificent composition.   There is less misanthropy in it than in any of the rest ; and the interest is made up of alternate representations of soft and solemn scenes and emotions, and of the tumult, and terrors, and intoxication of war.   These opposite pictures are, perhaps, too violently contrasted, and, in some parts, too harshly coloured ; but they are in general exquisitely designed, and executed with the utmost spirit and energy.— JEFFREY.]

PARISINA.

TO

SCROPE BERDMORE DAVIES, ESQ.

THE FOLLOWING POEM

Is Inscribed,

BY ONE WHO HAS LONG ADMIRED HIS TALENTS

AND VALUED HIS FRIENDSHIP.

January 22, 1816.

ADVERTISEMENT.

THE following poem is grounded on a circumstance mentioned in Gibbon's "Antiquities of the House of Brunswick." I am aware, that in modern times, the delicacy or fastidiousness of the reader may deem such subjects unfit for the purposes of poetry. The Greek dramatists, and some of the best of our old English writers, were of a different opinion: as Alfieri and Schiller have also been, more recently, upon the Continent. The following extract will explain the facts on which the story is founded. The name of *Azo* is substituted for Nicholas, as more metrical.

"Under the reign of Nicholas III. Ferrara was polluted with a domestic tragedy. By the testimony of an attendant, and his own observation, the Marquis of Este discovered the incestuous loves of his wife Parisina, and Hugo his bastard son, a beautiful and valiant youth. They were beheaded in the castle by the sentence of a father and husband, who published his shame, and survived their execution.* He was unfortunate, if they were guilty: if they were innocent, he was still more unfortunate; nor is there any possible situation in which I can sincerely approve the last act of the justice of a parent."—GIBBON's *Miscellaneous Works*, vol. iii. p. 470.

* ["Ferrara is much decayed and depopulated; but the castle still exists entire; and I saw the court where Parisina and Hugo were beheaded, according to the annal of Gibbon."—*B. Letters*, 1817.]

INTRODUCTION TO PARISINA.

"Parisina" is perhaps, the most sweetly versified of Lord Byron's tales. Although the beauties were at once acknowledged, and fragments of its music were soon on every lip, there was, at the period of its publication, a general expression of regret that the author should invite sympathy for incestuous lovers To this it may be replied, that the sympathy is for their sufferings and not for their sin So far from extenuating the crime, or apologising for the criminals, the poet maintains the justice of their dreadful doom. But no management can remove the objections to a subject which is naturally revolting, and in obedience to the feeling Lord Byron abandoned his original design of making Selim the brother of the "Bride of Abydos." Notwithstanding that the situation admits of powerful writing, and that the finest works of the Greeks, as well as many among the moderns, turn upon similar catastrophes, the time, he said, or such topics had long gone by In spite of the refinement with which he has conducted the narrative, it is to be regretted that he did not adhere to the opinion when he planned "Parisina," and devote the same amount of beautiful verse to a more legitimate theme   With respect to the evil tendency which has been sometimes ascribed to his tales in the mass, it has been well remarked by Sir E Brydges that the usages depicted in the "Giaour," and its companions, are too remote from our own to have a mischievous effect, while the sentiments they evoke are universally applicable, and convey delight to the mind In speaking of the collective stories, it may be interesting to add, that all his heroines were framed, as Lord Byron related to Lady Blessington, on an imaginative model which he had rarely or ever met with in life,—a union, as to their persons, of rounded forms with fairy hands and feet, and as to their manners, of refinement with want of education. In practice he found that untutored simplicity was allied to coarseness, and that diminutive hands and feet were joined to spare figures, which he held in abhorrence.   These contradictory characteristics, which he expected would vouch to posterity for his taste in beauty, are less distinctly defined in the poems than in the oral commentary.   The *mental* qualities of his favourites had a living original.   What he called "his *fables* about the celestial nature of women," were derived from his youthful ideas of Miss Chaworth , nor could his fancy conjure up richer colours than were reflected from "his bright morning-star of Annesley." He asserted, however, that most of the perfection was due to the illusions of love, and that if Miss Chaworth had something of the angel, she had not a little of the woman.

PARISINA.[1]

I.

It is the hour when from the boughs
The nightingale's high note is heard;
It is the hour when lovers' vows
Seem sweet in every whisper'd word;

[1] " This turned out a calamitous year for the people of Ferrara, for there occurred a
very tragical event in the court of their sovereign   Our annals, both printed and in
manuscript, with the exception of the unpolished and negligent work of Sardi, and one
other, have given the following relation of it,—from which, however, are rejected
many details, and especially the narrative of Bandelli, who wrote a century afterwards,
and who does not accord with the contemporary historians

"By the above-mentioned Stella dell' Assassino, the Marquis, in the year 1405,
had a son called Ugo, a beautiful and ingenuous youth.   Parisina Malatesta, second
wife of Niccolo, like the generality of step-mothers, treated him with little kindness,
to the infinite regret of the Marquis, who regarded him with fond partiality   One
day she asked leave of her husband to undertake a certain journey, to which he
consented, but upon condition that Ugo should bear her company , for he hoped by
these means to induce her, in the end, to lay aside the obstinate aversion which she
had conceived against him   And indeed his intent was accomplished but too well, since,
during the journey, she not only divested herself of all her hatred, but fell into the
opposite extreme   After their return, the Marquis had no longer any occasion to
renew his former reproofs   It happened one day that a servant of the Marquis,
named Zoese, or, as some call him, Giorgio, passing before the apartments of Parisina,
saw going out from them one of her chamber-maids, all terrified and in tears.
Asking the reason, she told him that her mistress, for some slight offence, had been
beating her ; and, giving vent to her rage, she added, that she could easily be revenged, if
she chose to make known the criminal familiarity which subsisted between Parisina
and her step-son.   The servant took note of the words, and related them to his
master   He was astounded thereat, but, scarcely believing his ears, he assured
himself of the fact, alas ! too clearly, on the 18th of May, by looking through a hole
made in the ceiling of his wife's chamber.   Instantly he broke into a furious rage, and
arrested both of them, together with Aldobrandino Rangoni, of Modena, her gentleman,
and also, as some say, two of the women of her chamber, as abettors of this sinful·
act   He ordered them to be brought to a hasty trial, desiring the judges to
pronounce sentence, in the accustomed forms, upon the culprits.   This sentence was

And gentle winds, and waters near,
Make music to the lonely ear.
Each flower the dews have lightly wet,
And in the sky the stars are met,
And on the wave is deeper blue,
And on the leaf a browner hue,

death. Some there were that bestirred themselves in favour of the delinquents, and, amongst others, Ugoccion Contrario, who was all-powerful with Niccolo, and also his aged and much deserving minister Alberto dal Sale. Both of these, their tears flowing down their cheeks, and upon their knees, implored him for mercy, adducing whatever reasons they could suggest for sparing the offenders, besides those motives of honour and decency which might persuade him to conceal from the public so scandalous a deed But his rage made him inflexible, and, on the instant, he commanded that the sentence should be put in execution

"It was, then, in the prisons of the castle, and exactly in those frightful dungeons which are seen at this day beneath the chamber called the Aurora, at the foot of the Lion's tower, at the top of the street Giovecca, that on the night of the 21st of May were beheaded, first, Ugo, and afterwards Parisina Zoese, he that accused her, conducted the latter under his arm to the place of punishment She, all along, fancied that she was to be thrown into a pit, and asked at every step, whether she was yet come to the spot? She was told that her punishment was the axe She enquired what was become of Ugo, and received for answer, that he was already dead, at which, sighing grievously, she exclaimed, 'Now, then, I wish not myself to live,' and, being come to the block, she stripped herself, with her own hands, of all her ornaments, and, wrapping a cloth round her head, submitted to the fatal stroke, which terminated the cruel scene. The same was done with Rangoni, who, together with the others, according to two calendars in the library of St Francesco, was buried in the cemetery of that convent. Nothing else is known respecting the women

"The Marquis kept watch the whole of that dreadful night, and, as he was walking backwards and forwards, enquired of the captain of the castle if Ugo was dead yet? who answered him, Yes. He then gave himself up to the most desperate lamentations, exclaiming, 'Oh! that I too were dead, since I have been hurried on to resolve thus against my own Ugo!' And then gnawing with his teeth a cane which he had in his hand, he passed the rest of the night in sighs and in tears, calling frequently upon his own dear Ugo. On the following day calling to mind that it would be necessary to make public his justification, seeing that the transaction could not be kept secret, he ordered the narrative to be drawn out upon paper, and sent it to all the courts of Italy.

"On receiving this advice, the Doge of Venice, Francesco Foscari, gave orders, but without publishing his reasons, that stop should be put to the preparations for a tournament, which, under the auspices of the Marquis, and at the expense of the city of Padua, was about to take place, in the square of St Mark, in order to celebrate his advancement to the ducal chair

"The Marquis, in addition to what he had already done, from some unaccountable burst of vengeance, commanded that as many of the married women as were well known to him to be faithless, like his Parisina, should, like her, be beheaded. Amongst others, Barberina, or, as some call her, Laodamia Romei, wife of the court judge, underwent this sentence, at the usual place of execution; that is to say, in the quarter of St Giacomo, opposite the present fortress, beyond St Paul's. It cannot be told how strange appeared this proceeding in a prince, who, considering his own disposition, should, as it seemed, have been in such cases most indulgent Some, however, there were who did not fail to commend him "*

---

* Frizzi—"History of Ferrara"

And in the heaven that clear obscure,
So softly dark, and darkly pure,
Which follows the decline of day,
As twilight melts beneath the moon away.[2]

II.

But it is not to list to the waterfall
That Parisina leaves her hall,
And it is not to gaze on the heavenly light
That the lady walks in the shadow of night;
And if she sits in Este's bower,
'Tis not for the sake of its full-blown flower;
She listens—but not for the nightingale—
Though her ear expects as soft a tale.
There glides a step through the foliage thick,
And her cheek grows pale, and her heart beats quick.
There whispers a voice through the rustling leaves,
And her blush returns, and her bosom heaves:
A moment more and they shall meet—
'Tis past—her lover's at her feet.

III.

And what unto them is the world beside,
With all its change of time and tide?
Its living things, its earth and sky,
Are nothing to their mind and eye.
And heedless as the dead are they
    Of aught around, above, beneath;
As if all else had passed away,
    They only for each other breathe;
Their very sighs are full of joy
    So deep, that did it not decay,
That happy madness would destroy
    The hearts which feel its fiery sway:
Of guilt, of peril, do they deem
In that tumultuous tender dream?

[2] The lines contained in this section were printed as set to music some time since, but belong to the poem where they now appear, the greater part of which was composed prior to "Lara"

Who that have felt that passion's power,
Or paused, or fear'd in such an hour?
Or thought how brief such moments last?
But yet—they are already past!
Alas! we must awake before
We know such vision comes no more.

IV.

With many a lingering look they leave
  The spot of guilty gladness past:
And though they hope, and vow, they grieve,
  As if that parting were the last.
The frequent sigh—the long embrace—
  The lip that there would cling for ever,
While gleams on Parisina's face
  The Heaven she fears will not forgive her,
As if each calmly conscious star
Beheld her frailty from afar—
The frequent sigh, the long embrace,
Yet binds them to their trysting place.
But it must come, and they must part
In fearful heaviness of heart,
With all the deep and shuddering chill
Which follows fast the deeds of ill.

V.

And Hugo is gone to his lonely bed,
  To covet there another's bride;
But she must lay her conscious head
  A husband's trusting heart beside.
But fever'd in her sleep she seems,
And red her cheek with troubled dreams,
  And mutters she in her unrest
A name she dare not breathe by day,
  And clasps her Lord unto the breast
Which pants for one away:
And he to that embrace awakes,
And, happy in the thought, mistakes
That dreaming sigh, and warm caress,
For such as he was wont to bless;

And could in very fondness weep
O'er her who loves him even in sleep.

VI.

He clasp'd her sleeping to his heart,
  And listened to each broken word:
He hears—Why doth Prince Azo start,
  As if the Archangel's voice he heard?
And well he may—a deeper doom
Could scarcely thunder o'er his tomb,
When he shall wake to sleep no more,
And stand the eternal throne before.
And well he may—his earthly peace
Upon that sound is doom'd to cease.
That sleeping whisper of a name
Bespeaks her guilt and Azo's shame.
And whose that name? that o'er his pillow
Sounds fearful as the breaking billow,
Which rolls the plank upon the shore,
  And dashes on the pointed rock
The wretch who sinks to rise no more,—
  So came upon his soul the shock.
And whose that name?—'tis Hugo's,—his—
In sooth he had not deem'd of this!—
'Tis Hugo's,—he, the child of one
He loved—his own all-evil son—
The offspring of his wayward youth,
When he betray'd Bianca's truth,
The maid whose folly could confide
In him who made her not his bride.

VII.

He pluck'd his poniard in its sheath,
  But sheath'd it ere the point was bare;
Howe'er unworthy now to breathe,
  He could not slay a thing so fair—
  At least, not smiling—sleeping—there:
Nay more:—he did not wake her then,
  But gazed upon her with a glance
  Which, had she roused her from her trance,

Had frozen her sense to sleep again;
And o'er his brow the burning lamp
Gleam'd on the dew-drops big and damp.
She spake no more—but still she slumber'd—
While, in his thought, her days are number'd.

VIII.

And with the morn he sought and found,
In many a tale from those around,
The proof of all he fear'd to know,
Their present guilt, his future woe;
The long-conniving damsels seek
    To save themselves, and would transfer
    The guilt—the shame—the doom—to her:
Concealment is no more—they speak
All circumstance which may compel
Full credence to the tale they tell:
And Azo's tortured heart and ear
Have nothing more to feel or hear.

IX.

He was not one who brook'd delay:
    Within the chamber of his state,
The chief of Este's ancient sway
    Upon his throne of judgment sate;
His nobles and his guards are there,—
Before him is the sinful pair;
Both young, and *one* how passing fair!
With swordless belt, and fetter'd hand,
Oh, Christ! that thus a son should stand
    Before a father's face!
Yet thus must Hugo meet his sire,
And hear the sentence of his ire,
    The tale of his disgrace!
And yet he seems not overcome,
Although, as yet, his voice be dumb.

X.

And still, and pale, and silently
    Did Parisina wait her doom;

How changed since last her speaking eye
  Glanced gladness round the glittering room,
Where high-born men were proud to wait,
Where Beauty watch'd to imitate
  Her gentle voice, her lovely mien,
And gather from her air and gait
  The graces of its queen :
Then,—had her eye in sorrow wept,
A thousand warriors forth had leapt,
A thousand swords had sheathless shone,
And made her quarrel all their own.
Now,—what is she? and what are they?
Can she command, or these obey?
All silent and unheeding now,
With downcast eyes and knitting brow,
And folded arms, and freezing air,
And lips that scarce their scorn forbear,
Her knights, her dames, her court—is there:
And he, the chosen one, whose lance
Had yet been couch'd before her glance,
Who—were his arm a moment free—
Had died or gain'd her liberty;
The minion of his father's bride,—
He, too, is fetter'd by her side;
Nor sees her swoln and full eye swim
Less for her own despair than him:
Those lids—o'er which the violet vein
Wandering, leaves a tender stain,
Shining through the smoothest white
That e'er did softest kiss invite—
Now seem'd with hot and livid glow
To press, not shade, the orbs below;
Which glance so heavily, and fill,
As tear on tear grows gathering still.

XI.

And he for her had also wept,
  But for the eyes that on him gazed:
His sorrow, if he felt it, slept;
  Stern and erect his brow was raised.

Whate'er the grief his soul avow'd,
He would not shrink before the crowd;
But yet he dared not look on her;
Remembrance of the hours that were—
His guilt, his love, his present state—
His father's wrath, all good men's hate—
His earthly, his eternal fate—
And hers,—oh, hers! he dared not throw
One look upon that death-like brow!
Else had his rising heart betray'd
Remorse for all the wreck it made.

XII.

And Azo spake:—"But yesterday
  I gloried in a wife and son;
That dream this morning pass'd away;
  Ere day declines, I shall have none.
My life must linger on alone;
Well,—let that pass,—there breathes not one
Who would not do as I have done:
Those ties are broken—not by me;
  Let that too pass;—the doom's prepared!
Hugo, the priest awaits on thee,
  And then—thy crime's reward!
Away! address thy prayers to Heaven;
  Before its evening stars are met
Learn if thou there canst be forgiven;
  Its mercy may absolve thee yet.
But here, upon the earth beneath,
  There is no spot where thou and I
Together for an hour could breathe:
  Farewell! I will not see thee die—
But thou, frail thing! shalt view his head—
  Away! I cannot speak the rest:
  Go! woman of the wanton breast;
Not I, but thou his blood dost shed:
Go! if that sight thou canst outlive,
And joy thee in the life I give."

XIII.

And here stern Azo hid his face—
  For on his brow the swelling vein
  Throbb'd as if back upon his brain
  The hot blood ebb'd and flow'd again;
And therefore bow'd he for a space,
  And pass'd his shaking hand along
  His eye, to veil it from the throng;
While Hugo raised his chained hands,
And for a brief delay demands
His father's ear: the silent sire
Forbids not what his words require.

  "It is not that I dread the death—
For thou hast seen me by thy side
All redly through the battle ride,
And that—not once a useless brand—
Thy slaves have wrested from my hand
Hath shed more blood in cause of thine,
Than e'er can stain the axe of mine:
  Thou gav'st, and may'st resume my breath,
A gift for which I thank thee not;
Nor are my mother's wrongs forgot,
Her slighted love and ruin'd name,
Her offspring's heritage of shame;
But she is in the grave, where he,
Her son, thy rival, soon shall be.
Her broken heart—my sever'd head—
Shall witness for thee from the dead
How trusty and how tender were
Thy youthful love—paternal care.
'Tis true that I have done thee wrong—
  But wrong for wrong:—this,—deem'd thy bride,
  The other victim of thy pride,—
Thou know'st for me was destined long;
Thou saw'st, and coveted'st her charms;
  And with thy very crime—my birth,—
  Thou taunted'st me, as little worth;
A match ignoble for her arms,
Because, forsooth, I could not claim

The lawful heirship of thy name,
Nor sit on Este's lineal throne;
   Yet, were a few short summers mine,
   My name should more than Este's shine
With honours all my own.
I had a sword—and have a breast
That should have won as haught[2] a crest
As ever waved along the line
Of all these sovereign sires of thine.
Not always knightly spurs are worn
The brightest by the better born;
And mine have lanced my courser's flank
Before proud chiefs of princely rank,
When charging to the cheering cry
Of ' Este and of Victory !'
I will not plead the cause of crime,
Nor sue thee to redeem from time
A few brief hours or days that must
At length roll o'er my reckless dust;—
Such maddening moments as my past,
They could not, and they did not, last.
Albeit my birth and name be base,
And thy nobility of race
Disdain'd to deck a thing like me—
   Yet in my lineaments they trace
   Some features of my father's face,
And in my spirit—all of thee.
From thee this tamelessness of heart—
From thee—nay, wherefore dost thou start?—
From thee in all their vigour came
My arm of strength, my soul of flame;
Thou didst not give me life alone,
But all that made me more thine own.
See what thy guilty love hath done !
Repaid thee with too like a son !
I am no bastard in my soul,
For that, like thine, abhorr'd control;
And for my breath, that hasty boon

---

[2] Haught—haughty.—"Away, *haught* man, thou art insulting me "—SHAK-
SPEARE.

Thou gav'st and wilt resume so soon,
I valued it no more than thou,
When rose thy casque above thy brow,
And we, all side by side, have striven,
And o'er the dead our coursers driven:
The past is nothing—and at last
The future can but be the past;
Yet would I that I then had died:
  For though thou work'dst my mother's ill,
And made thy own my destined bride,
  I feel thou art my father still
And harsh as sounds thy hard decree,
'Tis not unjust, although from thee.
Begot in sin, to die in shame,
My life begun and ends the same:
As err'd the sire, so err'd the son,
And thou must punish both in one.
My crime seems worst to human view,
But God must judge between us too!'"

XIV.

He ceased—and stood with folded arms,
  On which the circling fetters sounded;
  And not an ear but felt as wounded,
  Of all the chiefs that there were rank'd,
  When those dull chains in meeting clank'd:
Till Parisina's fatal charms [4]

[4] ["I sent for 'Marmion,' because it occurred to me, there might be a resemblance between part of 'Parisina' and a similar scene in the second canto of 'Marmion' I fear there is, though I never thought of it before, and could hardly wish to imitate that which is inimitable I had completed the story on the passage from Gibbon, which indeed leads to a like scene naturally, without a thought of the kind, but it comes upon me not very comfortably."—*Lord B to Mr. M*, Feb 3, 1816 —The scene in "Marmion" is the one where Constance de Beverley appears before the conclave—

"Her look composed, and steady eye,
Bespoke a matchless constancy;
And there she stood so calm and pale,
That, but her breathing did not fail,
And motion slight of eye and head,
And of her bosom, warranted,
That neither sense nor pulse she lacks,
You must have thought a form of wax,
Wrought to the very life, was there—
So still she was, so pale, so fair"]

Again attracted every eye—
Would she thus hear him doom'd to die!
She stood, I said, all pale and still,
The living cause of Hugo's ill.
Her eyes unmoved, but full and wide,
Not once had turn'd to either side—
Nor once did those sweet eyelids close,
Or shade the glance o'er which they rose,
But round their orbs of deepest blue
The circling white dilated grew—
And there with glassy gaze she stood
As ice were in her curdled blood;
But every now and then a tear
 So large and slowly gather'd slid
 From the long dark fringe of that fair lid,
It was a thing to see, not hear!
And those who saw, it did surprise,
Such drops could fall from human eyes.
To speak she thought—the imperfect note
Was choked within her swelling throat,
Yet seem'd in that low hollow groan
Her whole heart gushing in the tone.
It ceased—again she thought to speak,
Then burst her voice in one long shriek,
And to the earth she fell like stone
Or statue from its base o'erthrown,
More like a thing that ne'er had life,—
A monument of Azo's wife,—
Than her, that living guilty thing,
Whose every passion was a sting,
Which urged to guilt, but could not bear
That guilt's detection and despair.
But yet she lived—and all too soon
Recover'd from that death-like swoon—
But scarce to reason—every sense
Had been o'erstrung by pangs intense;
And each frail fibre of her brain
(As bowstrings, when relax'd by rain,
The erring arrow launch aside)
Sent forth her thoughts all wild and wide—

The past a blank, the future black,
With glimpses of a dreary track,
Like lightning on the desert path,
When midnight storms are mustering wrath.
She fear'd—she felt that something ill
Lay on her soul, so deep and chill;
That there was sin and shame she knew,
That some one was to die—but who?
She had forgotten :—did she breathe?
Could this be still the earth beneath,
The sky above, and men around;
Or were they fiends who now so frown'd
On one, before whose eyes each eye
Till then had smiled in sympathy?
All was confused and undefined
To her all-jarr'd and wandering mind;
A chaos of wild hopes and fears:
And now in laughter, now in tears,
But madly still in each extreme,
She strove with that convulsive dream:
For so it seem'd on her to break:
Oh ! vainly must she strive to wake !

XV.

The Convent bells are ringing,
  But mournfully and slow;
In the grey square turret swinging,
  With a deep sound, to and fro.
  Heavily to the heart they go !
Hark ! the hymn is singing—
  The song for the dead below,
  Or the living who shortly shall be so !
For a departed being's soul
The death-hymn peals and the hollow bells knoll:
He is near his mortal goal;
Kneeling at the Friar's knee,
Sad to hear, and piteous to see—
Kneeling on the bare cold ground,
With the block before and the guards around;

And the headsman with his bare arm ready,
That the blow may be both swift and steady,
Feels if the axe be sharp and true
Since he set its edge anew:
While the crowd in a speechless circle gather
To see the Son fall by the doom of the Father!

XVI.

It is a lovely hour as yet
Before the summer sun shall set,
Which rose upon that heavy day,
And mock'd it with his steadiest ray;
And his evening beams are shed
Full on Hugo's fated head,
As his last confession pouring
To the monk, his doom deploring
In penitential holiness,
He bends to hear his accents bless
With absolution such as may
Wipe our mortal stains away.
That high sun on his head did glisten
As he there did bow and listen,
And the rings of chestnut hair
Curl'd half down his neck so bare;
But brighter still the beam was thrown
Upon the axe which near him shone
With a clear and ghastly glitter——
Oh! that parting hour was bitter!
Even the stern stood chill'd with awe:
Dark the crime, and just the law—
Yet they shudder'd as they saw.

XVII.

The parting prayers are said and over
Of that false son, and daring lover!
His beads and sins are all recounted,
His hours to their last minute mounted;
His mantling cloak before was stripp'd,
His bright brown locks must now be clipp'd;

'Tis done—all closely are they shorn;
The vest which till this moment worn—
The scarf which Parisina gave—
Must not adorn him to the grave.
Even that must now be thrown aside,
And o'er his eyes the kerchief tied;
But no—that last indignity
Shall ne'er approach his haughty eye.
All feelings seemingly subdued,
In deep disdain were half renew'd,
When headsman's hands prepared to bind
Those eyes which would not brook such blind,
As if they dared not look on death.
"No—yours my forfeit blood and breath;
These hands are chain'd, but let me die
At least with an unshackled eye—
Strike:"—and as the word he said,
Upon the block he bow'd his head;
These the last accents Hugo spoke:
"Strike"—and flashing fell the stroke—
Roll'd the head—and, gushing, sunk
Back the stain'd and heaving trunk,
In the dust, which each deep vein
Slaked with its ensanguined rain;
His eyes and lips a moment quiver,
Convulsed and quick—then fix for ever.

He died, as erring man should die,
    Without display, without parade;
    Meekly had he bow'd and pray'd,
    As not disdaining priestly aid,
Nor desperate of all hope on high.
And while before the Prior kneeling,
His heart was wean'd from earthly feeling;
His wrathful sire, his paramour—
What were they in such an hour?
No more reproach, no more despair,
No thought but heaven, no word but prayer—
Save the few which from him broke,
When, bared to meet the headsman's stroke,

He claim'd to die with eyes unbound,
His sole adieu to those around.'

XVIII.

Still as the lips that closed in death,
Each gazer's bosom held his breath:
But yet, afar, from man to man,
A cold electric shiver ran,
As down the deadly blow descended
On him whose life and love thus ended;
And, with a hushing sound compress'd,
A sigh shrunk back on every breast;
But no more thrilling noise rose there,
    Beyond the blow that to the block
    Pierced through with forced and sullen shock,
Save one:—what cleaves the silent air
So madly shrill, so passing wild?
That, as a mother's o'er her child,
Done to death by sudden blow,
To the sky these accents go,
Like a soul's in endless woe.
Through Azo's palace-lattice driven,
That horrid voice ascends to heaven,
And every eye is turn'd thereon;
But sound and sight alike are gone!
It was a woman's shriek—and ne'er
In madlier accents rose despair;
And those who heard it, as it past,
In mercy wish'd it were the last.

XIX.

Hugo is fallen; and, from that hour,
No more in palace, hall, or bower,
Was Parisina heard or seen:
Her name—as if she ne'er had been—

' [The grand part of this poem is that which describes the execution of the rival
son; and in which, though there is no pomp, either of language or of sentiment, and
every thing, on the contrary, is conceived and expressed with studied simplicity and
directness, there is a spirit of pathos and poetry to which it would not be easy to find
many parallels.—JEFFREY.]

Was banish'd from each lip and ear,
Like words of wantonness or fear;
And from Prince Azo's voice, by none
Was mention heard of wife or son;
No tomb, no memory had they;
Theirs was unconsecrated clay—
At least the knight's who died that day.
But Parisina's fate lies hid
Like dust beneath the coffin lid:
Whether in convent she abode,
And won to heaven her dreary road,
By blighted and remorseful years
Of scourge, and fast, and sleepless tears;
Or if she fell by bowl or steel,
For that dark love she dared to feel;
Or if, upon the moment smote,
She died by tortures less remote,
Like him she saw upon the block,
With heart that shared the headsman's shock,
In quicken'd brokenness that came,
In pity o'er her shatter'd frame,
None knew—and none can ever know:
But whatsoe'er its end below,
Her life began and closed in woe!

xx.

And Azo found another bride,
And goodly sons grew by his side;
But none so lovely and so brave
As him who wither'd in the grave;
Or if they were—on his cold eye
Their growth but glanced unheeded by,
Or noticed with a smother'd sigh.
But never tear his cheek descended,
And never smile his brow unbended;
And o'er that fair broad brow were wrought
The intersected lines of thought;
Those furrows which the burning share
Of Sorrow ploughs untimely there;

Scars of the lacerating mind
Which the Soul's war doth leave behind.
He was past all mirth or woe:
Nothing more remain'd below
But sleepless nights and heavy days,
A mind all dead to scorn or praise,
A heart which shunn'd itself—and yet
That would not yield, nor could forget,
Which, when it least appear'd to melt,
Intensely thought, intensely felt:
The deepest ice which ever froze
Can only o'er the surface close;
The living stream lies quick below,
And flows, and cannot cease to flow.
Still was his seal'd-up bosom haunted
By thoughts which Nature hath implanted;
Too deeply rooted thence to vanish,
Howe'er our stifled tears we banish;
When struggling as they rise to start,
We check those waters of the heart,
They are not dried—those tears unshed
But flow back to the fountain head,
And resting in their spring more pure,
For ever in its depth endure,
Unseen, unwept, but uncongeal'd,
And cherish'd most where least reveal'd.
With inward starts of feeling left,
To throb o'er those of life bereft,
Without the power to fill again
The desert gap which made his pain;
Without the hope to meet them where
United souls shall gladness share;
With all the consciousness that he
Had only pass'd a just decree;
That they had wrought their doom of ill;
Yet Azo's age was wretched still.
The tainted branches of the tree,
    If lopp'd with care, a strength may give,
    By which the rest shall bloom and live
All greenly fresh and wildly free

But if the lightning, in its wrath,
The waving boughs with fury scathe,
The massy trunk the ruin feels,
And never more a leaf reveals.[6]

---

[6] [In Parisina there is no tumult or stir.   It is all sadness, and pity, and terror. There is too much of horror, perhaps, in the circumstances; but the writing is beautiful throughout, and the whole wrapped in a rich and redundant veil of poetry, where every thing breathes the pure essence of genius and sensibility.—JEFFREY.

THE PRISONER OF CHILLON.

SONNET ON CHILLON.

ETERNAL Spirit of the chainless Mind !*
   Brightest in dungeons, Liberty! thou art,
   For there thy habitation is the heart—
The heart which love of thee alone can bind;
And when thy sons to fetters are consign'd—
   To fetters, and the damp vault's dayless gloom,
   Their country conquers with their martyrdom,
And Freedom's fame finds wings on every wind.
Chillon! thy prison is a holy place,   ·
   And thy sad floor an altar—for 'twas trod,
Until his very steps have left a trace
   Worn, as if thy cold pavement were a sod,
By Bonnivard!   May none those marks efface!
   For they appeal from tyranny to God.

---

* [In the first draught, the sonnet opens thus—

   "Beloved Goddess of the chainless mind !
     Brightest in dungeons, Liberty ! thou art,
     Thy palace is within the Freeman's heart,
     Whose soul the love of thee alone can bind ,
     And when thy sons to fetters are consign'd—
      To fetters, and the damp vault's dayless gloom,
     Thy joy is with them still, and unconfined,
      Their country conquers with their martyrdom.]

ADVERTISEMENT.

WHEN this poem was composed, I was not sufficiently aware of the history of Bonnivard, or I should have endeavoured to dignify the subject by an attempt to celebrate his courage and his virtues With some account of his life I have been furnished, by the kindness of a citizen of that republic, which is still proud of the memory of a man worthy of the best age of ancient freedom :—

"François de Bonnivard, fils de Louis de Bonnivard, originaire de Seyssel et Seigneur de Lunes, naquit en 1496. Il fit ses études à Turin : en 1510 Jean Aimé de Bonnivard, son oncle, lui résigna le Prieuré de St. Victor, qui aboutissait aux murs de Genève, et qui formait un bénéfice considérable.

"Ce grand homme—(Bonnivard mérite ce titre par la force de son âme, la droiture de son cœur, la noblesse de ses intentions, la sagesse de ses conseils, le courage de ses démarches, l'étendue de ses connaissances, et la vivacité de son esprit),—ce grand homme, qui excitera l'admiration de tous ceux qu'une vertu héroïque peut encore émouvoir, inspirera encore la plus vive reconnaissance dans les cœurs des Génévois qui aiment Genève. Bonnivard en fut toujours un des plus fermes appuis : pour assurer la liberté de notre République, il ne craignit pas de perdre souvent la sienne; il oublia son repos; il méprisa ses richesses; il ne négligea rien pour affermir le bonheur d'une patrie qu'il honora de son choix : dès ce moment il la chérit comme le plus zélé de ses citoyens; il la servit avec l'intrépidité d'un héros, et il écrivit son Histoire avec la naiveté d'un philosophe et la chaleur d'un patriote.

"Il dit dans le commencement de son Histoire de Genève, que, *dès qu'il eut commencé de lire l'histoire des nations, il se sentit entraîné par son goût pour les Républiques, dont il épousa toujours les intérêts.* c'est ce goût pour la liberté qui lui fit sans doute adopter Genève pour sa patrie.

"Bonnivard, encore jeune, s'annonça hautement comme le défenseur de Genève contre le Duc de Savoye et l'Evêque.

"En 1519, Bonnivard devient le martyr de sa patrie : Le Duc de Savoye étant entré dans Genève avec cinq cent hommes, Bonnivard craint le ressentiment du Duc ; il voulut se retirer à Fribourg pour en éviter les suites ; mais il fut trahi par deux hommes qui l'accompagnaient, et conduit par ordre du Prince à Grolée, où il resta prisonnier pendant deux ans. Bonnivard était malheureux dans ses voyages : comme ses malheurs n'avaient point ralenti son zèle pour Genève, il était toujours un ennemi redoutable pour ceux qui la menaçaient, et par conséquent il devait être exposé à leurs coups. Il fut rencontré en 1530 sur le Jura par des voleurs, qui le dépouillèrent, et qui le mirent encore entre les mains du Duc de Savoye : ce Prince le fit enfermer dans le Château de Chillon, où il resta sans être interrogé jusques en 1536 ; il fut alors délivré par les Bernois, qui s'emparèrent du Pays de Vaud.

" Bonnivard, en sortant de sa captivité, eut le plaisir de trouver Genève libre et réformée : la République s'empressa de lui témoigner sa reconnaissance, et de le dédommager des maux qu'il avoit soufferts ; elle le reçut Bourgeois de la ville au mois de Juin, 1536 ; elle lui donna la maison habitée autrefois par le Vicaire-Général, et elle lui assigna une pension de deux cent écus d'or tant qu'il séjournerait à Genève. Il fut admis dans le Conseil de Deux-Cent en 1537.

"Bonnivard n'a pas fini d'être utile : après avoir travaillé à rendre Genève libre, il réussit à la rendre tolérante. Bonnivard engagea le Conseil à accorder aux ecclésiastiques et aux paysans un tems suffisant pour examiner les propositions qu'on leur faisait ; il réussit par sa douceur : on prêche toujours le Christianisme avec succès quand on le prêche avec charité.

"Bonnivard fut savant : ses manuscrits, qui sont dans la bibliothèque publique, prouvent qu'il avait bien lu les auteurs classiques Latins, et qu'il avait approfondi la théologie et l'histoire. Ce grand homme aimait les sciences, et il croyait qu'elles pouvaient faire la gloire de Genève ; aussi il ne négligea rien pour les fixer dans cette ville naissante ; en 1551 il donna sa bibliothèque au public ; elle fut le commencement de notre bibliothèque publique, et ces livres sont en partie les rares et belles éditions du quinzieme siècle qu'on voit dans notre collection. Enfin, pendant la même année, ce bon patriote institua la République son héritière, à condition qu'elle employerait ses biens à entretenir le collège dont on projettait la fondation.

"Il paraît que Bonnivard mourut en 1570 ; mais on ne peut l'assurer, parcequ'il y a une lacune dans le Nécrologe depuis le mois de Juillet, 1570, jusques en 1571."

INTRODUCTION TO THE PRISONER OF CHILLON.

Lord Byron said of the Castle of Chillon that all description must fall short of the impression it made. While this impression was fresh in his mind he was detained for two days by stress of weather (June 1816) at a small inn in the village of Ouchy, near Lausanne, and there he composed the pathetic poem, which, in the language of Moore, "has added another deathless association to the previously immortalised localities of the Lake" The piece was written contemporaneously with the third canto of "Childe Harold," and exhibits, like the latter, that modification in Lord Byron's mood which was produced by the rupture of his domestic ties The pilgrim of the first two cantos of "Childe Harold" is cursed with the loathing of satiety. He gazes about him with contempt, and seldom rouses himself except to vent his spleen upon the weakness or wickedness of his fellow-men The single thing which still has power to engage his sympathy and soothe his spirit, is the incorruptible glory of earth, sea, and sky In the third canto he is no longer drooping from lassitude. His heart is torn now by an active sorrow, which quickens his verse with deeper emotions and healthier humanity. He continues to inveigh against his species, but in sadness as well as scorn, and his reproaches of others are tempered by the indication of penitent self-regrets He is more than ever anxious to forget himself and the world in the beauties of nature, and shows a livelier sense of their soul-subduing power. The generous spark which seemed before on the verge of extinction is again reviving His cynicism is neither so sullen nor so bitter, and he leaves us with a hope that he will learn to pluck a flower out of the nettle which has stung him The "Prisoner of Chillon" is even a stronger proof of the chastened temper which possessed the poet at the time He has kept to that circle in which he always walked with a magician's power, and portrays the anguish of an agonised spirit But it is not here the bitterness of remorse, nor the conflicts of passion It is the grief of holy instincts and affections,—a grief as tender as it is intense The great defect is to have made the brothers martyrs for their religious faith, and to have nowhere assigned them the consolations of religion The belief which led them to prefer a prison to apostacy would have accompanied them to their dungeon, and lent triumphant dignity to deaths, which appear to grow in the poem out of the pinings of despair The copyright was purchased for 500 guineas.

THE PRISONER OF CHILLON.

I.

My hair is grey, but not with years,
Nor grew it white
    In a single night,[1]
As men's have grown from sudden fears:
My limbs are bow'd, though not with toil,
  But rusted with a vile repose,[2]
For they have been a dungeon's spoil,
  And mine has been the fate of those
To whom the goodly earth and air
Are bann'd, and barr'd—forbidden fare;
But this was for my father's faith
I suffer'd chains and courted death;
That father perish'd at the stake
For tenets he would not forsake;
And for the same his lineal race
In darkness found a dwelling place;
We were seven—who now are one,
  Six in youth, and one in age,

[1] Ludovico Sforza, and others.—The same is asserted of Marie Antoinette's, the wife of Louis the Sixteenth, though not in quite so short a period   Grief is said to have the same effect, to such, and not to fear, this change in *hers* was to be attributed [The transformation was effected in the brief transit from Varennes to Paris   Our own Charles I. was another instance of the phenomenon, his hair turning grey during his confinement at Carisbrooke]

[2]   ["But with the inward waste of grief "—MS]

Finish'd as they had begun,
　Proud of Persecution's rage;[3]
One in fire, and two in field,
Their belief with blood have seal'd,
Dying as their father died,
For the God their foes denied;
Three were in a dungeon cast,
Of whom this wreck is left the last.

II

There are seven pillars of Gothic mould,
In Chillon's dungeons deep and old,
There are seven columns, massy and grey,
Dim with a dull imprison'd ray,
A sunbeam which hath lost its way,
And through the crevice and the cleft
Of the thick wall is fallen and left;
Creeping o'er the floor so damp,
Like a marsh's meteor lamp: 　　·
And in each pillar there is a ring,
　And in each ring there is a chain;
That iron is a cankering thing,
　For in these limbs its teeth remain,
With marks that will not wear away,
Till I have done with this new day,
Which now is painful to these eyes,
Which have not seen the sun so rise
For years—I cannot count them o'er,
I lost their long and heavy score,
When my last brother droop'd and died,
And I lay living by his side.

III.

They chain'd us each to a column stone,
And we were three—yet, each alone:
We could not move a single pace,
We could not see each other's face.
But with that pale and livid light
That made us strangers in our sight:

---

[3] ["Braving rancour—chains —and rage."—MS.]

And thus together—yet apart,
Fetter'd in hand, but join'd in heart,
'Twas still some solace in the dearth
Of the pure elements of earth,
To hearken to each other's speech,
And each turn comforter to each
With some new hope, or legend old,
Or song heroically bold;
But even these at length grew cold.
Our voices took a dreary tone,
An echo of the dungeon stone,
    A grating sound, not full and free,
    As they of yore were wont to be:
    It might be fancy, but to me
They never sounded like our own.

IV.

I was the eldest of the three,
    And to uphold and cheer the rest
    I ought to do—and did my best—
And each did well in his degree.
    The youngest, whom my father loved,
Because our mother's brow was given
To him, with eyes as blue as heaven—
    For him my soul was sorely moved
And truly might it be distress'd
To see such bird in such a nest;
For he was beautiful as day—
    (When day was beautiful to me
    As to young eagles, being free)—
    A polar day, which will not see
A sunset till its summer's gone,
    Its sleepless summer of long light,
The snow-clad offspring of the sun:
    And thus he was as pure and bright,
And in his natural spirit gay,
With tears for nought but others' ills,
And then they flow'd like mountain rills,
Unless he could assuage the woe
Which he abhorr'd to view below.

V.

The other was as pure of mind,
But form'd to combat with his kind;
Strong in his frame, and of a mood
Which 'gainst the world in war had stood,
And perish'd in the foremost rank
    With joy:—but not in chains to pine:
His spirit wither'd with their clank,
    I saw it silently decline—
And so perchance in sooth did mine:
But yet I forced it on to cheer
Those relics of a home so dear.
He was a hunter of the hills,
    Had follow'd there the deer and wolf;
    To him this dungeon was a gulf,
And fetter'd feet the worst of ills.

VI.

Lake Leman lies by Chillon's walls:
A thousand feet in depth below
Its massy waters meet and flow;
Thus much the fathom-line was sent
From Chillon's snow-white battlement,[*]
    Which round about the wave inthralls:
A double dungeon wall and wave
Have made—and like a living grave.
Below the surface of the lake
The dark vault lies wherein we lay,
We heard it ripple night and day

[*] The Château de Chillon is situated between Clarens and Villeneuve, which last is at one extremity of the Lake of Geneva. On its left are the entrances of the Rhone, and opposite are the heights of Meillerie and the range of Alps above Boveret and St. Gingo. Near it, on a hill behind, is a torrent . below it, washing its walls, the lake has been fathomed to the depth of 800 feet French measure: within it are a range of dungeons, in which the early reformers, and subsequently prisoners of state, were confined. Across one of the vaults is a beam black with age, on which we were informed that the condemned were formerly executed. In the cells are seven pillars, or, rather, eight, one being half merged in the wall; in some of these are rings for the fetters and the fettered: in the pavement the steps of Bonnivard have left their traces He was confined here several years. It is by this castle that Rousseau has fixed the catastrophe of his Héloïse, in the rescue of one of her children by Julie from the water; the shock of which, and the illness produced by the immersion, is the cause of her death. The château is large, and seen along the lake for a great distance. The walls are white

Sounding o'er our heads it knock'd;
And I have felt the winter's spray
Wash through the bars when winds were high
And wanton in the happy sky;
    And then the very rock hath rock'd,
    And I have felt it shake, unshock'd,
Because I could have smiled to see
The death that would have set me **free.**

VII.

I said my nearer brother pined,
I said his mighty heart declined,
He loathed and put away his food;
It was not that 'twas coarse and rude,
For we were used to hunter's fare,
And for the like had little care:
The milk drawn from the mountain goat
Was changed for water from the moat,
Our bread was such as captives' tears
Have moisten'd many a thousand years,
Since man first pent his fellow men
Like brutes within an iron den;
But what were these to us or him?
These wasted not his heart or limb;
My brother's soul was of that mould
Which in a palace had grown cold,
Had his free breathing been denied
The range of the steep mountain's side;
But why delay the truth?—he died.[5]
I saw, and could not hold his head,
Nor reach his dying hand—nor dead,—
Though hard I strove, but strove in vain,
To rend and gnash[6] my bonds in twain.
He died, and they unlock'd his chain,
And scoop'd for him a shallow grave
Even from the cold earth of our cave.
I begg'd them, as a boon, to lay
His corse in dust whereon the day

[5] ["But why withhold the blow?—he died."—MS.]
[6]   ["To break or bite."—MS.]

T 2

Might shine—it was a foolish thought,
But then within my brain it wrought,
That even in death his freeborn breast
In such a dungeon could not rest.
I might have spared my idle prayer—
They coldly laugh'd, and laid him there:
The flat and turfless earth above
The being we so much did love;
His empty chain above it leant,
Such murder's fitting monument !

VIII.

But he, the favourite and the flower,
Most cherish'd since his natal hour,
His mother's image in fair face,
The infant love of all his race,
His martyr'd father's dearest thought,
My latest care, for whom I sought
To hoard my life, that his might be
Less wretched now, and one day free;
He, too, who yet had held untired
A spirit natural or inspired—
He, too, was struck, and day by day
Was wither'd on the stalk away.
Oh, God ! it is a fearful thing
To see the human soul take wing
In any shape, in any mood :
I've seen it rushing forth in blood,
I've seen it on the breaking ocean
Strive with a swoln convulsive motion,
I've seen the sick and ghastly bed
Of Sin delirious with its dread :
But these were horrors—this was woe
Unmix'd with such—but sure and slow :
He faded, and so calm and meek,
So softly worn, so sweetly weak,
So tearless, yet so tender, kind,
And grieved for those he left behind ;
With all the while a cheek whose bloom
Was as a mockery of the tomb,

Whose tints as gently sunk away
As a departing rainbow's ray;
An eye of most transparent light,
That almost made the dungeon bright,
And not a word of murmur, not
A groan o'er his untimely lot,—
A little talk of better days,
A little hope my own to raise,
For I was sunk in silence—lost
In this last loss, of all the most;
And then the sighs he would suppress
Of fainting nature's feebleness,
More slowly drawn, grew less and less:
I listen'd, but I could not hear;
I call'd, for I was wild with fear;
I knew 'twas hopeless, but my dread
Would not be thus admonished;
I call'd, and thought I heard a sound—
I burst my chain with one strong bound,
And rush'd to him :—I found him not,
I only stirr'd in this black spot,
I only lived, *I* only drew
The accursed breath of dungeon-dew;
The last, the sole, the dearest link
Between me and the eternal brink,
Which bound me to my failing race,
Was broken in this fatal place.'
One on the earth, and one beneath—
My brothers—both had ceased to breathe :
I took that hand which lay so still,
Alas! my own was full as chill;
I had not strength to stir, or strive,
But felt that I was still alive—
A frantic feeling, when we know
That what we love shall ne'er be so.
  I know not why
  I could not die,
I had no earthly hope but faith,
And that forbade a selfish death.

' [The gentle decay and gradual extinction of the youngest life is the most tender
and beautiful passage in the poem.—JEFFREY.]

IX

What next befell me then and there
　I know not well—I never knew—
First came the loss of light, and air,
　And then of darkness too:
I had no thought, no feeling—none—
Among the stones I stood a stone,
And was, scarce conscious what I wist,
As shrubless crags within the mist;
For all was blank, and bleak, and grey;
It was not night, it was not day;
It was not even the dungeon-light,
So hateful to my heavy sight,
But vacancy absorbing space,
And fixedness without a place;
There were no stars, no earth, no time,
No check, no change, no good, no crime,
But silence, and a stirless breath
Which neither was of life nor death;
A sea of stagnant idleness,
Blind, boundless, mute, and motionless!

x.

A light broke in upon my brain,
　It was the carol of a bird;
It ceased, and then it came again,
　The sweetest song ear ever heard,
And mine was thankful till my eyes
Ran over with the glad surprise,
And they that moment could not see
I was the mate of misery;
But then by dull degrees came back
My senses to their wonted track;
I saw the dungeon walls and floor
Close slowly round me as before,
I saw the glimmer of the sun
Creeping as it before had done,
But through the crevice where it came
That bird was perch'd, as fond and tame,

And tamer than upon the tree ;
A lovely bird, with azure wings,
And song that said a thousand things,
    And seem'd to say them all for me !
I never saw its like before,
I ne'er shall see its likeness more :
It seem'd like me to want a mate,
But was not half so desolate,
And it was come to love me when
None lived to love me so again,
And cheering from my dungeon's brink,
Had brought me back to feel and think.
I know not if it late were free,
    Or broke its cage to perch on mine,
But knowing well captivity,
    Sweet bird ! I could not wish for thine !
Or if it were, in winged guise,
A visitant from Paradise ;
For—Heaven forgive that thought ! the while
Which made me both to weep and smile—
I sometimes deem'd that it might be
My brother's soul come down to me ;
But then at last away it flew,
And then 'twas mortal well I knew,
For he would never thus have flown,
And left me twice so doubly lone,
Lone as the corse within its shroud,
Lone as a solitary cloud,—
    A single cloud on a sunny day,
While all the rest of heaven is clear,
A frown upon the atmosphere,
That hath no business to appear
    When skies are blue, and earth is gay.

XI.

A kind of change came in my fate,
My keepers grew compassionate ;
I know not what had made them so,
They were inured to sights of woe,

But so it was:—my broken chain
With links unfasten'd did remain,
And it was liberty to stride
Along my cell from side to side,
And up and down, and then athwart,
And tread it over every part;
And round the pillars one by one,
Returning where my walk begun,
Avoiding only, as I trod,
My brothers' graves without a sod;
For if I thought with heedless tread
My step profaned their lowly bed,
My breath came gaspingly and thick,
And my crush'd heart fell blind and sick.

XII.

I made a footing in the wall,
    It was not therefrom to escape,
For I had buried one and all,
    Who loved me in a human shape;
And the whole earth would henceforth be
A wider prison unto me:
No child, no sire, no kin had I,
No partner in my misery;
I thought of this, and I was glad,
For thought of them had made me mad;
But I was curious to ascend
To my barr'd windows, and to bend
Once more, upon the mountains high,
The quiet of a loving eye.

XIII.

I saw them, and they were the same,
They were not changed like me in frame;
I saw their thousand years of snow
On high—their wide long lake below,*
And the blue Rhone in fullest flow;

---

* ["I saw them with their lake below,
    And their three thousand years of snow."—MS.]

I heard the torrents leap and gush
O'er channell'd rock and broken bush;
I saw the white-wall'd distant town,
And whiter sails go skimming down;
And then there was a little isle,[9]
Which in my very face did smile,
   The only one in view;
A small green isle, it seem'd no more,
Scarce broader than my dungeon floor,
But in it there were three tall trees,
And o'er it blew the mountain breeze,
And by it there were waters flowing,
And on it there were young flowers growing,
   Of gentle breath and hue.
The fish swam by the castle wall,
And they seem'd joyous each and all;
The eagle rode the rising blast,
Methought he never flew so fast
As then to me he seem'd to fly;
And then new tears came in my eye,
And I felt troubled—and would fain
I had not left my recent chain;
And when I did descend again,
The darkness of my dim abode
Fell on me as a heavy load;
It was as is a new-dug grave,
Closing o'er one we sought to save,—
And yet my glance, too much opprest,
Had almost need of such a rest.

XIV.

It might be months, or years, or days,
   I kept no count, I took no note,
I had no hope my eyes to raise,
   And clear them of their dreary mote;

[9] Between the entrances of the Rhone and Villeneuve, not far from Chillon, is a very small island; the only one I could perceive, in my voyage round and over the lake, within its circumference. It contains a few trees (I think not above three), and from its singleness and diminutive size has a peculiar effect upon the view.

At last men came to set me free;
  I ask'd not why, and reck'd not where;
It was at length the same to me,
Fetter'd or fetterless to be,
  I learn'd to love despair.
And thus when they appear'd at last,
And all my bonds aside were cast,
These heavy walls to me had grown
A hermitage—and all my own!
And half I felt as they were come
To tear me from a second home:
With spiders I had friendship made,
And watch'd them in their sullen trade,
Had seen the mice by moonlight play,
And why should I feel less than they?
We were all inmates of one place,
And I, the monarch of each race,
Had power to kill—yet, strange to tell!
In quiet we had learn'd to dwell;[1]
My very chains and I grew friends,
So much a long communion tends
To make us what we are:—even I
Regain'd my freedom with a sigh.[2]

[1] [Here follows in the MS —

  "Nor slew I of my subjects one
What sovereign { hath so little } done?"]
             { yet so much hath }

[2] [It will readily be allowed that this singular poem is more powerful than pleasing.
The dungeon of Bonnivard is, like that of Ugolino, a subject too dismal for even the
power of the painter or poet to counteract its horrors   It is the more disagreeable as
affording human hope no anchor to rest upon, and describing the sufferer, though a
man of talents, and virtues, as altogether inert and powerless under his accumulated
sufferings, yet, as a picture, however gloomy the colouring, it may rival any which
Lord Byron has drawn; nor is it possible to read it without a sinking of the heart,
corresponding with that which he describes the victim to have suffered —SIR WALTER
SCOTT.]

BEPPO:

A VENETIAN STORY.

Rosalind. Farewell, Monsieur Traveller; Look, you lisp, and wear strange suits: disable all the benefits of your own country; be out of love with your Nativity, and almost chide God for making you that countenance you are · or I will scarce think you have swam in a *Gondola*

As You Like It, Act IV., Scene i.

Annotation of the Commentators.

That is, been at *Venice*, which was much visited by the young English gentlemen of those times, and was then what *Paris* is *now*—the seat of all dissoluteness.—S. A.*

* ["Although I was only nine days at Venice, I saw, in that little time, more liberty to sin than ever I heard tell of in the city of London in nine years "—ROGER ABCHAM]

INTRODUCTION TO BEPPO.

GALT had heard, but could not vouch for the truth of the anecdote, that the day Lord Byron received the "Prospectus and Specimen of an intended National Work by William and Robert Whistlecraft," he sat down to spin a web of the same airy texture and finished "Beppo" at a single sitting   Even in the first draught, the poem consisted of eighty-four octave stanzas, which would be at the rate of more than a line a minute for eleven consecutive hours   Though Galt considers the feat not improbable, we believe it *impossible*, and are confident that if Lord Byron had performed it he would have put the marvel upon record   What is certain in the story is that "Beppo" was suggested by the "Prospectus and Specimen" put forth by Hookham Frere under the name of Whistlecraft, as Whistlecraft's model was the *Bernesque* of the Italians , so called from Berni, the first distinguished cultivator of the style   "I have written," said Lord Byron at the beginning of October, which was immediately after the completion of the fourth Canto of Childe Harold, "a humorous poem, in the excellent manner of Mr. Whistlecraft, on a Venetian anecdote which amused me.   It is called '*Beppo*,' the short name for Giuseppe,—that is the *Joe* of the Italian Joseph   Mr Whistlecraft has no greater admirer than myself"   Whistle-craft, however, attracted little attention, and is now quite forgotten, while "Beppo," when published anonymously in May, 1818, obtained, without the advantage of Lord Byron's name, a signal success   The difference in the poems explains and justifies the difference in their reception.   The easy flow of Mr. Frere's "Specimen" showed a great command of idiomatic English, and was not without strokes of satirical wit, but was inferior in both to the "Beppo" of Byron   Mr Frere took for his subject the fabulous days of King Arthur, and, except in occasional allusions, has neglected to animate his obsolete fiction with permanent passions or passing follies   Lord Byron has devoted a hundred stanzas to the telling of a brief and trivial anecdote, which even for the purposes of common conversation has no superfluity of point, but he had the tact to embroider it with numerous sketches of modern manners, which do, in reality, constitute the poem, and please by their liveliness and truth.   The contrasted grouping of the characteristics of Italy and England, the criticisms of Laura upon her compeers at the Ball, the effect of the dawn upon the complexion of the dancers, the ludicrous mixture of feminine volatility, inquisitiveness, and loquacity in the crowd of incongruous questions with which the voluble wife greets her long lost husband, are all transcripts from familiar life, and are narrated in a style which combines the music of an elaborate metre with the freedom of colloquial prose   Lord Byron said the piece had "politics and ferocity," but the politics are confined to a few casual allusions, and there is nothing which deserves the name of ferocity, unless it is the ridicule of Sotheby,—appropriately dubbed Botherby,—and of the blue-stockings who believed in him. Wordsworth strangely alleged that Lord Byron was deficient in feeling, and no less strangely quoted a saying in support of the opinion, to the effect that "Beppo" was his best piece, because there all his faults are brought to a height. Gay feelings have always been permitted to poets as well as grave, lively verse as well as severe, and Wordsworth might as reasonably have maintained that Shakespeare was deficient in tragic passion, and instanced Dogberry to prove it "Beppo" was valued by Mr Murray at 500 guineas, which formed part of 2500 guineas demanded by the poet for the fourth Canto of Childe Harold. After striking the bargain he voluntarily threw in the Venetian Tale, "to help the publisher round to his money." His letters show that he attached no particular importance to the poem, and he certainly had not the remotest idea that he had opened a vein from which was to flow what is usually thought the greatest effort of his genius

BEPPO.[1]

I

'Tis known, at least it should be, that throughout
    All countries of the Catholic persuasion,
Some weeks before Shrove Tuesday comes about,
    The people take their fill of recreation,
And buy repentance, ere they grow devout,
    However high their rank, or low their station,
With fiddling, feasting, dancing, drinking, masquing,
And other things which may be had for asking.

II

The moment night with dusky mantle covers
    The skies (and the more duskily the better),
The time less liked by husbands than by lovers
    Begins, and prudery flings aside her fetter;
And gaiety on restless tiptoe hovers,
    Giggling with all the gallants who beset her;
And there are songs and quavers, roaring, humming,
Guitars, and every other sort of strumming.

III.

And there are dresses splendid, but fantastical,
    Masks of all times and nations, Turks and Jews,
And harlequins and clowns, with feats gymnastical,
    Greeks, Romans, Yankee-doodles, and Hindoos;
All kinds of dress, except the ecclesiastical,
    All people, as their fancies hit, may choose,
But no one in these parts may quiz the clergy,—
Therefore take heed, ye Freethinkers! I charge ye.

IV.

You'd better walk about begirt with briars,
   Instead of coat and smallclothes, than put on
A single stitch reflecting upon friars,
   Although you swore it only was in fun;
They'd haul you o'er the coals, and stir the fires
   Of Phlegethon with every mother's son,
Nor say one mass to cool the caldron's bubble
That boil'd your bones, unless you paid them double.

V.

But saving this, you may put on whate'er
   You like by way of doublet, cape, or cloak,
Such as in Monmouth-street, or in Rag Fair,
   Would rig you out in seriousness or joke;
And even in Italy such places are,
   With prettier name in softer accents spoke,
For, bating Covent Garden, I can hit on
No place that's called "Piazza" in Great Britain.

VI

This feast is named the Carnival,' which being
   Interpreted, implies "farewell to flesh:"
So call'd, because the name and thing agreeing,
   Through Lent they live on fish both salt and fresh.
But why they usher Lent with so much glee in,
   Is more than I can tell, although I guess
'Tis as we take a glass with friends at parting,
In the stage-coach or packet just at starting.

VII

And thus they bid farewell to carnal dishes,
   And solid meats, and highly spiced ragouts,
To live for forty days on ill-dress'd fishes,
   Because they have no sauces to their stews;
A thing which causes many "poohs" and "pishes,"
   And several oaths (which would not suit the Muse),
From travellers accustom'd from a boy
To eat their salmon, at the least, with soy;

VIII.

And therefore humbly I would recommend
  "The curious in fish-sauce," before they cross
The sea, to bid their cook, or wife, or friend,
  Walk or ride to the Strand, and buy in gross
(Or if set out beforehand, these may send
  By any means least liable to loss),
Ketchup, Soy, Chili-vinegar, and Harvey,
Or, by the Lord! a Lent will well nigh starve ye;

IX.

That is to say, if your religion's Roman,
  And you at Rome would do as Romans do,
According to the proverb,—although no man,
  If foreign, is obliged to fast; and you,
If Protestant, or sickly, or a woman,
  Would rather dine in sin on a ragout—
Dine and be d—d! I don't mean to be coarse,
But that's the penalty, to say no worse.

X.

Of all the places where the Carnival
  Was most facetious in the days of yore,
For dance, and song, and serenade, and ball,
  And masque, and mime, and mystery, and more
Than I have time to tell now, or at all,
  Venice the bell from every city bore,—
And at the moment when I fix my story,
That sea-born city was in all her glory.

XI.

They've pretty faces yet, those same Venetians,
  Black eyes, arch'd brows, and sweet expressions still;
Such as of old were copied from the Grecians,
  In ancient arts by moderns mimick'd ill;
And like so many Venuses of Titian's
  (The best's at Florence—see it, if ye will,)
They look when leaning over the balcony,
Or stepp'd from out a picture by Giorgione,²

XII.

Whose tints are truth and beauty at their best;
  And when you to Manfrini's palace go,[4]
That picture (howsoever fine the rest)
  Is loveliest to my mind of all the show;
It may perhaps be also to *your* zest,
  And that's the cause I rhyme upon it so:
'Tis but a portrait of his son, and wife,
And self; but *such* a woman! love in life![5]

XIII.

Love in full life and length, not love ideal,
  No, nor ideal beauty, that fine name,
But something better still, so very real,
  That the sweet model must have been the same;
A thing that you would purchase, beg, or steal,
  Wer't not impossible, besides a shame:
The face recalls some face, as 'twere with pain,
You once have seen, but ne'er will see again;

XIV.

One of those forms which flit by us, when we
  Are young, and fix our eyes on every face;
And, oh! the loveliness at times we see
  In momentary gliding, the soft grace,
The youth, the bloom, the beauty which agree,
  In many a nameless being we retrace,
Whose course and home we knew not, nor shall know,
Like the lost Pleiad[6] seen no more below.

XV.

I said that like a picture by Giorgione
  Venetian women were, and so they *are*,
Particularly seen from a balcony,
  (For beauty's sometimes best set off afar)
And there, just like a heroine of Goldoni,
  They peep from out the blind, or o'er the bar;
And truth to say, they're mostly very pretty,
And rather like to show it, more's the pity!

XVI.

For glances beget ogles, ogles sighs,
　Sighs wishes, wishes words, and words a letter,
Which flies on wings of light-heel'd Mercuries,
　Who do such things because they know no better;
And then, God knows what mischief may arise,
　When love links two young people in one fetter,
Vile assignations, and adulterous beds,
Elopements, broken vows, and hearts, and heads.

XVII.

Shakspeare described the sex in Desdemona
　As very fair, but yet suspect in fame,'
And to this day from Venice to Verona
　Such matters may be probably the same,
Except that since those times was never known a
　Husband whom mere suspicion could inflame
To suffocate a wife no more than twenty,
Because she had a " cavalier servente."

XVIII.

Their jealousy (if they are ever jealous)
　Is of a fair complexion altogether,
Not like that sooty devil of Othello's,
　Which smothers women in a bed of feather,
But worthier of these much more jolly fellows,
　When weary of the matrimonial tether
His head for such a wife no mortal bothers,
But takes at once another, or another's.*

XIX.

Didst ever see a Gondola?　For fear
　You should not, I'll describe it you exactly:
'Tis a long cover'd boat that's common here,
　Carved at the prow, built lightly, but compactly,
Row'd by two rowers, each call'd " Gondolier,"
　It glides along the water looking blackly,
Just like a coffin clapt in a canoe,
Where none can make out what you say or do.

XX

And up and down the long canals they go,
   And under the Rialto * shoot along,
By night and day, all paces, swift or slow,
   And round the theatres, a sable throng,
They wait in their dusk livery of woe,—
   But not to them do woeful things belong,
For sometimes they contain a deal of fun,
Like mourning coaches when the funeral's done.

XXI

But to my story.—'Twas some years ago,
   It may be thirty, forty, more or less,
The Carnival was at its height, and so
   Were all kinds of buffoonery and dress;
A certain lady went to see the show,
   Her real name I know not, nor can guess,
And so we'll call her Laura, if you please,
Because it slips into my verse with ease.

XXII.

She was not old, nor young, nor at the years
   Which certain people call a "*certain age,*"
Which yet the most uncertain age appears,
   Because I never heard, nor could engage
A person yet by prayers, or bribes, or tears,
   To name, define by speech, or write on page,
The period meant precisely by that word,—
Which surely is exceedingly absurd.

XXIII.

Laura was blooming still, had made the best
   Of time, and time return'd the compliment,
And treated her genteelly, so that, dress'd,
   She look'd extremely well where'er she went;
A pretty woman is a welcome guest,
   And Laura's brow a frown had rarely bent;
Indeed, she shone all smiles, and seem'd to flatter
Mankind with her black eyes for looking at her.

XXIV.

She was a married woman; 'tis convenient,
  Because in Christian countries 'tis a rule
To view their little slips with eyes more lenient;
  Whereas if single ladies play the fool,
(Unless within the period intervenient
  A well-timed wedding makes the scandal cool)
I don't know how they ever can get over it,
Except they manage never to discover it.

XXV.

Her husband sail'd upon the Adriatic,
  And made some voyages, too, in other seas,
And when he lay in quarantine for pratique
  (A forty days' precaution 'gainst disease),
His wife would mount, at times, her highest attic,
  For thence she could discern the ship with ease:
He was a merchant trading to Aleppo,
His name Giuseppe, call'd more briefly, Beppo.

XXVI.

He was a man as dusky as a Spaniard,
  Sunburnt with travel, yet a portly figure;
Though colour'd, as it were, within a tanyard,
  He was a person both of sense and vigour—
A better seaman never yet did man yard;
  And she, although her manners show'd no rigour,
Was deem'd a woman of the strictest principle,
So much as to be thought almost invincible.

XXVII.

But several years elapsed since they had met;
  Some people thought the ship was lost, and some
That he had somehow blunder'd into debt,
  And did not like the thought of steering home;
And there were several offer'd any bet,
  Or that he would, or that he would not come;
For most men (till by losing render'd sager)
Will back their own opinions with a wager.

XXVIII.

'Tis said that their last parting was pathetic,
    As partings often are, or ought to be,
And their presentiment was quite prophetic,
    That they should never more each other see,
(A sort of morbid feeling, half poetic,
    Which I have known occur in two or three,)
When kneeling on the shore upon her sad knee
He left this Adriatic Ariadne.

XXIX.

And Laura waited long, and wept a little,
    And thought of wearing weeds, as well she might;
She almost lost all appetite for victual,
    And could not sleep with ease alone at night;
She deem'd the window-frames and shutters brittle
    Against a daring housebreaker or sprite,
And so she thought it prudent to connect her
With a vice-husband, *chiefly* to *protect her.*

XXX.

She chose, (and what is there they will not choose,
    If only you will but oppose their choice?)
Till Beppo should return from his long cruise,
    And bid once more her faithful heart rejoice,
A man some women like, and yet abuse—
    A coxcomb was he by the public voice;
A Count of wealth, they said, as well as quality,
And in his pleasures of great liberality.¹⁰

XXXI.

And then he was a Count, and then he knew
    Music, and dancing, fiddling, French and Tuscan;
The last not easy, be it known to you,
    For few Italians speak the right Etruscan.
He was a critic upon operas, too,
    And knew all niceties of sock and buskin;
And no Venetian audience could endure a
Song, scene, or air, when he cried "seccatura!"

XXXII.

His "bravo" was decisive, for that sound
  Hush'd "Academie" sigh'd in silent awe;
The fiddlers trembled as he look'd around,
  For fear of some false note's detected flaw;
The "prima donna's" tuneful heart would bound,
  Dreading the deep damnation of his "bah!"
Soprano, basso, even the contra-alto,
Wish'd him five fathom under the Rialto.

XXXIII.

He patronised the Improvisatori,
  Nay, could himself extemporise some stanzas,
Wrote rhymes, sang songs, could also tell a story,
  Sold pictures, and was skilful in the dance as
Italians can be, though in this their glory
  Must surely yield the palm to that which France has;
In short, he was a perfect cavaliero,
And to his very valet seem'd a hero.

XXXIV.

Then he was faithful too, as well as amorous;
  So that no sort of female could complain,
Although they're now and then a little clamorous,
  He never put the pretty souls in pain;
His heart was one of those which most enamour us,
  Wax to receive, and marble to retain:
He was a lover of the good old school,
Who still become more constant as they cool.

XXXV.

No wonder such accomplishments should turn
  A female head, however sage and steady—
With scarce a hope that Beppo could return,
  In law he was almost as good as dead, he
Nor sent, nor wrote, nor show'd the least concern,
  And she had waited several years already;
And really if a man won't let us know
That he's alive, he's *dead*, or should be so.

XXXVI.

Besides, within the Alps, to every woman,
  (Although, God knows, it is a grievous sin,)
'Tis, I may say, permitted to have *two* men;
  I can't tell who first brought the custom in,
But " Cavalier Serventes" are quite common,
  And no one notices nor cares a pin;
And we may call this (not to say the worst)
A *second* marriage which corrupts the *first.*"

XXXVII.

The word was formerly a " Cicisbeo,"
  But *that* is now grown vulgar and indecent;
The Spaniards call the person a "*Cortejo,*" [12]
  For the same mode subsists in Spain, though **recent;**
In short it reaches from the Po to Teio,
  And may perhaps at last be o'er the sea sent:
But Heaven preserve Old England from such courses!
Or what becomes of damage and divorces?

XXXVIII

However, I still think, with all due deference
  To the fair *single* part of the creation,
That married ladies should preserve the preference
  In *tête à tête* or general conversation—
And this I say without peculiar reference
  To England, France, or any other nation—
Because they know the world, and are at ease,
And being natural, naturally please.

XXXIX.

'Tis true, your budding Miss is very charming,
  But shy and awkward at first coming out,
So much alarm'd, that she is quite alarming,
  All Giggle, Blush; half Pertness, and half Pout;
And glancing at *Mamma,* for fear there's harm in
  What you, she, it, or they, may be about,
The Nursery still lisps out in all they utter—
Besides, they always smell of bread and butter.

XL.

But "Cavalier Servente" is the phrase
  Used in politest circles to express
This supernumerary slave, who stays
  Close to the lady as a part of dress,
Her word the only law which he obeys.
  His is no sinecure, as you may guess;
Coach, servants, gondola, he goes to call,
And carries fan and tippet, gloves and shawl.

XLI.

With all its sinful doings, I must say,
  That Italy's a pleasant place to me,
Who love to see the Sun shine every day,
  And vines (not nail'd to walls) from tree to tree
Festoon'd, much like the back scene of a play,
  Or melodrame, which people flock to see,
When the first act is ended by a dance
In vineyards copied from the south of France.

XLII

I like on Autumn evenings to ride out,
  Without being forced to bid my groom be sure
My cloak is round his middle strapp'd about,
  Because the skies are not the most secure;
I know too that, if stopp'd upon my route,
  Where the green alleys windingly allure,
Reeling with grapes red wagons choke the way,—
In England 'twould be dung, dust, or a dray.

XLIII.

I also like to dine on becaficas,
  To see the Sun set, sure he'll rise to-morrow,
Not through a misty morning twinkling weak as
  A drunken man's dead eye in maudlin sorrow,
But with all Heaven t'himself; the day will break as
  Beauteous as cloudless, nor be forced to borrow
That sort of farthing candlelight which glimmers
Where reeking London's smoky caldron simmers.

XLIV.

I love the language, that soft bastard Latin,
  Which melts like kisses from a female mouth,
And sounds as if it should be writ on satin,
  With syllables which breathe of the sweet South,
And gentle liquids gliding all so pat in,
  That not a single accent seems uncouth,
Like our harsh northern whistling, grunting guttural,
Which we're obliged to hiss, and spit, and sputter all.

XLV.

I like the women too (forgive my folly),
  From the rich peasant cheek of ruddy bronze,[13]
And large black eyes that flash on you a volley
  Of rays that say a thousand things at once,
To the high dama's brow, more melancholy,
  But clear, and with a wild and liquid glance,
Heart on her lips, and soul within her eyes,
Soft as her clime,[14] and sunny as her skies.

XLVI.

Eve of the land which still is Paradise!
  Italian beauty didst thou not inspire
Raphael,[15] who died in thy embrace, and vies
  With all we know of Heaven, or can desire,
In what he hath bequeath'd us?—in what guise,
  Though flashing from the fervour of the lyre,
Would *words* describe thy past and present glow,
While yet Canova can create below?[16]

XLVII.

"England! with all thy faults I love thee still,"
  I said at Calais, and have not forgot it;
I like to speak and lucubrate my fill;
  I like the government (but that is not it);
I like the freedom of the press and quill;
  I like the Habeas Corpus (when we've got it)
I like a parliamentary debate,
Particularly when 'tis not too late;

XLVIII.

1 like the taxes, when they're not too many
    I like a seacoal fire, when not too dear ;
I like a beef-steak, too, as well as any ;
    Have no objection to a pot of beer ;
I like the weather, when it is not rainy,
    That is, I like two months of every year.
And so God save the Regent, Church, and King !
Which means that I like all and every thing.

XLIX

Our standing army, and disbanded seamen,
    Poor's rate, Reform, my own, the nation's debt,
Our little riots just to show we're free men,
    Our trifling bankruptcies in the Gazette,
Our cloudy climate, and our chilly women,
    All these I can forgive, and those forget,
And greatly venerate our recent glories,
And wish they were not owing to the Tories.

L.

But to my tale of Laura,— for I find
    Digression is a sin, that by degrees
Becomes exceeding tedious to my mind,
    And, therefore, may the reader too displease—
The gentle reader, who may wax unkind,
    And caring little for the author's ease,
Insist on knowing what he means, a hard
And hapless situation for a bard.

LI.

Oh that I had the art of easy writing
    What should be easy reading ! could I scale
Parnassus, where the Muses sit inditing
    Those pretty poems never known to fail,
How quickly would I print (the world delighting)
    A Grecian, Syrian, or Assyrian tale ;
And sell you, mix'd with western sentimentalism,
Some samples of the finest Orientalism.

LII.

But I am but a nameless sort of person,
  (A broken Dandy lately on my travels)
And take for rhyme, to hook my rambling verse on,
  The first that Walker's Lexicon unravels,
And when I can't find that, I put a worse on,
  Not caring as I ought for critics' cavils;
I've half a mind to tumble down to prose,
But verse is more in fashion—so here goes.

LIII

The Count and Laura made their new arrangement,
  Which lasted, as arrangements sometimes do,
For half a dozen years without estrangement;
  They had their little differences, too;
Those jealous whiffs, which never any change meant;
  In such affairs there probably are few
Who have not had this pouting sort of squabble,
From sinners of high station to the rabble.

LIV.

But, on the whole, they were a happy pair,
  As happy as unlawful love could make them:
The gentleman was fond, the lady fair,
  Their chains so slight, 'twas not worth while to break them:
The world beheld them with indulgent air;
  The pious only wish'd "the devil take them!"
He took them not; he very often waits,
And leaves old sinners to be young ones' baits.

LV.

But they were young: Oh! what without our youth
  Would love be! What would youth be without love!
Youth lends its joy, and sweetness, vigour, truth,
  Heart, soul, and all that seems as from above;
But, languishing with years, it grows uncouth—
  One of few things experience don't improve,
Which is, perhaps, the reason why old fellows
Are always so preposterously jealous.

LVI.

It was the Carnival, as I have said
    Some six and thirty stanzas back, and so
Laura the usual preparations made,
    Which you do when your mind's made up to go
To-night to Mrs. Boehm's masquerade,
    Spectator, or partaker in the show;
The only difference known between the cases
Is—*here*, we have six weeks of " varnished faces."

LVII.

Laura, when dress'd, was (as I sang before)
    A pretty woman as was ever seen,
Fresh as the Angel o'er a new inn door,
    Or frontispiece of a new Magazine,
With all the fashions which the last month wore,
    Colour'd, and silver paper leaved between
That and the title-page, for fear the press
Should soil with parts of speech the parts of dress.

LVIII

They went to the Ridotto,—'tis a hall
    Where people dance, and sup, and dance again;
Its proper name, perhaps, were a masqued ball,
    But that's of no importance to my strain;
'Tis (on a smaller scale) like our Vauxhall,
    Excepting that it can't be spoilt by rain;
The company is " mix'd " (the phrase I quote is
As much as saying, they're below your notice);

LIX

For a " mix'd company" implies that, save
    Yourself and friends, and half a hundred more,
Whom you may bow to without looking grave,
    The rest are but a vulgar set, the bore
Of public places, where they basely brave
    The fashionable stare of twenty score
Of well-bred persons, call'd " *The World;*" but I,
Although I know them, really don't know why.

LX.

This is the case in England; at least was
    During the dynasty of Dandies," now
Perchance succeeded by some other class
    Of imitated imitators :—how
Irreparably soon decline, alas !
    The demagogues of fashion : all below
Is frail; how easily the world is lost
By love, or war, and now and then by frost !

LXI.

Crush'd was Napoleon by the northern Thor,
    Who knock'd his army down with icy hammer,
Stopp'd by the *elements*,¹⁸ like a whaler, or
    A blundering novice in his new French grammar;
Good cause had he to doubt the chance of war,
    And as for Fortune—but I dare not d—n her,
Because, were I to ponder to infinity,
The more I should believe in her divinity.¹⁹

LXII.

She rules the present, past, and all to be yet,
    She gives us luck in lotteries, love, and marriage;
I cannot say that she's done much for me yet;
    Not that I mean her bounties to disparage,
We've not yet closed accounts, and we shall see yet
    How much she'll make amends for past miscarriage
Meantime the Goddess I'll no more importune,
Unless to thank her when she's made my fortune.

LXIII.

To turn,—and to return ;—the devil take it !
    This story slips for ever through my fingers,
Because, just as the stanza likes to make it,
    It needs must be—and so it rather lingers;
This form of verse began, I can't well break it,
    But must keep time and tune like public singers;
But if I once get through my present measure,
I'll take another when I'm next at leisure.

LXIV.

They went to the Ridotto ('tis a place
 To which 1 mean to go myself to-morrow,*
Just to divert my thoughts a little space
 Because I'm rather hippish, and may borrow
Some spirits, guessing at what kind of face
 May lurk beneath each mask; and as my sorrow
Slackens its pace sometimes, I'll make, or find,
Something shall leave it half an hour behind.)

LXV.

Now Laura moves along the joyous crowd,
 Smiles in her eyes, and simpers on her lips;
To some she whispers, others speaks aloud;
 To some she curtsies, and to some she dips,
Complains of warmth, and this complaint avow'd,
 Her lover brings the lemonade, she sips;
She then surveys, condemns, but pities still
Her dearest friends for being dress'd so ill.

LXVI.

One has false curls, another too much paint,
 A third—where did she buy that frightful turban?
A fourth's so pale she fears she's going to faint,
 A fifth's look's vulgar, dowdyish, and suburban,
A sixth's white silk has got a yellow taint,
 A seventh's thin muslin surely will be her bane,
And lo! an eighth appears,—" I'll see no more!"
For fear, like Banquo's kings, they reach a score.

LXVII

Meantime, while she was thus at others gazing,
 Others were levelling their looks at her;
She heard the men's half-whisper'd mode of praising,
 And, till 'twas done, determined not to stir;
The women only thought it quite amazing
 That, at her time of life, so many were
Admirers still,—but men are so debased,
Those brazen creatures always suit their taste.

LXVIII

For my part, now, I ne'er could understand
    Why naughty women—but I won't discuss
A thing which is a scandal to the land,
    I only don't see why it should be thus;
And if I were but in a gown and band,
    Just to entitle me to make a fuss,
I'd preach on this till Wilberforce and Romilly
Should quote in their next speeches from my homily.

LXIX

While Laura thus was seen, and seeing, smiling,
    Talking, she knew not why, and cared not what,
So that her female friends, with envy broiling,
    Beheld her airs and triumph, and all that;
And well-dress'd males still kept before her filing,
    And passing bow'd and mingled with her chat;
More than the rest one person seem'd to stare
With pertinacity that's rather rare.

LXX.

He was a Turk, the colour of mahogany;
    And Laura saw him, and at first was glad,
Because the Turks so much admire philogyny,
    Although their usage of their wives is sad;
'Tis said they use no better than a dog any
    Poor woman, whom they purchase like a pad:
They have a number, though they ne'er exhibit 'em,
Four wives by law, and concubines "ad libitum."

LXXI.

They lock them up, and veil, and guard them daily,
    They scarcely can behold their male relations,
So that their moments do not pass so gaily
    As is supposed the case with northern nations;
Confinement, too, must make them look quite palely;
    And as the Turks abhor long conversations,
Their days are either pass'd in doing nothing,
Or bathing, nursing, making love, and clothing.

LXXII.

They cannot read, and so don't lisp in criticism ;
　　Nor write, and so they don't affect the muse ;
Were never caught in epigram or witticism,
　　Have no romances, sermons, plays, reviews,—
In harams learning soon would make a pretty schism,
　　But luckily these beauties are no " Blues ; "
No bustling Botherbys have they to show 'em
" That charming passage in the last new poem : "

LXXIII

No solemn, antique gentleman of rhyme,
　　Who having angled all his life for fame,
And getting but a nibble at a time,
　　Still fussily keeps fishing on, the same
Small " Triton of the minnows," the subline
　　Of mediocrity, the furious tame,
The echo's echo, usher of the school
Of female wits, boy bards—in short, a fool !

LXXIV.

A stalking oracle of awful phrase,
　　The approving " *Good!* " (by no means GOOD in law)
Humming like flies around the newest blaze,
　　The bluest of bluebottles you e'er saw,
Teasing with blame, excruciating with praise,
　　Gorging the little fame he gets all raw,
Translating tongues he knows not even by letter,
And sweating plays so middling, bad were better.

LXXV.

One hates an author that's *all author*, fellows
　　In foolscap uniforms turn'd up with ink,
So very anxious, clever, fine, and jealous,
　　One don't know what to say to them, or think,
Unless to puff them with a pair of bellows ;
　　Of coxcombry's worst coxcombs e'en the pink
Are preferable to these shreds of paper,
These unquench'd snuffings of the midnight taper.

LXXVI.

Of these same we see several, and of others,
   Men of the world, who know the world like men,
Scott, Rogers, Moore, and all the better brothers,
   Who think of something else besides the pen ;
But for the children of the " mighty mother's,"
   The would-be wits, and can't-be gentlemen,
I leave them to their daily " tea is ready,"
Smug coterie, and literary lady.

LXXVII.

The poor dear Mussulwomen whom I mention
   Have none of these instructive pleasant people,
And *one* would seem to them a new invention,
   Unknown as bells within a Turkish steeple ;
I think 'twould almost be worth while to pension
   (Though best-sown projects very often reap ill)
A missionary author, just to preach
Our Christian usage of the parts of speech.

LXXVIII.

No chemistry for them unfolds her gases,
   No metaphysics are let loose in lectures,
No circulating library amasses
   Religious novels, moral tales, and strictures
Upon the living manners, as they pass us ;
   No exhibition glares with annual pictures ;
They stare not on the stars from out their attics,
Nor deal (thank God for that !) in mathematics.

LXXIX

Why I thank God for that is no great matter,
   I have my reasons, you no doubt suppose,
And as, perhaps, they would not highly flatter,
   I'll keep them for my life (to come) in prose ;
I fear I have a little turn for satire,
   And yet methinks the older that one grows
Inclines us more to laugh than scold, though laughter
Leaves us so doubly serious shortly after.

LXXX

Oh, mirth and innocence ! Oh, milk and water !
  Ye happy mixtures of more happy days !
In these sad centuries of sin and slaughter,
  Abominable Man no more allays
His thirst with such pure beverage. No matter,
  I love you both, and both shall have my praise :
Oh, for old Saturn's reign of sugar-candy !—
Meantime I drink to your return in brandy.

LXXXI

Our Laura's Turk still kept his eyes upon her,
  Less in the Mussulman than Christian way,
Which seems to say, " Madam, I do you honour,
  " And while I please to stare, you'll please to stay."
Could staring win a woman, this had won her,
  But Laura could not thus be led astray ;
She had stood fire too long and well, to boggle
Even at this stranger's most outlandish ogle.

LXXXII.

The morning now was on the point of breaking,
  A turn of time at which I would advise
Ladies who have been dancing, or partaking
  In any other kind of exercise,
To make their preparations for forsaking
  The ball-room ere the sun begins to rise,
Because when once the lamps and candles fail,
His blushes make them look a little pale.

LXXXIII.

I've seen some balls and revels in my time,
  And stay'd them over for some silly reason,
And then I look'd (I hope it was no crime)
  To see what lady best stood out the season ;
And though I've seen some thousands in their prime,
  Lovely and pleasing, and who still may please on,
I never saw but one (the stars withdrawn)
Whose bloom could after dancing dare the dawn.

LXXXIV.

The name of this Aurora I'll not mention,
   Although I might, for she was nought to me
More than that patent work of God's invention,
   A charming woman, whom we like to see;
But writing names would merit reprehension,
   Yet if you like to find out this fair *she,*
At the next London or Parisian ball
You still may mark her cheek, out-blooming all.

LXXXV.

Laura, who knew it would not do at all
   To meet the daylight after seven hours' sitting
Among three thousand people at a ball,
   To make her curtsy thought it right and fitting;
The Count was at her elbow with her shawl,
   And they the room were on the point of quitting,
When lo! those cursed gondoliers had got
Just in the very place where they *should not.*

LXXXVI

In this they're like our coachmen, and the cause
   Is much the same—the crowd, and pulling, hauling,
With blasphemies enough to break their jaws,
   They make a never intermitted bawling.
At home, our Bow-street gemmen keep the laws,
   And here a sentry stands within your calling;
But for all that, there is a deal of swearing,
And nauseous words past mentioning or bearing.

LXXXVII.

The Count and Laura found their boat at last,
   And homeward floated o'er the silent tide,
Discussing all the dances gone and past;
   The dancers and their dresses, too, beside;
Some little scandals eke; but all aghast
   (As to their palace-stairs the rowers glide)
Sate Laura by the side of her Adorer,[21]
When lo! the Mussulman was there before her.

LXXXVIII.

" Sir," said the Count, with brow exceeding grave,
    " Your unexpected presence here will make
It necessary for myself to crave
    Its import ?   But perhaps 'tis a mistake;
I hope it is so; and, at once to waive
    All compliment, I hope so for *your* sake;
You understand my meaning, or you *shall*."
" Sir," (quoth the Turk) " 'tis no mistake at all:

LXXXIX.

" That lady is *my wife !* "   Much wonder paints
    The lady's changing cheek, as well it might;
But where an Englishwoman sometimes faints,
    Italian females don't do so outright ,
They only call a little on their saints,
    And then come to themselves, almost or quite;
Which saves much hartshorn, salts, and sprinkling faces,
And cutting stays, as usual in such cases.

XC.

She said,—what could she say?   Why, not a word
    But the Count courteously invited in
The stranger, much appeased by what he heard :
    " Such things, perhaps, we'd best discuss within,"
Said he; " don't let us make ourselves absurd
    In public, by a scene, nor raise a din,
For then the chief and only satisfaction
Will be much quizzing on the whole transaction."

XCI.

They enter'd, and for coffee call'd—it came,
    A beverage for Turks and Christians both,
Although the way they make it's not the same.
    Now Laura, much recover'd, or less loth
To speak, cries " Beppo ! what's your pagan name?
    Bless me ! your beard is of amazing growth !
And how came you to keep away so long
Are you not sensible 'twas very wrong?

xcii.

"And are you *really*, *truly*, now a Turk?
 With any other women did you wive?
Is't true they use their fingers for a fork?
 Well, that's the prettiest shawl—as I'm alive!
You'll give it me? They say you eat no pork.
 And how so many years did you contrive
To—Bless me! did I ever? No, I never
Saw a man grown so yellow! How's your liver?

xciii

" Beppo! that beard of yours becomes you not;
 It shall be shaved before you're a day older.
Why do you wear it? Oh! I had forgot—
 Pray don't you think the weather here is colder?
How do I look? You shan't stir from this spot
 In that queer dress, for fear that some beholder
Should find you out, and make the story known.
How short your hair is! Lord! how grey it's grown!"

xciv

What answer Beppo made to these demands
 Is more than I know. He was cast away
About where Troy stood once, and nothing stands;
 Became a slave of course, and for his pay
Had bread and bastinadoes, till some bands
 Of pirates landing in a neighbouring bay,
He join'd the rogues and prosper'd, and became
A renegado of indifferent fame.

xcv.

But he grew rich, and with his riches grew so
 Keen the desire to see his home again,
He thought himself in duty bound to do so,
 And not be always thieving on the main;
Lonely he felt, at times, as Robin Crusoe,
 And so he hired a vessel come from Spain,
Bound for Corfu. she was a fine polacca,
Mann'd with twelve hands, and laden with tobacco.

XCVI

Himself, and much (heaven knows how gotten!) cash,
  He then embark'd, with risk of life and limb,
And got clear off, although the attempt was rash;
  He said that *Providence* protected him—
For my part, I say nothing—lest we clash
  In our opinions:—well, the ship was trim,
Set sail, and kept her reckoning fairly on,
Except three days of calm when off Cape Bonn.

XCVII

They reach'd the island, he transferr'd his lading,
  And self and live stock to another bottom,
And pass'd for a true Turkey-merchant, trading
  With goods of various names, but I've forgot 'em.
However, he got off by this evading,
  Or else the people would perhaps have shot him,
And thus at Venice landed to reclaim
His wife, religion, house, and Christian name.

XCVIII.

His wife received, the patriarch re-baptised him,
  (He made the church a present, by the way;)
He then threw off the garments which disguised him,
  And borrow'd the Count's smallclothes for a day:
His friends the more for his long absence prized him,
  Finding he'd wherewithal to make them gay,
With dinners, where he oft became the laugh of them,
For stories—but *I* don't believe the half of them.

XCIX

Whate'er his youth had suffer'd, his old age
  With wealth and talking made him some amends;
Though Laura sometimes put him in a rage,
  I've heard the Count and he were always friends.
My pen is at the bottom of a page,
  Which being finish'd, here the story ends;
'Tis to be wish'd it had been sooner done,
But stories somehow lengthen when begun."

NOTES TO BEPPO.

———•———

[1] [An extract from Mr Frere's Specimen, which has long been out of print, will show how closely the versification resembles that of "Beppo."

"I've often wish'd that I could write a book,
    Such as all English people might peruse ,
I never shall regret the pains it took,
    That's just the sort of fame that I should choose :
To sail about the world like Captain Cook,
    I'd sling a cot up for my favourite Muse,
And we'd take verses out to Demarara,
To New South Wales, and up to Niagara.

"Poets consume exciseable commodities,
    They raise the nation's spirit when victorious,
They drive an export trade in whims and oddities,
    Making our commerce and revenue glorious ;
As an industrious and pains taking body 'tis
    That Poets should be reckon d meritorious .
And therefore I submissively propose
To erect one Board for Verse and one for Prose.

"Princes protecting Sciences and Art
    I've often seen in copper-plate and print ,
I never saw them elsewhere, for my part,
    And therefore I conclude there's nothing in't :
But every body knows the Regent's heart ,
    I trust he won't reject a well-meant hint ;
Each Board to have twelve members, with a seat
To bring them in per ann. five hundred neat .—

"From Princes I descend to the Nobility .
    In former times all persons of high stations,
Lords, Baronets, and Persons of gentility,
    Paid twenty guineas for the dedications ;
This practice was attended with utility ,
    The patrons lived to future generations,
The poets lived by their industrious earning,—
So men alive and dead could live by Learning.

"Then twenty guineas was a little fortune ,
    Now, we must starve unless the times should mend :
Our poets now-a-days are deem'd importune
    If their addresses are diffusely penn'd ,

Most fashionable authors make a short one
  To their own wife, or child, or private friend,
To show their independence, I suppose ;
  And that may do for Gentlemen like those.

"Lastly, the common people I beseech—
  Dear people ! if you think my verses clever,
Preserve with care your noble parts of speech,
  And take it as a maxim to endeavour
To talk as your good mothers used to teach,
  And then these lines of mine may last for ever ;
And don't confound the language of the nation
With long-tail'd words in *osity* and *ation*."]

2 ["The Carnival," says Mr. Rose, "though it is gayer or duller, according to the genius of the nations which celebrate it, is, in its general character, nearly the same all over the peninsula. The beginning is like any other season ; towards the middle you begin to meet masques and mummers in sunshine : in the last fifteen days the plot thickens ; and during *the three last* all is hurly-burly. The shops are shut, all business is at a stand, and the drunken cries heard at night afford a clear proof of the pleasures to which these days of leisure are dedicated."]

3 [The Venus is in the Medici gallery. Giorgione was Lord Byron's favourite artist. "I know nothing," he wrote in 1820, "of pictures myself, and care almost as little, but to me there are none like the Venetian,—above all, Giorgione."]

4 [The following is Lord Byron's account of his visit to this palace, in April, 1817.— "To-day, I have been over the Manfrini palace, famous for its pictures. What struck me most in the general collection, was the extreme resemblance of the style of the female faces in the mass of pictures, so many centuries or generations old, to those you see and meet every day among the existing Italians. The Queen of Cyprus and Giorgione's wife, particularly the latter, are Venetians as it were of yesterday ; the same eyes and expression, and, to my mind, there is none finer."]

5 [This appears to be an incorrect description of the picture ; as, according to Vasari and others, Giorgione never was married, and died young.]

6   ["Quæ septem dici sex tamen esse solent."—OVID.]

7   ["Look to't :
In Venice they do let heaven see the pranks
They dare not show their husbands ; their best conscience
Is—not to leave undone, but keep unknown."—*Othello*.]

8 ["Jealousy is not the order of the day in Venice, and daggers are out of fashion, while duels on love matters are unknown—at least, with the husbands."—*Byron Letters*.]

9 [An English abbreviation. Rialto is the name, not of the bridge, but of the island from which it is called ; and the Venetians say, il ponte di Rialto, as we say Westminster Bridge. In that island is the Exchange. It was there that the Christian held discourse with the Jew ; and Shylock refers to it, when he says,

"Signor Antonio, many a time and oft,
  In the Rialto, you have rated me."—ROGERS.]

10   ["A Count of wealth inferior to his quality,
  Which somewhat limited his liberality."—MS.]

11 ["The general state of morals here is much the same as in the Doges' time : a woman is virtuous (according to the code) who limits herself to her husband and one lover ; those who have two, three, or more, are a little wild ; but it is only those who

are indiscriminately diffuse, and form a low connection, who are considered as overstepping the modesty of marriage   There is no convincing a woman here, that she is in the smallest degree deviating from the rule of right or the fitness of things, in having an *amoroso*.   The great sin seems to lie in concealing it, or having more than one, that is, unless such an extension of the prerogative is understood and approved of by the prior claimant."—*Byron Letters*, 1817]

[12] Cortejo is pronounced Cortе*k*o, with an aspirate, according to the Arabesque guttural   It means what there is as yet no precise name for in England, though the practice is as common as in any tramontane country whatever

[13]   ["From the tall peasant with her ruddy bronze"—MS.]

[14]   ["Like her own clime, all sun, and bloom, and skies"—MS.]

[15] For the received accounts of the cause of Raphael's death, see his Lives.

[16]   (In talking thus, the writer, more especially
                        Of women, would be understood to say,
                        He speaks as a spectator, not officially,
                        And always, reader, in a modest way,
                        Perhaps, too, in no very great degree shall he
                        Appear to have offended in this lay,
                        Since, as all know, without the sex, our sonnets
                        Would seem unfinish'd, like their untrimm'd bonnets)
                                        (Signed)   PRINTER'S DEVIL.

[17] ["I liked the Dandies   they were always very civil to me ; though, in general, they disliked literary people, and persecuted and mystified Madame de Staël, Lewis, Horace Twiss, and the like.   The truth is, that though I gave up the business early, I had a tinge of Dandyism in my minority, and probably retained enough of it to conciliate the great ones at four and twenty "—*Byron Diary*, 1821]

[18] ["When Brummell was obliged to retire to France, he knew no French ; and having obtained a grammar for the purpose of study, our friend Scrope Davies was asked what progress Brummell had made in French , he responded, 'that Brummell had been stopped, like Bonaparte in Russia, by the *elements*'   I have put this pun into Beppo, which is 'a fair exchange and no robbery ,' for Scrope made his fortune at several dinners (as he owned himself), by repeating occasionally, as his own, some of the buffooneries with which I had encountered him in the morning "—*Byron Diary*, 1821]

[19] ["Like Sylla, I have always believed that all things depend upon Fortune, and nothing upon ourselves.   I am not aware of any one thought or action, worthy of being called good to myself or others, which is not to be attributed to the good goddess —Fortune ! "—*Byron Diary*, 1821]

[20] In the margin of the original MS Lord Byron has written—"January, 19th, 1818.   To-morrow will be a Sunday, and full Ridotto ")]

[21]   ["Sate Laura with a kind of comic horror "—MS]

[22] [This extremely clever and amusing performance affords a very curious and complete specimen of a kind of diction and composition of which our English literature has hitherto presented very few examples   It is, in itself, absolutely a thing of nothing —without story, characters, sentiments, or intelligible object ,—a mere piece of lively and loquacious prattling, in short, upon all kinds of frivolous subjects,—a sort of gay and desultory babbling about Italy and England, Turks, balls, literature, and fish sauces.   But still there is something very engaging in the uniform gaiety, politeness, and good humour of the author, and something still more striking and admirable in the matchless facility with which he has cast into regular, and even difficult, versification the unmingled, unconstrained, and unselected language of the

most light, familiar, and ordinary conversation   With great skill and felicity, he has furnished us with an example of about one hundred stanzas of good verse, entirely composed of common words, in their common places ; never presenting us with one sprig of what is called poetical diction, or even making use of a single inversion, either to raise the style or assist the rhyme, but running on in an inexhaustible series of good, easy colloquial phrases, and finding them fall into verse by some unaccountable and happy fatality.   In this great and characteristic quality it is almost invariably excellent   In some other respects, it is more unequal   About one half is as good as possible, in the style to which it belongs , the other half bears, perhaps, too many marks of that haste with which such a work must necessarily be written.   Some passages are rather too snappish, and some run too much on the cheap and rather plebeian humour of out-of-the-way rhymes, and strange-sounding words and epithets. But the greater part is extremely pleasant, amiable, and gentlemanlike.—JEFFREY.]

MAZEPPA.

ADVERTISEMENT.

"CELUI qui remplissait alors cette place était un gentilhomme Polonais, nommé Mazeppa, né dans le palatinat de Padolie : il avait été élevé page de Jean Casimir, et avait pris à sa cour quelque teinture des belles-lettres. Une intrigue qu'il eut dans sa jeunesse avec la femme d'un gentilhomme Polonais ayant été découverte, le mari le fit lier tout nu sur un cheval farouche, et le laissa aller en cet état. Le cheval, qui était du pays de l'Ukraine, y retourna, et y porta Mazeppa, demi-mort de fatigue et de faim Quelques paysans le secoururent : il resta longtems parmi eux, et se signala dans plusieurs courses contre les Tartares. La supériorité de ses lumières lui donna une grande considération parmi les Cosaques : sa réputation s'augmentant de jour en jour, obligea le Czar à le faire Prince de l'Ukraine."—VOLTAIRE, *Hist. de Charles XII.* p. 196.

"Le roi fuyant, et poursuivi, eut son cheval tué sous lui ; le Colonel Gieta, blessé, et perdant tout son sang, lui donna le sien. Ainsi on remit deux fois à cheval, dans la fuite, ce conquérant qui n'avait pu y monter pendant la bataille."—P. 216.

"Le roi alla par un autre chemin avec quelques cavaliers. Le carrosse, où il était, rompit dans la marche ; on le remit à cheval. Pour comble de disgrace, il s'égara pendant la nuit dans un bois ; là, son courage ne pouvant plus suppléer à ses forces épuisées, les douleurs de sa blessure devenues plus insupportables par la fatigue, son cheval étant tombé de lassitude, il se coucha quelques heures au pied d'un arbre, en danger d'être surpris à tout moment par les vainqueurs, qui le cherchaient de tous côtés."—P. 218.

INTRODUCTION TO MAZEPPA.

"MAZEPPA" was begun at Venice at least as early as July, 1818, and, contrary to the poet's ordinary practice of striking off his works at a heat, was not completed till October Its historical frame-work cannot hinder the conviction that the jealous rage of the old Count Palatine against the youthful lover of the fair Theresa was filled up from the personal experience of the author Mr. Gifford terms it, on the margin of the MS , "a lively, spirited, and pleasant tale ;" and M Villemain, the eminent French critic, declares that, sublime in its substance and finishing with a joke, it is at once the master-piece and symbol of Byron The poet himself did not consider that it was in his best manner. It must be admitted that the narrative sometimes flags, yet the tale is uncommonly animated and impressive, and the finest passages equal any which ever proceeded from his pen. If the poem falls below the panegyric of M. Villemain, it more than maintains the description of Mr. Gifford An able critic of the day commended the manner in which the story was introduced, and thought that the calm resignation of Mazeppa to defeat,—the heroic thoughtlessness of his royal auditor, with the perilous accompaniments of their desolate bivouac—all contributed to throw a striking charm both of preparation and contrast over the wild adventures related by the Hetman. No one will deny that there is considerable gracefulness in the comic portions of the tale, and it is quite in keeping with an old soldier's character that he should enliven a history of bygone dangers with strokes of humour. But, through the power of the poet, the reader feels himself placed nearer to the event than a narrator who calls to memory his long-past perils ; and thus the main story is, to our thinking, much too impassioned to harmonise with the jesting prelude and conclusion The end, especially, sounds a mockery of the emotions which are excited by the Hetman's fearful ride However natural it might be for the Swedish madman to fall asleep after the terrible labours of Pultowa's day, we, who have not participated in his fatigues, give up our sympathies to Mazeppa, and are offended at a pleasantry which dissipates, in a measure, the romance of his recitation Lord Byron received for "Mazeppa" the 500 guineas which was paid for most of his tales.

MAZEPPA.

I.

'Twas after dread Pultowa's day,
  When fortune left the royal Swede,
Around a slaughter'd army lay,
  No more to combat and to bleed.
The power and glory of the war,
  Faithless as their vain votaries, men,
Had pass'd to the triumphant Czar,
  And Moscow's walls were safe again,
Until a day more dark and drear,
And a more memorable year,
Should give to slaughter and to shame
A mightier host and haughtier name;
A greater wreck, a deeper fall,
A shock to one—a thunderbolt to all.

II

Such was the hazard of the die;
The wounded Charles was taught to fly—
By day and night through field and flood,
Stain'd with his own and subjects' blood;
For thousands fell that flight to aid:
And not a voice was heard t'upbraid
Ambition in his humbled hour,
When truth had nought to dread from power.

His horse was slain, and Gieta gave
His own—and died the Russians' slave.
This too sinks after many a league
Of well sustain'd, but vain fatigue;
And in the depth of forests darkling,
The watch-fires in the distance sparkling—
    The beacons of surrounding foes—
A king must lay his limbs at length.
    Are these the laurels and repose
For which the nations strain their strength?
They laid him by a savage tree,
In outworn nature's agony;
His wounds were stiff, his limbs were stark;
The heavy hour was chill and dark;
The fever in his blood forbade
A transient slumber's fitful aid:
And thus it was; but yet through all,
Kinglike the monarch bore his fall,
And made, in this extreme of ill,
His pangs the vassals of his will:
All silent and subdued were they,
As once the nations round him lay.

                         III

A band of chiefs!—alas! how few,
    Since but the fleeting of a day
Had thinn'd it; but this wreck was true
    And chivalrous: upon the clay
Each sate him down, all sad and mute,
    Beside his monarch and his steed;
For danger levels man and brute,
    And all are fellows in their need.
Among the rest, Mazeppa made
His pillow in an old oak's shade—
Himself as rough, and scarce less old,
The Ukraine's Hetman, calm and bold;
But first, outspent with this long course,
The Cossack prince rubb'd down his horse,
And made for him a leafy bed,
    And smooth'd his fetlocks and his mane,

And slack'd his girth, and stripp'd his rein,
And joy'd to see how well he fed;
For until now he had the dread
His wearied courser might refuse
To browse beneath the midnight dews:
But he was hardy as his lord,
And little cared for bed and board;
But spirited and docile too,
Whate'er was to be done, would do.
Shaggy and swift, and strong of limb,
All Tartar-like he carried him;
Obey'd his voice, and came to call,
And knew him in the midst of all:
Though thousands were around,—and Night,
Without a star, pursued her flight,—
That steed from sunset until dawn
His chief would follow like a fawn.

IV.

This done, Mazeppa spread his cloak,
And laid his lance beneath his oak,
Felt if his arms in order good
The long day's march had well withstood—
If still the powder fill'd the pan,
    And flints unloosen'd kept their lock—
His sabre's hilt and scabbard felt,
And whether they had chafed his belt;
And next the venerable man,
From out his havresack and can,
    Prepared and spread his slender stock;
And to the monarch and his men
The whole or portion offer'd then
With far less of inquietude
Than courtiers at a banquet would.
And Charles of this his slender share
With smiles partook a moment there,
To force of cheer a greater show,
And seem above both wounds and woe;
And then he said—" Of all our band,
Though firm of heart and strong of hand,

In skirmish, march, or forage, none
Can less have said or more have done
Than thee, Mazeppa! On the earth
So fit a pair had never birth,
Since Alexander's days till now,
As thy Bucephalus and thou:
All Scythia's fame to thine should yield
For pricking on o'er flood and field."
Mazeppa answer'd—" Ill betide
The school wherein I learn'd to ride!"
Quoth Charles—" Old Hetman, wherefore so,
Since thou hast learn'd the art so well?"
Mazeppa said—" 'Twere long to tell;
And we have many a league to go,
With every now and then a blow,
And ten to one at least the foe,
Before our steeds may graze at ease,
Beyond the swift Borysthenes:
And, Sire, your limbs have need of rest,
And I will be the sentinel
Of this your troop "—" But I request,"
Said Sweden's monarch, "thou wilt tell
This tale of thine, and I may reap,
Perchance, from this the boon of sleep;
For at this moment from my eyes
The hope of present slumber flies."

" Well, Sire, with such a hope, I'll track
My seventy years of memory back:
I think 'twas in my twentieth spring,—
Ay, 'twas,—when Casimir was king—
John Casimir,—I was his page
Six summers, in my earlier age:
A learned monarch, faith! was he,
And most unlike your majesty;
He made no wars, and did not gain
New realms to lose them back again;
And (save debates in Warsaw's diet)
He reign'd in most unseemly quiet;
Not that he had no cares to vex;

He loved the muses and the sex;
And sometimes these so froward are,
They made him wish himself at war;
But soon his wrath being o'er, he took
Another mistress, or new book:
And then he gave prodigious fêtes—
All Warsaw gather'd round his gates
To gaze upon his splendid court,
And dames, and chiefs, of princely port.
He was the Polish Solomon,
So sung his poets, all but one,
Who, being unpension'd, made a satire,
And boasted that he could not flatter.
It was a court of jousts and mimes,
Where every courtier tried at rhymes;
Even I for once produced some verses,
And sign'd my odes ' Despairing Thyrsis.'
There was a certain Palatine,
    A count of far and high descent,
Rich as a salt or silver mine;[1]
And he was proud, ye may divine,
    As if from heaven he had been sent;
He had such wealth in blood and ore
    As few could match beneath the throne;
And he would gaze upon his store,
And o'er his pedigree would pore,
Until by some confusion led,
Which almost look'd like want of head,
    He thought their merits were his own.
His wife was not of his opinion;
    His junior she by thirty years,
Grew daily tired of his dominion;
    And, after wishes, hopes, and fears,
    To virtue a few farewell tears,
A restless dream or two, some glances
At Warsaw's youth, some songs, and dances,
Awaited but the usual chances,

---

[1] This comparison of a "*salt* mine" may, perhaps, be permitted to a Pole, as the wealth of the country consists greatly in the salt mines.

Those happy accidents which render
The coldest dames so very tender,
To deck her Count with titles given,
'Tis said, as passports into heaven;
But, strange to say, they rarely boast
Of these, who have deserved them most.

v.

" I was a goodly stripling then;
    At seventy years I so may say,
That there were few, or boys or men,
    Who, in my dawning time of day,
Of vassal or of knight's degree,
Could vie in vanities with me;
For I had strength, youth, gaiety,
A port, not like to this ye see,
But smooth, as all is rugged now;
    For time, and care, and war, have plough'd
My very soul from out my brow;
    And thus I should be disavow'd
By all my kind and kin, could they
Compare my day and yesterday;
This change was wrought, too, long ere age
Had ta'en my features for his page:
With years, ye know, have not declined
My strength, my courage, or my mind,
Or at this hour I should not be
Telling old tales beneath a tree,
With starless skies my canopy.
    But let me on: Theresa's form—
Methinks it glides before me now,
Between me and yon chestnut's bough,
    The memory is so quick and warm;
And yet I find no words to tell
The shape of her I loved so well:
She had the Asiatic eye,
    Such as our Turkish neighbourhood
    Hath mingled with our Polish blood,
Dark as above us is the sky;

But through it stole a tender light,
Like the first moonrise of midnight;
Large, dark, and swimming in the stream,
Which seem'd to melt to its own beam;
All love, half languor, and half fire,
Like saints that at the stake expire,
And lift their raptured looks on high,
As though it were a joy to die.[2]
A brow like a midsummer lake,
   Transparent with the sun therein,
When waves no murmur dare to make,
   And heaven beholds her face within.
A cheek and lip—but why proceed?
   I loved her then, I love her still;
And such as I am, love indeed
   In fierce extremes—in good and ill.
But still we love even in our rage,
And haunted to our very age
With the vain shadow of the past,
As is Mazeppa to the last.

          VI.

" We met—we gazed—I saw, and sigh'd,
She did not speak, and yet replied;
There are ten thousand tones and signs
We hear and see, but none defines—
Involuntary sparks of thought,
Which strike from out the heart o'erwrought,
And form a strange intelligence,
Alike mysterious and intense,
Which link the burning chain that binds,
Without their will, young hearts and minds;
Conveying, as the electric wire,
We know not how, the absorbing fire.
I saw, and sigh'd—in silence wept,
And still reluctant distance kept,
Until I was made known to her,
And we might then and there confer

    [2] [" Until it proves a joy to die."—MS]

Without suspicion—then, even then,
   I long'd, and was resolved to speak;
But on my lips they died again,
   The accents tremulous and weak,
Until one hour.—There is a game,
   A frivolous and foolish play,
   Wherewith we while away the day;
It is—I have forgot the name—
And we to this, it seems, were set,
By some strange chance, which I forget:
I reck'd not if I won or lost,
   It was enough for me to be
   So near to hear, and oh! to see
The being whom I loved the most.
I watch'd her as a sentinel,
(May ours this dark night watch as well!)
   Until I saw, and thus it was,
That she was pensive, nor perceived
Her occupation, nor was grieved
Nor glad to lose or gain; but still
Play'd on for hours, as if her will
Yet bound her to the place, though not
That hers might be the winning lot.[3]
   Then through my brain the thought did pass,
Even as a flash of lightning there,
That there was something in her air
Which would not doom me to despair;
And on the thought my words broke forth,
   All incoherent as they were;
Their eloquence was little worth,
But yet she listen'd—'tis enough—
   Who listens once will listen twice;
   Her heart, be sure, is not of ice,
And one refusal no rebuff.

VII.

"I loved, and was beloved again—
   They tell me, Sire, you never knew

[3]   [——"but not
     For that which we had both forgot "—MS]

Those gentle frailties; if 'tis true,
I shorten all my joy or pain;
To you 'twould seem absurd as vain;
But all men are not born to reign,
Or o'er their passions, or as you
Thus o'er themselves and nations too.
I am—or rather *was*—a prince,
  A chief of thousands, and could lead
  Them on where each would foremost bleed;
But could not o'er myself evince
The like control—But to resume:
  I loved, and was beloved again;
In sooth, it is a happy doom,
  But yet where happiest ends in pain.
We met in secret, and the hour
Which led me to that lady's bower
Was fiery Expectation's dower.
My days and nights were nothing—all
Except that hour, which doth recall
In the long lapse from youth to age,
  No other like itself: I'd give
  The Ukraine back again to live
It o'er once more, and be a page,
The happy page, who was the lord
Of one soft heart, and his own sword,
And had no other gem nor wealth
Save Nature's gift of youth and health.
We met in secret—doubly sweet,
Some say, they find it so to meet;
I know not that—I would have given
  My life but to have call'd her mine
In the full view of earth and heaven;
  For I did oft and long repine
That we could only meet by stealth.

VIII.

" For lovers there are many eyes,
  And such there were on us; the devil
  On such occasions should be civil—
The devil!—I'm loth to do him wrong,

It might be some untoward saint,
Who would not be at rest too long,
 But to his pious bile gave vent—
But one fair night, some lurking spies
Surprised and seized us both.
The Count was something more than wroth—
I was unarm'd; but if in steel,
All cap-à-pie from head to heel,
What 'gainst their numbers could I do?
'Twas near his castle, far away
 From city or from succour near,
And almost on the break of day;
I did not think to see another,
 My moments seem'd reduced to few;
And with one prayer to Mary Mother,
 And, it may be, a saint or two,
As I resign'd me to my fate,
They led me to the castle gate:
 Theresa's doom I never knew,
Our lot was henceforth separate.
An angry man, ye may opine,
Was he, the proud Count Palatine;
And he had reason good to be,
 But he was most enraged lest such
 An accident should chance to touch
Upon his future pedigree;
Nor less amazed, that such a blot
His noble 'scutcheon should have got,
While he was highest of his line;
 Because unto himself he seem'd
 The first of men, nor less he deem'd
In others' eyes, and most in mine.
'Sdeath! with a *page*—perchance a king
Had reconciled him to the thing;
But with a stripling of a page—
I felt—but cannot paint his rage.

IX.

 " 'Bring forth the horse!'—the horse was brought;
 In truth, he was a noble steed,

A Tartar of the Ukraine breed,
Who look'd as though the speed of thought
Were in his limbs; but he was wild,
   Wild as the wild deer, and untaught,
With spur and bridle undefiled—
   'Twas but a day he had been caught;
And snorting, with erected mane,
And struggling fiercely, but in vain,
In the full foam of wrath and dread
To me the desert-born was led:
They bound me on, that menial throng,
Upon his back with many a thong;
Then loosed him with a sudden lash—
Away!—away!—and on we dash!
Torrents less rapid and less rash.

x.

" Away!—away!—My breath was gone,
I saw not where he hurried on:
'Twas scarcely yet the break of day,
And on he foam'd—away!—away!
The last of human sounds which rose,
As I was darted from my foes,
Was the wild shout of savage laughter,
Which on the wind came roaring after
A moment from that rabble rout:
With sudden wrath I wrench'd my head,
   And snapp'd the cord, which to the mane
   Had bound my neck in lieu of rein,
And, writhing half my form about,
Howl'd back my curse; but 'midst the tread,
The thunder of my courser's speed,
Perchance they did not hear nor heed:
It vexes me—for I would fain
Have paid their insult back again.
I paid it well in after days:
There is not of that castle gate,
Its drawbridge and portcullis' weight,
Stone, bar, moat, bridge, or barrier left;

Nor of its fields a blade of grass,
　　Save what grows on a ridge of wall,
　　Where stood the hearth-stone of the hall;
And many a time ye there might pass,
Nor dream that e'er the fortress was.
I saw its turrets in a blaze,
Their crackling battlements all cleft,
　　And the hot lead pour down like rain
From off the scorch'd and blackening roof,
Whose thickness was not vengeance-proof.
　　They little thought that day of pain,
When launch'd, as on the lightning's flash,
They bade me to destruction dash,
　　That one day I should come again,
With twice five thousand horse, to thank
　　The Count for his uncourteous ride.
They play'd me then a bitter prank,
　　When, with the wild horse for my guide,
They bound me to his foaming flank:
At length I play'd them one as frank—
For time at last sets all things even—
　　And if we do but watch the hour,
　　There never yet was human power
Which could evade, if unforgiven,
The patient search and vigil long
Of him who treasures up a wrong.

XI.

" Away, away, my steed and I,
　　Upon the pinions of the wind,
　　All human dwellings left behind;
We sped like meteors through the sky,
When with its crackling sound the night
Is chequer'd with the northern light:
Town—village—none were on our track,
　　But a wild plain of far extent,
And bounded by a forest black;
　　And, save the scarce seen battlement
On distant heights of some strong hold,
Against the Tartars built of old,

No trace of man. The year before
A Turkish army had march'd o'er ;
And where the Spahi's hoof hath trod,
The verdure flies the bloody sod :
The sky was dull, and dim, and gray,
   And a low breeze crept moaning by—
I could have answer'd with a sigh—
But fast we fled, away, away,
And I could neither sigh nor pray ;
And my cold sweat-drops fell like rain
Upon the courser's bristling mane ;
But, snorting still with rage and fear,
He flew upon his far career :
At times I almost thought, indeed,
He must have slacken'd in his speed ;
But no—my bound and slender frame
   Was nothing to his angry might,
And merely like a spur became :
Each motion which I made to free
My swoln limbs from their agony
   Increased his fury and affright :
I tried my voice,—'twas faint and low,
But yet he swerved as from a blow ;
And, starting to each accent, sprang
As from a sudden trumpet's clang :
Meantime my cords were wet with gore,
Which, oozing through my limbs, ran o'er ;
And in my tongue the thirst became
A something fiercer far than flame.

XII.

" We near'd the wild wood—'twas so wide,
I saw no bounds on either side ;
'Twas studded with old sturdy trees,
That bent not to the roughest breeze
Which howls down from Siberia's waste,
And strips the forest in its haste,—
But these were few, and far between
Set thick with shrubs more young and green,

Luxuriant with their annual leaves,
Ere strown by those autumnal eves
That nip the forest's foliage dead,
Discolour'd with a lifeless red,
Which stands thereon like stiffen'd gore
Upon the slain when battle's o'er,
And some long winter's night hath shed
Its frost o'er every tombless head,
So cold and stark the raven's beak
May peck unpierced each frozen cheek:
'Twas a wild waste of underwood,
And here and there a chestnut stood,
The strong oak, and the hardy pine;
 But far apart—and well it were,
Or else a different lot were mine—
 The boughs gave way, and did not tear
My limbs; and I found strength to bear
My wounds, already scarr'd with cold;
My bonds forbade to loose my hold.
We rustled through the leaves like wind,
Left shrubs, and trees, and wolves behind;
By night I heard them on the track,
Their troop came hard upon our back,
With their long gallop, which can tire
The hound's deep hate, and hunter's fire:
Where'er we flew they follow'd on,
Nor left us with the morning sun;
Behind I saw them, scarce a rood,
At day-break winding through the wood,
And through the night had heard their feet
Their stealing, rustling step repeat.
Oh! how I wish'd for spear or sword,
At least to die amidst the horde,
And perish—if it must be so—
At bay, destroying many a foe.
When first my courser's race begun,
I wish'd the goal already won;
But now I doubted strength and speed.
Vain doubt! his swift and savage breed
Had nerved him like the mountain-roe;

Nor faster falls the blinding snow
Which whelms the peasant near the door
Whose threshold he shall cross no more,
Bewilder'd with the dazzling blast,
Than through the forest-paths he past—
Untired, untamed, and worse than wild;
All furious as a favour'd child
Balk'd of its wish; or fiercer still—
A woman piqued—who has her will.

XIII.

"The wood was past; 'twas more than noon,
But chill the air, although in June;
Or it might be my veins ran cold—
Prolong'd endurance tames the bold;
And I was then not what I seem,
But headlong as a wintry stream,
And wore my feelings out before
I well could count their causes o'er:
And what with fury, fear, and wrath,
The tortures which beset my path,
Cold, hunger, sorrow, shame, distress,
Thus bound in nature's nakedness;
Sprung from a race whose rising blood
When stirr'd beyond its calmer mood,
And trodden hard upon, is like
The rattle-snake's, in act to strike,
What marvel if this worn-out trunk
Beneath its woes a moment sunk?
The earth gave way, the skies roll'd round,
I seem'd to sink upon the ground;
But err'd, for I was fastly bound.
My heart turn'd sick, my brain grew sore,
And throbb'd awhile, then beat no more:
The skies spun like a mighty wheel;
I saw the trees like drunkards reel,
And a slight flash sprang o'er my eyes,
Which saw no farther: he who dies
Can die no more than then I died.
O'ertortured by that ghastly ride,

I felt the blackness come and go,
   And strove to wake; but could not make
My senses climb up from below:
I felt as on a plank at sea,
When all the waves that dash o'er thee,
At the same time upheave and whelm,
And hurl thee towards a desert realm.
My undulating life was as
The fancied lights that flitting pass
Our shut eyes in deep midnight, when
Fever begins upon the brain;
But soon it pass'd, with little pain,
   But a confusion worse than such:
   I own that I should deem it much,
Dying, to feel the same again;
And yet I do suppose we must
Feel far more ere we turn to dust:
No matter; I have bared my brow
Full in Death's face—before—and now.

XIV.

"My thoughts came back; where was I?   Cold,
   And numb, and giddy: pulse by pulse
Life reassumed its lingering hold,
And throb by throb,—till grown a pang
   Which for a moment would convulse,
   My blood reflow'd, though thick and chill;
My ear with uncouth noises rang,
   My heart began once more to thrill;
My sight return'd, though dim; alas!
And thicken'd, as it were, with glass.
Methought the dash of waves was nigh;
There was a gleam too of the sky,
Studded with stars;—it is no dream;
The wild horse swims the wilder stream!
The bright broad river's gushing tide
Sweeps, winding onward, far and wide,
And we are half-way, struggling o'er
To yon unknown and silent shore.

The waters broke my hollow trance,
And with a temporary strength
　　My stiffen'd limbs were rebaptised.
My courser's broad breast proudly braves,
And dashes off the ascending waves,
And onward we advance !
We reach the slippery shore at length,
　　A haven I but little prized,
For all behind was dark and drear,
And all before was night and fear.
How many hours of night or day
In those suspended pangs I lay,
I could not tell; I scarcely knew
If this were human breath I drew.

xv.

" With glossy skin, and dripping mane,
　　And reeling limbs, and reeking flank,
The wild steed's sinewy nerves still strain
　　Up the repelling bank.
We gain the top: a boundless plain
Spreads through the shadow of the night,
　　And onward, onward, onward, seems,
　　Like precipices in our dreams,
To stretch beyond the sight;
And here and there a speck of white,
　　Or scatter'd spot of dusky green,
In masses broke into the light,
As rose the moon upon my right:
　　But nought distinctly seen
In the dim waste would indicate
The omen of a cottage gate;
No twinkling taper from afar
Stood like a hospitable star;
Not even an ignis-fatuus rose
To make him merry with my woes:
　　That very cheat had cheer'd me then !
Although detected, welcome still,
Reminding me, through every ill,
　　Of the abodes of men.

XVI.

"Onward we went—but slack and slow;
   His savage force at length o'erspent,
The drooping courser, faint and low,
   All feebly foaming went.
A sickly infant had had power
To guide him forward in that hour;
   But useless all to me:
His new-born tameness nought avail'd—
My limbs were bound; my force had fail'd,
   Perchance, had they been free.
With feeble effort still I tried
To rend the bonds so starkly tied,
   But still it was in vain;
My limbs were only wrung the more,
And soon the idle strife gave o'er,
   Which but prolong'd their pain:
The dizzy race seem'd almost done,
Although no goal was nearly won:
Some streaks announced the coming sun—
   How slow, alas! he came!
Methought that mist of dawning gray
Would never dapple into day;
How heavily it roll'd away—
   Before the eastern flame
Rose crimson, and deposed the stars,
And call'd the radiance from their cars,[4]
And fill'd the earth, from his deep throne,
With lonely lustre, all his own.

XVII.

"Up rose the sun; the mists were curl'd
Back from the solitary world
Which lay around, behind, before.
What booted it to traverse o'er
Plain, forest, river?   Man nor brute,
Nor dint of hoof, nor print of foot,

---

[4] ["Rose crimson, and forbade the stars
    To sparkle in their radiant cars."—MS]

Lay in the wild luxuriant soil;
No sign of travel, none of toil;
The very air was mute;
And not an insect's shrill small horn,
Nor matin bird's new voice was borne
From herb nor thicket.   Many a werst,
Panting as if his heart would burst,
The weary brute still stagger'd on;
And still we were—or seem'd—alone:
At length, while reeling on our way,
Methought I heard a courser neigh,
From out yon tuft of blackening firs.
Is it the wind those branches stirs?
No, no! from out the forest prance
    A trampling troop; I see them come!
In one vast squadron they advance!
    I strove to cry—my lips were dumb.
The steeds rush on in plunging pride;
But where are they the reins to guide?
A thousand horse, and none to ride!
With flowing tail, and flying mane,
Wide nostrils never stretch'd by pain,
Mouths bloodless to the bit or rein,
And feet that iron never shod,
And flanks unscarr'd by spur or rod,
A thousand horse, the wild, the free,
Like waves that follow o'er the sea,
    Came thickly thundering on,
As if our faint approach to meet;
The sight re-nerved my courser's feet,
A moment staggering, feebly fleet,
A moment, with a faint low neigh,
    He answer'd, and then fell;
With gasps and glazing eyes he lay,
    And reeking limbs immoveable,
    His first and last career is done!
On came the troop—they saw him stoop,
    They saw me strangely bound along
    His back with many a bloody thong:
They stop, they start, they snuff the air,

Gallop a moment here and there,
Approach, retire, wheel round and round,
Then plunging back with sudden bound,
Headed by one black mighty steed,
Who seem'd the patriarch of his breed,
   Without a single speck or hair
Of white upon his shaggy hide ;
They snort, they foam, neigh, swerve aside,
And backward to the forest fly,
By instinct, from a human eye.
   They left me there to my despair,
Link'd to the dead and stiffening wretch,
Whose lifeless limbs beneath me stretch,
Relieved from that unwonted weight,
From whence I could not extricate
Nor him nor me—and there we lay,
   The dying on the dead !
I little deem'd another day
   Would see my houseless, helpless head.

"And there from morn to twilight bound,
I felt the heavy hours toil round,
With just enough of life to see
My last of suns go down on me,
In hopeless certainty of mind,
That makes us feel at length resign'd
To that which our foreboding years
Present the worst and last of fears :
Inevitable—even a boon,
Nor more unkind for coming soon,
Yet shunn'd and dreaded with such care,
As if it only were a snare
   That prudence might escape :
At times both wish'd for and implored,
At times sought with self-pointed sword,
Yet still a dark and hideous close
To even intolerable woes,
   And welcome in no shape.
And, strange to say, the sons of pleasure,
They who have revell'd beyond measure

In beauty, wassail, wine, and treasure,
Die calm, or calmer, oft than he
Whose heritage was misery:
For he who hath in turn run through
All that was beautiful and new,
    Hath nought to hope, and nought to leave:
And, save the future, (which is view'd
Not quite as men are base or good,
But as their nerves may be endued,)
    With nought perhaps to grieve:
The wretch still hopes his woes must end,
And Death, whom he should deem his friend,
Appears, to his distemper'd eyes,
Arrived to rob him of his prize,
The tree of his new Paradise.
To-morrow would have given him all,
Repaid his pangs, repair'd his fall,
To-morrow would have been the first
Of days no more deplored or curst,
But bright, and long, and beckoning years,
Seen dazzling through the mist of tears,
Guerdon of many a painful hour;
To-morrow would have given him power
To rule, to shine, to smite, to save—
And must it dawn upon his grave?

XVIII.

"The sun was sinking—still I lay
   Chain'd to the chill and stiffening steed,
I thought to mingle there our clay,
   And my dim eyes of death had need,
   No hope arose of being freed:
I cast my last looks up the sky,
   And there between me and the sun
I saw the expecting raven fly,
Who scarce would wait till both should die,
   Ere his repast begun;
He flew, and perch'd, then flew once more,
And each time nearer than before;

I saw his wing through twilight flit,
And once so near me he alit
  I could have smote, but lack'd the strength;
But the slight motion of my hand,
And feeble scratching of the sand,
The exerted throat's faint struggling noise,
Which scarcely could be called a voice,
  Together scared him off at length.
I know no more—my latest dream
  Is something of a lovely star
  Which fix'd my dull eyes from afar,
And went and came with wandering beam,
And of the cold, dull, swimming, dense
Sensation of recurring sense,
And then subsiding back to death,
And then again a little breath,
A little thrill, a short suspense,
  An icy sickness curdling o'er
My heart, and sparks that cross'd my brain—
A gasp, a throb, a start of pain,
  A sigh, and nothing more.

XIX.

"I woke—where was I?—Do I see
A human face look down on me?
And doth a roof above me close?
Do these limbs on a couch repose?
Is this a chamber where I lie?
And is it mortal yon bright eye,
That watches me with gentle glance?
  I closed my own again once more,
As doubtful that my former trance
  Could not as yet be o'er.
A slender girl, long-hair'd, and tall,
Sate watching by the cottage wall;
The sparkle of her eye I caught,
Even with my first return of thought;
For ever and anon she threw
  A prying, pitying glance on me
  With her black eyes so wild and free:

I gazed, and gazed, until I knew
　　No vision it could be,—
But that I lived, and was released
From adding to the vulture's feast :
And when the Cossack maid beheld
My heavy eyes at length unseal'd,
She smiled—and I essay'd to speak,
　　But fail'd—and she approach'd, and made
　　With lip and finger signs that said,
I must not strive as yet to break
The silence, till my strength should be
Enough to leave my accents free ;
And then her hand on mine she laid,
And smooth'd the pillow for my head,
And stole along on tiptoe tread,
　　And gently oped the door, and spake
In whispers—ne'er was voice so sweet !
Even music follow'd her light feet ,
　　But those she call'd were not awake,
And she went forth ; but, ere she pass'd,
Another look on me she cast,
　　Another sign she made, to say,
That I had nought to fear, that all
Were near, at my command or call,
　　And she would not delay
Her due return :—while she was gone,
Methought I felt too much alone.

XX

" She came with mother and with sire—
What need of more ?—I will not tire
With long recital of the rest,
Since I became the Cossack's guest.
They found me senseless on the plain,
　　They bore me to the nearest hut,
They brought me into life again—
Me—one day o'er their realm to reign !
　　Thus the vain fool who strove to glut
His rage, refining on my pain,

Sent me forth to the wilderness,
Bound, naked, bleeding, and alone,
To pass the desert to a throne,—
 What mortal his own doom may guess?
 Let none despond, let none despair!
To-morrow the Borysthenes
May see our coursers graze at ease
Upon his Turkish bank, and never
Had I such welcome for a river
 As I shall yield when safely there.[5]
Comrades, good night!"—The Hetman threw
 His length beneath the oak-tree shade,
 With leafy couch already made,
A bed nor comfortless nor new
To him, who took his rest whene'er
The hour arrived, no matter where:
 His eyes the hastening slumbers steep.
And if ye marvel Charles forgot
To thank his tale, *he* wonder'd not,—
 The king had been an hour asleep.

[5] ["Charles, having perceived that the day was lost, fled to a place called Pere-wolochna, situated in the angle formed by the junction of the Vorskla and the Porysthenes Here, accompanied by Mazeppa, and a few hundreds of his followers, Charles swam over the latter great river, and at length reached the Bog, where he was kindly received by the Turkish pacha The Russian envoy at the Sublime Porte demanded that Mazeppa should be delivered up to Peter, but the old Hetman of the Cossacks escaped this fate by taking a disease which hastened his death."—BARROW'S *Peter the Great*, pp 196—203.]

THE ISLAND;

OR.

CHRISTIAN AND HIS COMRADES.

ADVERTISEMENT.

THE foundation of the following story will be found partly in Lieutenant Bligh's "Narrative of the Mutiny and Seizure of the Bounty, in the South Seas, in 1789;" and partly in "Mariner's Account of the Tonga Islands."

GENOA, 1823.

INTRODUCTION TO THE ISLAND.

On the 28th of April, 1789, the Bounty was on its way from Otaheite with a cargo of bread-fruit trees, which the English Government wished to naturalise in the West Indies, when the larger part of the crew, headed by Christian, the mate, seized the commander, Captain Bligh, and launched him, together with eighteen others, who remained faithful to their duty, in an open boat upon the wide ocean. The remainder, twenty-eight in number, of whom four were detained against their will, set sail to Toobonai, one of the Friendly Islands Thence they returned to Otaheite, where Christian landed the majority of the mutineers, while himself and eight of his comrades went back to Toobonai, with the intention of settling there. The natives regarding them as intruders, Christian and his company again put to sea, and established themselves, in 1790, upon Pitcairn's Island, which was then uninhabited Captain Bligh, with twelve of his men, got safe to England, and the Pandora was despatched to Otaheite to apprehend the mutineers Fourteen were captured, and of these four were drowned on the voyage, and three executed in England It was in anticipation of the search for them at Otaheite that Christian and his party sought a securer home, and they took the further precaution to burn the ship as soon as they were settled upon Pitcairn's Island No one guessed what had become of them, till the captain of an American vessel chanced, in 1809, to stop at their place of retreat, and learnt their curious story They had carried with them from Otaheite six Tahitian men and twelve women. Quarrels broke out, a war of races commenced, and ultimately the nine Englishmen were killed or died, with the exception of one Smith, who assumed the name of Adams, and was the patriarch of the colony, which amounted in all to thirty-five Adams, touched by the tragedies he had witnessed, had trained up the half-caste children of himself and his countrymen in the way they should go, and they presented the singular spectacle of a moral, a united, and a happy family, sprung from a colony of ferocious mutineers Such was the romance upon which the poet founded the tale of "The Island," though he has injudiciously interwoven with the central narrative a marvellous incident from Mariner, which relates to an entirely different adventure. It will be seen that Lord Byron has often departed from his authorities, and we share the general opinion in thinking that the piece would have gained in poetic effect if he had adhered more closely to historic truth. The opening lines, descriptive of sunrise at sea, and the twelfth section of the second canto, are worthy of the author, but the bulk of the tale is feebly versified, and seldom reminds us of the master-hand which penned the heroics of "The Corsair" and "Lara." "The Island" was written at Genoa, early in 1823, and published in June

THE ISLAND.

CANTO THE FIRST.

I.

The morning watch was come; the vessel lay
Her course, and gently made her liquid way;
The cloven billow flash'd from off her prow
In furrows form'd by that majestic plough;
The waters with their world were all before;
Behind, the South Sea's many an islet shore.
The quiet night, now dappling, 'gan to wane,
Dividing darkness from the dawning main:
The dolphins, not unconscious of the day,
Swam high, as eager of the coming ray;
The stars from broader beams began to creep,
And lift their shining eyelids from the deep,
The sail resumed its lately shadow'd white,
And the wind flutter'd with a freshening flight;
The purpling ocean owns the coming sun,
But ere he break—a deed is to be done.

II

The gallant chief within his cabin slept,
Secure in those by whom the watch was kept·
His dreams were of Old England's welcome shore,
Of toils rewarded, and of dangers o'er;

His name was added to the glorious roll
Of those who search the storm-surrounded Pole.
The worst was over, and the rest seem'd sure,[1]
And why should not his slumber be secure?
Alas! his deck was trod by unwilling feet,
And wilder hands would hold the vessel's sheet;
Young hearts, which languish'd for some sunny isle,
Where summer years and summer women smile;
Men without country, who, too long estranged,
Had found no native home, or found it changed,
And, half uncivilised, preferr'd the cave
Of some soft savage to the uncertain wave—
The gushing fruits that nature gave untill'd;
The wood without a path but where they will'd;
The field o'er which promiscuous Plenty pour'd
Her horn; the equal land without a lord;
The wish—which ages have not yet subdued
In man—to have no master save his mood;[2]
The earth, whose mine was on its face, unsold,
The glowing sun and produce all its gold;
The freedom which can call each grot a home;
The general garden, where all steps may roam,
Where Nature owns a nation as her child,
Exulting in the enjoyment of the wild;
Their shells, their fruits, the only wealth they know,
Their unexploring navy, the canoe;
Their sport, the dashing breakers and the chase;
Their strangest sight, an European face:—
Such was the country which these strangers yearn'd
To see again; a sight they dearly earn'd.

---

[1] ["A few hours before, my situation had been peculiarly flattering: I had a ship
in the most perfect order, stored with every necessary, both for health and service;
the object of the voyage was attained, and two thirds of it now completed   The
remaining part had every prospect of success "—BLIGH.]

[2] ["The women of Otaheite are handsome, mild, and cheerful in manners and
conversation, possessed of great sensibility, and have sufficient delicacy to make them
be admired and beloved   The chiefs were so much attached to our people, that they rather
encouraged their stay among them than otherwise, and even made them promises of large
possessions   Under these and many other concomitant circumstances, it ought hardly
to be the subject of surprise that a set of sailors, most of them void of connections,
should be led away, where they had the power of fixing themselves, in the midst of
plenty, in one of the finest islands in the world, where there was no necessity to labour,
and where the allurements of dissipation are beyond any conception that can be formed
of it "—BLIGH]

III.

Awake, bold Bligh! the foe is at the gate!
Awake! awake!——Alas! it is too late!
Fiercely beside thy cot the mutineer
Stands, and proclaims the reign of rage and fear.
Thy limbs are bound, the bayonet at thy breast;
The hands, which trembled at thy voice, arrest;
Dragg'd o'er the deck, no more at thy command
The obedient helm shall veer, the sail expand;
That savage spirit, which would lull by wrath
Its desperate escape from duty's path,
Glares round thee, in the scarce believing eyes
Of those who fear the chief they sacrifice:
For ne'er can man his conscience all assuage,
Unless he drain the wine of passion—rage.

IV.

In vain, not silenced by the eye of death,
Thou call'st the loyal with thy menaced breath:—
They come not; they are few, and, overawed,
Must acquiesce, while sterner hearts applaud.
In vain thou dost demand the cause: a curse
Is all the answer, with the threat of worse.
Full in thine eyes is waved the glittering blade,
Close to thy throat the pointed bayonet laid.
The levell'd muskets circle round thy breast
In hands as steel'd to do the deadly rest.
Thou dar'st them to their worst, exclaiming—" Fire!"
But they who pitied not could yet admire;
Some lurking remnant of their former awe
Restrain'd them longer than their broken law;
They would not dip their souls at once in blood,
But left thee to the mercies of the flood.[3]

---

[3] [" Just before sunrise, while I was yet asleep, Mr Christian, with the master at arms, gunner's mate, and Thomas Burkitt, seaman, came into my cabin, and, seizing me, tied my hands with a cord behind my back, threatening me with instant death if I spoke or made the least noise. I nevertheless called out as loud as I could, in hopes of assistance, but the officers not of their party were already secured by sentinels at their doors. At my own cabin door were three men, besides the four within, all except Christian had muskets and bayonets; he had only a cutlass. I was dragged

V.

"Hoist out the boat!" was now the leader's cry;
And who dare answer "No!" to Mutiny,
In the first dawning of the drunken hour,
The Saturnalia of unhoped-for power?
The boat is lower'd with all the haste of hate,
With its slight plank between thee and thy fate;
Her only cargo such a scant supply
As promises the death their hands deny;
And just enough of water and of bread
To keep, some days, the dying from the dead:
Some cordage, canvass, sails, and lines, and twine,
But treasures all to hermits of the brine,
Were added after, to the earnest prayer
Of those who saw no hope, save sea and air;
And last, that trembling vassal of the Pole—
The feeling compass—Navigation's soul.[4]

VI.

And now the self-elected chief finds time
To stun the first sensation of his crime,
And raise it in his followers—"Ho! the bowl!"[5]
Lest passion should return to reason's shoal.
"Brandy for heroes!"[6] Burke could once exclaim—
No doubt a liquid path to epic fame;

eat of bed, and forced on deck in my shirt. On demanding the reason of such
violence, the only answer was abuse for not holding my tongue The boatswain was
then ordered to hoist out the launch, accompanied by a threat, if he did not do it
instantly, to take care of himself The boat being hoisted out, Mr. Heyward and
Mr Hallet, two of the midshipmen, and Mr. Samuel, the clerk, were ordered into it
I demanded the intention of giving this order, and endeavoured to persuade the people
near me not to persist in such acts of violence; but it was to no effect, for the
constant answer was, 'Hold your tongue, or you are dead this moment!'"—BLIGH.]

[4] ["The boatswain, and those seamen who were to be put in the boat, were
allowed to collect twine, canvass, lines, sails, cordage, and an eight and-twenty gallon
cask of water, and Mr Samuel got one hundred and fifty pounds of bread with a
small quantity of rum and wine; also a quadrant and compass "—BLIGH]

[5] ["The mutineers having thus forced those of the seamen whom they wished to
get rid of into the boat, Christian directed a dram to be served to each of his crew."—
BLIGH]

[6] [It was Dr Johnson who thus gave honour to Cognac —"He was persuaded,"
says Boswell, "to take one glass of claret. He shook his head, and said, 'Poor
stuff!—No, Sir, claret is the liquor for boys; port for men, but he who aspires to be
a hero (smiling) must drink brandy '"]

And such the new-born heroes found it here,
And drain'd the draught with an applauding cheer.
"Huzza! for Otaheite!" was the cry.
How strange such shouts from sons of Mutiny!
The gentle island, and the genial soil,
The friendly hearts, the feasts without a toil,
The courteous manners but from nature caught,
The wealth unhoarded, and the love unbought;
Could these have charms for rudest sea-boys, driven
Before the mast by every wind of heaven?
And now, even now prepared with others' woes
To earn mild Virtue's vain desire, repose?
Alas! such is our nature! all but aim
At the same end by pathways not the same;
Our means, our birth, our nation, and our name,
Our fortune, temper, even our outward frame,
Are far more potent o'er our yielding clay
Than aught we know beyond our little day.
Yet still there whispers the small voice within,
Heard through Gain's silence, and o'er Glory's din:
Whatever creed be taught, or land be trod,
Man's conscience is the oracle of God.

VII

The launch is crowded with the faithful few
Who wait their chief, a melancholy crew:
But some remain'd reluctant on the deck
Of that proud vessel—now a moral wreck—
And view'd their captain's fate with piteous eyes;
While others scoff'd his augur'd miseries,
Sneer'd at the prospect of his pigmy sail,
And the slight bark so laden and so frail.
The tender nautilus, who steers his prow,
The sea-born sailor of his shell canoe,
The ocean Mab, the fairy of the sea,
Seems far less fragile, and, alas! more free.
He, when the lightning-wing'd tornados sweep
The surge, is safe—his port is in the deep—
And triumphs o'er the armadas of mankind,
Which shake the world, yet crumble in the wind.

VIII.

When all was now prepared, the vessel clear
Which hail'd her master in the mutineer,
A seaman, less obdurate than his mates,
Show'd the vain pity which but irritates;
Watch'd his late chieftain with exploring eye,
And told, in signs, repentant sympathy;
Held the moist shaddock to his parched mouth,
Which felt exhaustion's deep and bitter drouth.
But soon observed, this guardian was withdrawn,
Nor further mercy clouds rebellion's dawn.'
Then forward stepp'd the bold and froward boy
His chief had cherish'd only to destroy,
And, pointing to the helpless prow beneath,
Exclaim'd, "Depart at once! delay is death!"
Yet then, even then, his feelings ceased not all:
In that last moment could a word recall
Remorse for the black deed as yet half done,
And what he hid from many show'd to one:
When Bligh in stern reproach demanded where
Was now his grateful sense of former care?
Where all his hopes to see his name aspire,
And blazon Britain's thousand glories higher?
His feverish lips thus broke their gloomy spell,
"'Tis that! 'tis that! I am in hell! in hell!"[8]
No more he said; but urging to the bark
His chief, commits him to his fragile ark;
These the sole accents from his tongue that fell,
But volumes lurk'd below his fierce farewell.

---

[7] ["Isaac Martin, I saw, had an inclination to assist me, and as he fed me with shaddock, my lips being quite parched, we explain'd each other's sentiments by looks. But this was observed, and he was removed   He then got into the boat, but was compelled to return."—BLIGH]

[8] ["Christian then said, 'Come, Captain Bligh, your officers and men are now in the boat, and you must go with them ' Without further ceremony, I was forced over the side by a tribe of armed ruffians, where they untied my hands   After having been kept for some time to make sport for these unfeeling wretches, and having undergone much ridicule, we were at length cast adrift in the open ocean.   When we were sent away, 'Huzza for Otaheite!' was frequently heard among the mutineers   While they were forcing me out of the ship, I asked Christian whether this was a proper return for the many instances he had experienced of my friendship? He appeared disturbed at the question, and answered, with much emotion, 'That – Captain Bligh   that is the thing—I am in hell—I am in hell!'"—BLIGH.]

IX

The arctic sun rose broad above the wave ;
The breeze now sank, now whisper'd from his cave ;
As on the Æolian harp, his fitful wings
Now swell'd, now flutter'd o'er his ocean strings.
With slow, despairing oar, the abandon'd skiff
Ploughs its drear progress to the scarce seen cliff,
Which lifts its peak a cloud above the main :
That boat and ship shall never meet again !

But 'tis not mine to tell their tale of grief,
Their constant peril, and their scant relief ;
Their days of danger, and their nights of pain ;
Their manly courage even when deem'd in vain ;
The sapping famine, rendering scarce a son
Known to his mother in the skeleton ;
The ills that lessen'd still their little store,
And starved even Hunger till he wrung no more,
The varying frowns and favours of the deep,
That now almost ingulfs, then leaves to creep
With crazy oar and shatter'd strength along
The tide that yields reluctant to the strong ;
The incessant fever of that arid thirst
Which welcomes, as a well, the clouds that burst
Above their naked bones, and feels delight
In the cold drenching of the stormy night,
And from the outspread canvass gladly wrings
A drop to moisten life's all-gasping springs ,
The savage foe escaped, to seek again
More hospitable shelter from the main ;
The ghastly spectres which were doom'd at last
To tell as true a tale of dangers past,
As ever the dark annals of the deep
Disclosed for man to dread or woman weep.

X.

We leave them to their fate, but not unknown
Nor unredress'd.   Revenge may have her own :
Roused discipline aloud proclaims their cause,
And injured navies urge their broken laws.

Pursue we on his track the mutineer,
Whom distant vengeance had not taught to fear.
Wide o'er the wave—away! away! away!
Once more his eyes shall hail the welcome bay;
Once more the happy shores without a law
Receive the outlaws whom they lately saw;
Nature, and Nature's goddess—woman—woos
To lands where, save their conscience, none accuse;
Where all partake the earth without dispute,
And bread itself is gather'd as a fruit; [9]
Where none contest the fields, the woods, the streams:—
The goldless age, where gold disturbs no dreams,
Inhabits or inhabited the shore,
Till Europe taught them better than before:
Bestow'd her customs, and amended theirs,
But left her vices also to their heirs.
Away with this! behold them as they were,
Do good with Nature, or with Nature err.
"Huzza! for Otaheite!" was the cry,
As stately swept the gallant vessel by.
The breeze springs up; the lately flapping sail
Extends its arch before the growing gale;
In swifter ripples stream aside the seas,
Which her bold bow flings off with dashing ease.
Thus Argo [10] plough'd the Euxine's virgin foam,
But those she wafted still look'd back to home;
These spurn their country with their rebel bark,
And fly her as the raven fled the ark;
And yet they seek to nestle with the dove,
And tame their fiery spirits down to love.

[9] The now celebrated bread-fruit, to transplant which Captain Bligh's expedition was undertaken.
[10] [The vessel in which Jason embarked in quest of the golden fleece.]

CANTO THE SECOND.

—◆—

I.

How pleasant were the songs of Toobonai,[1]
When summer's sun went down the coral bay!
Come, let us to the islet's softest shade,
And hear the warbling birds! the damsels said:
The wood-dove from the forest depth shall coo,
Like voices of the gods from Bolotoo;
We'll cull the flowers that grow above the dead,
For these most bloom where rests the warrior's head;
And we will sit in twilight's face, and see
The sweet moon glancing through the tooa tree,
The lofty accents of whose sighing bough
Shall sadly please us as we lean below;
Or climb the steep, and view the surf in vain
Wrestle with rocky giants o'er the main,
Which spurn in columns back the baffled spray.
How beautiful are these! how happy they,
Who, from the toil and tumult of their lives,
Steal to look down where nought but ocean strives!
Even he too loves at times the blue lagoon,
And smooths his ruffled mane beneath the moon.

II.

Yes—from the sepulchre we'll gather flowers,
Then feast like spirits in their promised bowers,

[1] The first three sections are taken from an actual song of the Tonga Islanders, of which a prose translation is given in "Mariner's Account of the Tonga Islands." Toobonai is *not* however one of them; but was one of those where Christian and the mutineers took refuge. I have altered and added, but have retained as much as possible of the original.

Then plunge and revel in the rolling surf,
Then lay our limbs along the tender turf,
And, wet and shining from the sportive toil,
Anoint our bodies with the fragrant oil,
And plait our garlands gather'd from the grave,
And wear the wreaths that sprung from out the brave.
But lo! night comes, the Mooa woos us back,
The sound of mats are heard along our track;
Anon the torchlight dance shall fling its sheen
In flashing mazes o'er the Marly's green;
And we too will be there; we too recall
The memory bright with many a festival,
Ere Fiji blew the shell of war, when foes
For the first time were wafted in canoes.
Alas! for them the flower of mankind bleeds;
Alas! for them our fields are rank with weeds:
Forgotten is the rapture, or unknown,
Of wandering with the moon and love alone.
But be it so.—*they* taught us how to wield
The club, and rain our arrows o'er the field:
Now let them reap the harvest of their art!
But feast to-night! to-morrow we depart.
Strike up the dance! the cava bowl fill high!
Drain every drop!—to-morrow we may die.
In summer garments be our limbs array'd;
Around our waists the tappa's white display'd;
Thick wreaths shall form our coronal, like spring's,
And round our necks shall glance the hooni strings;
So shall their brighter hues contrast the glow
Of the dusk bosoms that beat high below.

                                III

But now the dance is o'er—yet stay awhile;
Ah, pause! nor yet put out the social smile.
To-morrow for the Mooa we depart,
But not to-night—to-night is for the heart.
Again bestow the wreaths we gently woo,
Ye young enchantresses of gay Licoo!
How lovely are your forms! how every sense
Bows to your beauties, soften'd, but intense.

Like to the flowers on Mataloco's steep,
Which fling their flagrance far athwart the deep!—
We too will see Licoo; but—oh! my heart!—
What do I say?—to-morrow we depart!

IV

Thus rose a song—the harmony of times
Before the winds blew Europe o'er these climes.
True, they had vices—such are Nature's growth—
But only the barbarian's—we have both;
The sordor of civilisation, mix'd
With all the savage which man's fall hath fix'd.
Who hath not seen Dissimulation's reign,
The prayers of Abel link'd to deeds of Cain?
Who such would see may from his lattice view
The Old World more degraded than the New,—
Now *new* no more, save where Columbia rears
Twin giants, born by Freedom to her spheres,
Where Chimborazo, over air, earth, wave,
Glares with his Titan eye, and sees no slave.

V

Such was this ditty of Tradition's days,
Which to the dead a lingering fame conveys
In song, where fame as yet hath left no sign
Beyond the sound whose charm is half divine;
Which leaves no record to the sceptic eye,
But yields young history all to harmony;
A boy Achilles, with the centaur's lyre
In hand, to teach him to surpass his sire.
For one long-cherish'd ballad's simple stave,
Rung from the rock, or mingled with the wave,
Or from the bubbling streamlet's grassy side,
Or gathering mountain echoes as they glide,
Hath greater power o'er each true heart and ear,
Than all the columns Conquest's minions rear;
Invites, when hieroglyphics are a theme
For sages' labours, or the student's dream;
Attracts, when History's volumes are a toil,—
The first, the freshest bud of Feeling's soil.

Such was this rude rhyme—rhyme is of the rude—
But such inspired the Norseman's solitude,
Who came and conquer'd; such, wherever rise
Lands which no foes destroy or civilise,
Exist: and what can our accomplish'd art
Of verse do more than reach the awaken'd heart?

VI.

And sweetly now those untaught melodies
Broke the luxurious silence of the skies,
The sweet siesta of a summer day,
The tropic afternoon of Toobonai,
When every flower was bloom, and air was balm,
And the first breath began to stir the palm,
The first yet voiceless wind to urge the wave
All gently to refresh the thirsty cave,   ·
Where sat the songstress with the stranger boy,
Who taught her passion's desolating joy,
Too powerful over every heart, but most
O'er those who know not how it may be lost;
O'er those who, burning in the new-born fire,
Like martyrs revel in their funeral pyre,
With such devotion to their ecstacy,
That life knows no such rapture as to die:
And die they do; for earthly life has nought
Match'd with that burst of nature, even in thought;
And all our dreams of better life above
But close in one eternal gush of love.

VII.

There sat the gentle savage of the wild,
In growth a woman, though in years a child,
As childhood dates within our colder clime,
Where nought is ripen'd rapidly save crime;
The infant of an infant world, as pure
From nature—lovely, warm, and premature;
Dusky like night, but night with all her stars;
Or cavern sparkling with its native spars;
With eyes that were a language and a spell,
A form like Aphrodite's in her shell,

With all her loves around her on the deep,
Voluptuous as the first approach of sleep;
Yet full of life—for through her tropic cheek
The blush would make its way, and all but speak;
The sun-born blood suffused her neck, and threw
O'er her clear nut-brown skin a lucid hue,
Like coral reddening through the darken'd wave,
Which draws the diver to the crimson cave.
Such was this daughter of the southern seas,
Herself a billow in her energies,
To bear the bark of others' happiness,
Nor feel a sorrow till their joy grew less:
Her wild and warm yet faithful bosom knew
No joy like what it gave; her hopes ne'er drew
Aught from experience, that chill touchstone, whose
Sad proof reduces all things from their hues:
She fear'd no ill, because she knew it not,
Or what she knew was soon—too soon—forgot:
Her smiles and tears had pass'd, as light winds pass
O'er lakes to ruffle, not destroy, their glass,
Whose depths unsearch'd, and fountains from the hill,
 Restore their surface, in itself so still,
Until the earthquake tear the naiad's cave,
Root up the spring, and trample on the wave,
And crush the living waters to a mass,
The amphibious desert of the dank morass!
And must their fate be hers? The eternal change
But grasps humanity with quicker range;
And they who fall but fall as worlds will fall,
To rise, if just, a spirit o'er them all.

VIII.

And who is he? the blue-eyed northern child [2]
Of isles more known to man, but scarce less wild;
The fair-hair'd offspring of the Hebrides,
Where roars the Pentland with its whirling seas;

[2] [George Stewart. "He was," says Bligh, "a young man of creditable parents in tne Orkneys, at which place, on the return of the Resolution from the South Seas, in 1780, we received so many civilities, that, on that account only, I should gladly have taken him with me but, independent of this recommendation, he was a seaman, and had always borne a good character "]

Rock'd in his cradle by the roaring wind,
The tempest-born in body and in mind,
His young eyes opening on the ocean-foam,
Had from that moment deem'd the deep his home,
The giant comrade of his pensive moods,
The sharer of his craggy solitudes,
The only Mentor of his youth, where'er
His bark was borne; the sport of wave and air;
A careless thing, who placed his choice in chance,
Nursed by the legends of his land's romance;
Eager to hope, but not less firm to bear,
Acquainted with all feelings save despair.
Placed in the Arab's clime he would have been
As bold a rover as the sands have seen,
And braved their thirst with as enduring lip
As Ishmael, wafted on his desert-ship;[3]
Fix'd upon Chili's shore, a proud cacique;
On Hellas' mountains, a rebellious Greek;
Born in a tent, perhaps a Tamerlane;
Bred to a throne, perhaps unfit to reign.
For the same soul that rends its path to sway,
If rear'd to such, can find no further prey
Beyond itself, and must retrace its way,[4]
Plunging for pleasure into pain: the same
Spirit which made a Nero, Rome's worst shame,
A humbler state and discipline of heart,
Had form'd his glorious namesake's counterpart;[5]
But grant his vices, grant them all his own,
How small their theatre without a throne!

---

[3] The "ship of the desert" is the Oriental figure for the camel or dromedary, and they deserve the metaphor well,—the former for his endurance, the latter for his swiftness

[4]   "Lucullus, when frugality could charm,
                    Had roasted turnips in the Sabine farm."—POPE.

[5] The consul Nero, who made the unequalled march which deceived Hannibal, and defeated Asdrubal; thereby accomplishing an achievement almost unrivalled in military annals   The first intelligence of his return, to Hannibal, was the sight of Asdrubal's head thrown into his camp   When Hannibal saw this, he exclaimed with a sigh, that "Rome would now be the mistress of the world"   And yet to this victory of Nero's it might be owing that his imperial namesake reigned at all.   But the infamy of the one has eclipsed the glory of the other   When the name of "Nero" is heard, who thinks of the consul ?—But such are human things !

IX.

Thou smilest :—these comparisons seem high
To those who scan all things with dazzled eye;
Link'd with the unknown name of one whose doom
Has nought to do with glory or with Rome,
With Chili, Hellas, or with Araby;—
Thou smilest?—Smile; 'tis better thus than sigh;
Yet such he might have been; he was a man,
A soaring spirit, ever in the van,
A patriot hero or despotic chief,
To form a nation's glory or its grief,
Born under auspices which make us more
Or less than we delight to ponder o'er.
But these are visions; say, what was he here?
A blooming boy, a truant mutineer.
The fair-hair'd Torquil, free as ocean's spray,
The husband of the bride of Toobonai.

X.

By Neuha's side he sate, and watch'd the waters,—
Neuha, the sun-flower of the island daughters,
Highborn, (a birth at which the herald smiles,
Without a scutcheon for these secret isles,)
Of a long race, the valiant and the free,
The naked knights of savage chivalry,
Whose grassy cairns ascend along the shore;
And thine—I've seen—Achilles ¹ do no more.
She, when the thunder-bearing strangers came,
In vast canoes, begirt with bolts of flame,
Topp'd with tall trees, which, loftier than the palm,
Seem'd rooted in the deep amidst its calm:
But when the winds awaken'd, shot forth wings
Broad as the cloud along the horizon flings,
And sway'd the waves, like cities of the sea,
Making the very billows look less free;—
She, with her paddling oar and dancing prow,
Shot through the surf, like reindeer through the snow,
Swift-gliding o'er the breaker's whitening edge,
Light as a nereid in her ocean sledge,

And gazed and wonder'd at the giant hulk,
Which heaved from wave to wave its trampling bulk.
The anchor dropp'd; it lay along the deep,
Like a huge lion in the sun asleep,
While round it swarm'd the proas' flitting chain,
Like summer bees that hum around his mane.

XI.

The white man landed!—need the rest be told?
The New World stretch'd its dusk hand to the Old;
Each was to each a marvel, and the tie
Of wonder warm'd to better sympathy.
Kind was the welcome of the sun-born sires,
And kinder still their daughters' gentler fires.
Their union grew: the children of the storm
Found beauty link'd with many a dusky form;
While these in turn admired the paler glow,
Which seem'd so white in climes that knew no snow.
The chace, the race, the liberty to roam,
The soil where every cottage show'd a home;
The sea-spread net, the lightly launch'd canoe,
Which stemm'd the studded archipelago,
O'er whose blue bosom rose the starry isles;
The healthy slumber, earn'd by sportive toils;
The palm, the loftiest dryad of the woods,
Within whose bosom infant Bacchus broods,
While eagles scarce build higher than the crest
Which shadows o'er the vineyard in her breast;
The cava feast, the yam, the cocoa's root,
Which bears at once the cup, and milk, and fruit;
The bread-tree, which, without the ploughshare, yields
The unreap'd harvest of unfurrow'd fields,
And bakes its unadulterated loaves
Without a furnace in unpurchased groves,
And flings off famine from its fertile breast,
A priceless market for the gathering guest;—
These, with the luxuries of seas and woods,
The airy joys of social solitudes,
Tamed each rude wanderer to the sympathies
Of those who were more happy, if less wise,

Did more than Europe's discipline had done.
And civilised Civilisation's son !

XII.

Of these, and there was many a willing pair,
Neuha and Torquil were not the least fair :
Both children of the isles, though distant far ;
Both born beneath a sea-presiding star ;
Both nourish'd amidst nature's native scenes,
Loved to the last, whatever intervenes
Between us and our childhood's sympathy,
Which still reverts to what first caught the eye.
He who first met the Highlands' swelling blue
Will love each peak that shows a kindred hue,
Hail in each crag a friend's familiar face,
And clasp the mountain in his mind's embrace.
Long have I roam'd through lands which are not mine,
Adored the Alp, and loved the Apennine,
Revered Parnassus, and beheld the steep
Jove's Ida and Olympus crown the deep:
But 'twas not all long ages' lore, nor all
Their nature held me in their thrilling thrall ;
The infant rapture still survived the boy,
And Loch-na-gar with Ida look'd o'er Troy,[6]
Mix'd Celtic memories with the Phrygian mount,
And Highland linns with Castalie's clear fount.
Forgive me, Homer's universal shade !
Forgive me, Phœbus ! that my fancy stray'd ;
The north and nature taught me to adore
Your scenes sublime, from those beloved before.

XIII.

The love which maketh all things fond and fair,
The youth which makes one rainbow of the air,

[6] When very young, about eight years of age, after an attack of the scarlet fever at Aberdeen, I was removed by medical advice into the Highlands Here I passed occasionally some summers, and from this period I date my love of mountainous countries I can never forget the effect, a few years afterwards, in England, of the only thing I had long seen, even in miniature, of a mountain, in the Malvern Hills After I returned to Cheltenham, I used to watch them every afternoon. at sunset, with a sensation which I cannot describe. This was boyish enough but I was then only thirteen years of age, and it was in the holidays

The dangers past, that make even man enjoy
The pause in which he ceases to destroy,
The mutual beauty, which the sternest feel
Strike to their hearts like lightning to the steel,
United the half savage and the whole,
The maid and boy, in one absorbing soul.
No more the thundering memory of the fight
Wrapp'd his wean'd bosom in its dark delight;
No more the irksome restlessness of rest
Disturb'd him like the eagle in her nest,
Whose whetted beak and far-pervading eye
Darts for a victim over all the sky :
His heart was tamed to that voluptuous state,
. At once Elysian and effeminate,
Which leaves no laurels o'er the hero's urn ;—
These wither when for aught save blood they burn ;
Yet when their ashes in their nook are laid,
Doth not the myrtle leave as sweet a shade ?
Had Cæsar known but Cleopatra's kiss,
Rome had been free, the world had not been his.
And what have Cæsar's deeds and Cæsar's fame
Done for the earth ?   We feel them in our shame.
The gory sanction of his glory stains
The rust which tyrants cherish on our chains.
Though Glory, Nature, Reason, Freedom, bid
Roused millions do what single Brutus did—
Sweep these mere mock-birds of the despot's song
From the tall bough where they have perch'd so long,—
Still are we hawk'd at by such mousing owls,
And take for falcons those ignoble fowls,
When but a word of freedom would dispel
These bugbears, as their terrors show too well.

XIV.

Rapt in the fond forgetfulness of life,
Neuha, the South Sea girl, was all a wife,
With no distracting world to call her off
From love; with no society to scoff
At the new transient flame; no babbling crowd
Of coxcombry in admiration loud,

Or with adulterous whisper to alloy
Her duty, and her glory, and her joy:
With faith and feelings naked as her form,
She stood as stands a rainbow in a storm,
Changing its hues with bright variety,
But still expanding lovelier o'er the sky,
Howe'er its arch may swell, its colours move,
The cloud-compelling harbinger of love.

xv.

Here, in this grotto of the wave-worn shore,
They pass'd the tropic's red meridian o'er;
Nor long the hours—they never paused o'er time,
Unbroken by the clock's funereal chime,
Which deals the daily pittance of our span,
And points and mocks with iron laugh at man.
What deem'd they of the future or the past?
The present, like a tyrant, held them fast:
Their hour-glass was the sea-sand, and the tide,
Like her smooth billow, saw their moments glide;
Their clock the sun, in his unbounded tow'r;
They reckon'd not, whose day was but an hour;
The nightingale, their only vesper-bell,
Sung sweetly to the rose the day's farewell;[7]
The broad sun set, but not with lingering sweep,
. As in the north he mellows o'er the deep;
But fiery, full, and fierce, as if he left
The world for ever, earth of light bereft,
Plunged with red forehead down along the wave,
As dives a hero headlong to his grave.
Then rose they, looking first along the skies,
And then for light into each other's eyes,
Wondering that summer show'd so brief a sun,
And asking if indeed the day were done.

xvi.

And let not this seem strange. the devotee
Lives not in earth, but in his ecstasy;

---

[7] The now well-known story of the loves of the nightingale and rose need not be
more than alluded to, being sufficiently familiar to the Western as to the Eastern reader

Around him days and worlds are heedless driven,
His soul is gone before his dust to heaven.
Is love less potent?   No—his path is trod,
Alike uplifted gloriously to God ;
Or link'd to all we know of heaven below,
The other better self, whose joy or woe
Is more than ours ; the all-absorbing flame
Which, kindled by another, grows the same,
Wrapt in one blaze ; the pure, yet funeral pile,
Where gentle hearts, like Bramins, sit and smile.
How often we forget all time, when lone,
Admiring Nature's universal throne,
Her woods, her wilds, her waters, the intense
Reply of *hers* to our intelligence !
Live not the stars and mountains ?   Are the waves
Without a spirit ?   Are the dropping caves
Without a feeling in their silent tears ?
No, no ;—they woo and clasp us to their spheres,
Dissolve this clog and clod of clay before
Its hour, and merge our soul in the great shore.
Strip off this fond and false identity !—
Who thinks of self when gazing on the sky ?
And who, though gazing lower, ever thought,
In the young moments ere the heart is taught
Time's lesson, of man's baseness or his own ?
All nature is his realm, and love his throne.

XVII.

Neuha arose, and Torquil : twilight's hour
Came sad and softly to their rocky bower,
Which, kindling by degrees its dewy spars,
Echoed their dim light to the mustering stars.
Slowly the pair, partaking nature's calm,
Sought out their cottage, built beneath the palm ;
Now smiling and now silent, as the scene ;
Lovely as Love—the spirit !—when serene.
The Ocean scarce spoke louder with his swell,
Than breathes his mimic murmurer in the shell,[8]

---

[8] If the reader will apply to his ear the sea-shell on his chimney piece, he will be
aware of what is alluded to. If the text should appear obscure, he will find in

As, far divided from his parent deep,
The sea-born infant cries, and will not sleep,
Raising his little plaint in vain, to rave
For the broad bosom of his nursing wave :
The woods droop'd darkly, as inclined to rest,
The tropic bird wheel'd rockward to his nest,
And the blue sky spread round them like a lake
Of peace, where Piety her thirst might slake.

XVIII

But through the palm and plantain, hark, a voice !
Not such as would have been a lover's choice,
In such an hour, to break the air so still ;
No dying night-breeze, harping o'er the hill,
Striking the strings of nature, rock and tree,
Those best and earliest lyres of harmony,
With Echo for their chorus ; nor the alarm
Of the loud war-whoop to dispel the charm ;
Nor the soliloquy of the hermit owl,
Exhaling all his solitary soul,
The dim though large-eyed winged anchorite,
Who peals his dreary pæan o'er the night ;
But a loud, long, and naval whistle, shrill
As ever started through a sea-bird's bill ;
And then a pause, and then a hoarse, "Hillo !
Torquil, my boy ! what cheer? Ho ! brother, ho ! "
"Who hails ? " cried Torquil, following with his eye
The sound. "Here's one," was all the brief reply.

"Gebir" the same idea better expressed in two lines The poem I never read, but
have heard the lines quoted, by a more recondite reader—who seems to be of a
different opinion from the editor of the Quarterly Review, who qualified it in his
answer to the Critical Reviewer of his Juvenal, as trash of the worst and most insane
description It is to Mr Landor, the author of "Gebir," so qualified, and of some
Latin poems, which vie with Martial or Catullus in obscenity, that the immaculate
Mr. Southey addresses his declamation against impurity !

[These are the lines in "Gebir" to which Lord Byron alludes —

"But I have sinuous shells of pearly hue
Shake one and it awakens, then apply
Its polisht lips to your attentive ear,
And it remembers its august abodes,
And murmurs as the ocean murmurs there."]

XIX.

But here the herald of the self-same mouth
Came breathing o'er the aromatic south,
Not like a " bed of violets " on the gale,
But such as wafts its cloud o'er grog or ale,
Borne from a short frail pipe, which yet had blown
Its gentle odours over either zone,
And, puff'd where'er winds rise or waters roll,
Had wafted smoke from Portsmouth to the Pole,
Opposed its vapour as the lightning flash'd,
And reek'd, 'midst mountain-billows, unabash'd,
To Æolus a constant sacrifice,
Through every change of all the varying skies.
And what was he who bore it ?—I may err,
But deem him sailor or philosopher.[*]
Sublime tobacco ! which from east to west
Cheers the tar's labour or the Turkman's rest ;
Which on the Moslem's ottoman divides
His hours, and rivals opium and his brides ;
Magnificent in Stamboul, but less grand,
Though not less loved, in Wapping or the Strand ;
Divine in hookas, glorious in a pipe,
When tipp'd with amber, mellow, rich, and ripe ;
Like other charmers, wooing the caress,
More dazzlingly when daring in full dress ;
Yet thy true lovers more admire by far
Thy naked beauties—Give me a cigar !

XX.

Through the approaching darkness of the wood
A human figure broke the solitude,
Fantastically, it may be, array'd,
A seaman in a savage masquerade ;
Such as appears to rise out from the deep
When o'er the line the merry vessels sweep,

---

[*] Hobbes, the father of Locke's and other philosophy, was an inveterate smoker,—
even to pipes beyond computation.
["Soon after dinner Mr. Hobbes retired to his study, and had his candle, with ten
or twelve pipes of tobacco laid by him ; then, shutting the door, he fell to smoking,
thinking, and writing for several hours."—DR. KENNET.]

And the rough Saturnalia of the tar
Flock o'er the deck, in Neptune's borrow'd car; [1]
And, pleased, the god of ocean sees his name
Revive once more, though but in mimic game
Of his true sons, who riot in the breeze
Undreamt of in his native Cyclades.
Still the old god delights, from out the main,
To snatch some glimpses of his ancient reign.
Our sailor's jacket, though in ragged trim,
His constant pipe, which never yet burn'd dim,
His foremast air, and somewhat rolling gait,
Like his dear vessel, spoke his former state;
But then a sort of kerchief round his head,
Not over tightly bound, nor nicely spread;
And, 'stead of trowsers (ah! too early torn!
For even the mildest woods will have their thorn)
A curious sort of somewhat scanty mat
Now served for inexpressibles and hat;
His naked feet and neck, and sunburnt face,
Perchance might suit alike with either race.
His arms were all his own, our Europe's growth,
Which two worlds bless for civilising both;
The musket swung behind his shoulders broad,
And somewhat stoop'd by his marine abode,
But brawny as the boar's; and hung beneath,
His cutlass droop'd, unconscious of a sheath,
Or lost or worn away; his pistols were
Link'd to his belt, a matrimonial pair—
(Let not this metaphor appear a scoff,
Though one miss'd fire, the other would go off);
These, with a bayonet, not so free from rust
As when the arm-chest held its brighter trust,
Completed his accoutrements, as Night
Survey'd him in his garb heteroclite.

XXI

"What cheer, Ben Bunting?" cried (when in full view
Our new acquaintance) Torquil. "Aught of new?"

---

[1] This rough but jovial ceremony, used in crossing the line, has been so often and
so well described, that it need not be more than alluded to

"Ey, ey!" quoth Ben, "not new, but news enow;
A strange sail in the offing."—"Sail! and how?
What! could you make her out? It cannot be;
I've seen no rag of canvass on the sea."
"Belike," said Ben, "you might not from the bay,
But from the bluff-head, where I watch'd to-day,
I saw her in the doldrums; for the wind
Was light and baffling."—"When the sun declined
Where lay she? had she anchor'd?"—"No, but still
She bore down on us, till the wind grew still."
"Her flag?"—"I had no glass: but fore and aft,
Egad! she seem'd a wicked-looking craft."
"Arm'd?"—"I expect so;—sent on the look-out:
'Tis time, belike, to put our helm about."
"About?—Whate'er may have us now in chase,
We'll make no running fight, for that were base;
We will die at our quarters, like true men."
"Ey, ey! for that 'tis all the same to Ben."
"Does Christian know this?"—"Ay; he has piped all hands
To quarters. They are furbishing the stands
Of arms; and we have got some guns to bear,
And scaled them. You are wanted."—"That's but fair;
And if it were not, mine is not the soul
To leave my comrades helpless on the shoal.
My Neuha! ah! and must my fate pursue
Not me alone, but one so sweet and true?
But whatsoe'er betide, ah, Neuha! now
Unman me not; the hour will not allow
A tear; I am thine whatever intervenes!"
"Right," quoth Ben; "that will do for the marines."[2]

---

[2] "That will do for the marines, but the sailors won't believe it," is an old saying and one of the few fragments of former jealousies which still survive (in jest only) between these gallant services.

CANTO THE THIRD.

THE fight was o'er; the flashing through the gloom,
Which robes the cannon as he wings a tomb,
Had ceased; and sulphury vapours upward driven
Had left the earth, and but polluted heaven:
The rattling roar which rung in every volley
Had left the echoes to their melancholy;
No more they shriek'd their horror, boom for boom;
The strife was done, the vanquish'd had their doom;
The mutineers were crush'd, dispersed, or ta'en,
Or lived to deem the happiest were the slain.
Few, few escaped, and these were hunted o'er
The isle they loved beyond their native shore.
No further home was theirs, it seem'd, on earth,
Once renegades to that which gave them birth;
Track'd like wild beasts, like them they sought the wild,
As to a mother's bosom flies the child;
But vainly wolves and lions seek their den,
And still more vainly men escape from men.

II

Beneath a rock whose jutting base protrudes
Far over ocean in its fiercest moods,
When scaling his enormous crag the wave
Is hurl'd down headlong, like the foremost brave,
And falls back on the foaming crowd behind,
Which fight beneath the banners of the wind,
But now at rest, a little remnant drew
Together, bleeding, thirsty, faint, and few;

But still their weapons in their hands, and still
With something of the pride of former will,
As men not all unused to meditate,
And strive much more than wonder at their fate.
Their present lot was what they had foreseen,
And dared as what was likely to have been;
Yet still the lingering hope, which deem'd their lot
Not pardon'd, but unsought for or forgot,
Or trusted that, if sought, their distant caves
Might still be miss'd amidst the world of waves,
Had wean'd their thoughts in part from what they saw
And felt, the vengeance of their country's law.
Their sea-green isle, their guilt-won paradise,
No more could shield their virtue or their vice:
Their better feelings, if such were, were thrown
Back on themselves,—their sins remain'd alone.
Proscribed even in their second country, they
Were lost; in vain the world before them lay;
All outlets seem'd secured.   Their new allies
Had fought and bled in mutual sacrifice;
But what avail'd the club and spear, and arm
Of Hercules, against the sulphury charm,
The magic of the thunder, which destroy'd
The warrior ere his strength could be employ'd?
Dug, like a spreading pestilence, the grave
No less of human bravery than the brave![1]
Their own scant numbers acted all the few
Against the many oft will dare and do;
But though the choice seems native to die free,
Even Greece can boast but one Thermopylæ,
Till *now*, when she has forged her broken chain
Back to a sword, and dies and lives again!

III.

Beside the jutting rock the few appear'd,
Like the last remnant of the red-deer's herd;

[1] Archidamus, King of Sparta, and son of Agesilaus, when he saw a machine invented for the casting of stones and darts, exclaimed that it was the "grave of valour." The same story has been told of some knights on the first application of gunpowder; but the original anecdote is in Plutarch.

Their eyes were feverish, and their aspect worn,
But still the hunter's blood was on their horn.
A little stream came tumbling from the height,
And straggling into ocean as it might,
Its bounding crystal frolick'd in the ray,
And gush'd from cliff to crag with saltless spray;
Close on the wild, wide ocean, yet as pure
And fresh as innocence, and more secure,
Its silver torrent glitter'd o'er the deep,
As the shy chamois' eye o'erlooks the steep,
While far below the vast and sullen swell
Of ocean's alpine azure rose and fell
To this young spring they rush'd,—all feelings first
Absorb'd in passion's and in nature's thirst,—
Drank as they do who drink their last, and threw
Their arms aside to revel in its dew;
Cool'd their scorch'd throats, and wash'd the gory stains
From wounds whose only bandage might be chains;
Then, when their drought was quench'd, look'd sadly round,
As wondering how so many still were found
Alive and fetterless :—but silent all,
Each sought his fellow's eyes, as if to call
On him for language which his lips denied,
As though their voices with their cause had died.

IV.

Stern, and aloof a little from the rest,
Stood Christian, with his arms across his chest.
The ruddy, reckless, dauntless hue once spread
Along his cheek was livid now as lead;
His light-brown locks, so graceful in their flow,
Now rose like startled vipers o'er his brow.
Still as a statue, with his lips comprest
To stifle even the breath within his breast,
Fast by the rock, all menacing, but mute,
He stood, and, save a slight beat of his foot,
Which deepen'd now and then the sandy dint
Beneath his heel, his form seem'd turn'd to flint.
Some paces further Torquil lean'd his head
Against a bank, and spoke not, but he bled,—

Not mortally :—his worst wound was within;
His brow was pale, his blue eyes sunken in,
And blood-drops, sprinkled o'er his yellow hair,
Show'd that his faintness came not from despair,
But nature's ebb.　Beside him was another,
Rough as a bear, but willing as a brother,—
Ben Bunting, who essay'd to wash, and wipe,
And bind his wound—then calmly lit his pipe,
A trophy which survived a hundred fights,
A beacon which had cheer'd ten thousand nights.
The fourth and last of this deserted group
Walk'd up and down—at times would stand, then stoop
To pick a pebble up—then let it drop—
Then hurry as in haste—then quickly stop—
Then cast his eyes on his companions—then
Half whistle half a tune, and pause again—
And then his former movements would redouble,
With something between carelessness and trouble.
This is a long description, but applies
To scarce five minutes pass'd before the eyes;
But yet *what* minutes!　Moments like to these
Rend men's lives into immortalities.

v.

At length Jack Skyscrape, a mercurial man,
Who flutter'd over all things like a fan,
More brave than firm, and more disposed to dare
And die at once than wrestle with despair,
Exclaim'd, " G—d damn !"—those syllables intense,—
Nucleus of England's native eloquence,
As the Turk's " Allah !" or the Roman's more
Pagan " Proh Jupiter !" was wont of yore
To give their first impressions such a vent,
By way of echo to embarrassment.
Jack was embarrass'd,—never hero more,
And as he knew not what to say, he swore:
Nor swore in vain; the long congenial sound
Revived Ben Bunting from his pipe profound;
He drew it from his mouth, and look'd full wise,
But merely added to the oath his *eyes;*

Thus rendering the imperfect phrase complete,
A peroration I need not repeat.

VI

But Christian, of a higher order, stood
Like an extinct volcano in his mood;
Silent, and sad, and savage,—with the trace
Of passion reeking from his clouded face;
Till lifting up again his sombre eye,
It glanced on Torquil, who lean'd faintly by.
"And is it thus?" he cried, "unhappy boy!
And thee, too, *thee*—my madness must destroy!"
He said, and strode to where young Torquil stood,
Yet dabbled with his lately flowing blood;
Seized his hand wistfully, but did not press,
And shrunk as fearful of his own caress;
Enquired into his state; and when he heard
The wound was slighter than he deem'd or fear'd,
A moment's brightness pass'd along his brow,
As much as such a moment would allow.
"Yes," he exclaim'd, "we are taken in the toil,
But not a coward or a common spoil;
Dearly they have bought us—dearly still may buy,—
And I must fall; but have you strength to fly?
'Twould be some comfort still, could you survive;
Our dwindled band is now too few to strive.
Oh! for a sole canoe! though but a shell,
To bear you hence to where a hope may dwell!
For me, my lot is what I sought, to be,
In life or death, the fearless and the free."

VII.

Even as he spoke, around the promontory,
Which nodded o'er the billows high and hoary,
A dark speck dotted ocean: on it flew
Like to the shadow of a roused sea-mew;
Onward it came—and, lo! a second follow'd—
Now seen—now hid—where ocean's vale was hollow'd;
And near, and nearer, till the dusky crew
Presented well-known aspects to the view,

'Till on the surf their skimming paddles play,
Buoyant as wings, and flitting through the spray;—
Now perching on the wave's high curl, and now
Dash'd downward in the thundering foam below,
Which flings it broad and boiling sheet on sheet,
And slings its high flakes, shiver'd into sleet:
But floating still through surf and swell, drew nigh
The barks, like small birds through a lowering sky.
Their art seem'd nature—such the skill to sweep
The wave of these born playmates of the deep.

VIII.

And who the first that, springing on the strand,
Leap'd like a nereid from her shell to land,
With dark but brilliant skin, and dewy eye
Shining with love, and hope, and constancy?
Neuha—the fond, the faithful, the adored—
Her heart on Torquil's like a torrent pour'd;
And smiled, and wept, and near, and nearer clasp'd,
As if to be assured 'twas *him* she grasp'd;
Shudder'd to see his yet warm wound, and then,
To find it trivial, smiled and wept again.
She was a warrior's daughter, and could bear
Such sights, and feel, and mourn, but not despair.
Her lover lived,—nor foes nor fears could blight
That full-blown moment in its all delight:
Joy trickled in her tears, joy fill'd the sob
That rock'd her heart till almost HEARD to throb;
And paradise was breathing in the sigh
Of nature's child in nature's ecstasy.

IX

The sterner spirits who beheld that meeting
Were not unmoved; who are, when hearts are greeting?
Even Christian gazed upon the maid and boy
With tearless eye, but yet a gloomy joy
Mix'd with those bitter thoughts the soul arrays
In hopeless visions of our better days,
When all's gone—to the rainbow's latest ray.
"And but for me!" he said, and turn'd away;

Then gazed upon the pair, as in his den
A lion looks upon his cubs again;
And then relapsed into his sullen guise,
As heedless of his further destinies.

X.

But brief their time for good or evil thought;
The billows round the promontory brought
The plash of hostile oars —Alas ! who made
That sound a dread ?　All around them seem'd array'd
Against them, save the bride of Toobonai :
She, as she caught the first glimpse o'er the bay
Of the arm'd boats, which hurried to complete
The remnant's ruin with their flying feet,
Beckon'd the natives round her to their prows,
Embark'd their guests and launch'd their light canoes,
In one placed Christian and his comrades twain ;
But she and Torquil must not part again.
She fix'd him in her own.—Away ! away !
They clear the breakers, dart along the bay,
And towards a group of islets, such as bear
The sea-bird's nest and seal's surf-hollow'd lair,
They skim the blue tops of the billows ; fast
They flew, and fast their fierce pursuers chased.
They gain upon them—now they lose again,—
Again make way and menace o'er the main ;
And now the two canoes in chase divide,
And follow different courses o'er the tide,
To baffle the pursuit.—Away ! away !
As life is on each paddle's flight to-day,
And more than life or lives to Neuha : Love
Freights the frail bark and urges to the cove ;
And now the refuge and the foe are nigh—
Yet, yet a moment !　Fly, thou light ark, fly !

CANTO THE FOURTH.

————◆————

I.

WHITE as a white sail on a dusky sea,
When half the horizon's clouded and half free,
Fluttering between the dun wave and the sky,
Is hope's last gleam in man's extremity.
Her anchor parts; but still her snowy sail
Attracts our eye amidst the rudest gale:
Though every wave she climbs divides us more,
The heart still follows from the loneliest shore.

II.

Not distant from the isle of Toobonai,
A black rock rears its bosom o'er the spray,
The haunt of birds, a desert to mankind,
Where the rough seal reposes from the wind,
And sleeps unwieldy in his cavern dun,
Or gambols with huge frolic in the sun:
There shrilly to the passing oar is heard
The startled echo of the ocean bird,
Who rears on its bare breast her callow brood,
The feather'd fishers of the solitude.
A narrow segment of the yellow sand
On one side forms the outline of a strand;
Here the young turtle, crawling from his shell,
Steals to the deep wherein his parents dwell;
Chipp'd by the beam, a nursling of the day,
But hatch'd for ocean by the fostering ray;

The rest was one bleak precipice, as e'er
Gave mariners a shelter and despair ;
A spot to make the saved regret the deck
Which late went down, and envy the lost wreck.
Such was the stern asylum Neuha chose
To shield her lover from his following foes;
But all its secret was not told; she knew
In this a treasure hidden from the view.

III.

Ere the canoes divided, near the spot,
The men that mann'd what held her Torquil's lot,
By her command removed, to strengthen more
The skiff which wafted Christian from the shore.
This he would have opposed; but with a smile
She pointed calmly to the craggy isle,
And bade him "speed and prosper." *She* would take
The rest upon herself for Torquil's sake.
They parted with this added aid; afar
The proa darted like a shooting star,
And gain'd on the pursuers, who now steer'd
Right on the rock which she and Torquil near'd.
They pull'd ; her arm, though delicate, was free
And firm as ever grappled with the sea,
And yielded scarce to Torquil's manlier strength.
The prow now almost lay within its length
Of the crag's steep, inexorable face,
With nought but soundless waters for its base;
Within a hundred boats' length was the foe,
And now what refuge but their frail canoe?
This Torquil ask'd with half upbraiding eye,
Which said—"Has Neuha brought me here to die ?
Is this a place of safety, or a grave,
And yon huge rock the tombstone of the wave?"

IV.

They rested on their paddles, and uprose
Neuha, and pointing to the approaching foes,
Cried, "Torquil, follow me, and fearless follow !"
Then plunged at once into the ocean's hollow.

There was no time to pause—the foes were near—
Chains in his eye, and menace in his ear;
With vigour they pull'd on, and as they came,
Hail'd him to yield, and by his forfeit name.
Headlong he leapt—to him the swimmer's skill
Was native, and now all his hope from ill:
But how, or where? He dived, and rose no more,
The boat's crew look'd amazed o'er sea and shore.
There was no landing on that precipice,
Steep, harsh, and slippery as a berg of ice.
They watch'd awhile to see him float again,
But not a trace rebubbled from the main:
The wave roll'd on, no ripple on its face,
Since their first plunge recall'd a single trace;
The little whirl which eddied, and slight foam,
That whiten'd o'er what seem'd their latest home,
White as a sepulchre above the pair
Who left no marble (mournful as an heir)
The quiet proa wavering o'er the tide
Was all that told of Torquil and his bride;
And but for this alone the whole might seem
The vanish'd phantom of a seaman's dream.
They paused and search'd in vain, then pull'd away;
Even superstition now forbade their stay.
Some said he had not plunged into the wave,
But vanish'd like a corpse-light from a grave;
Others, that something supernatural
Glared in his figure, more than mortal tall;
While all agreed that in his cheek and eye
There was a dead hue of eternity.
Still as their oars receded from the crag,
Round every weed a moment would they lag,
Expectant of some token of their prey;
But no—he had melted from them like the spray.

v.

And where was he the pilgrim of the deep,
Following the nereid? Had they ceased to weep
For ever? or, received in coral caves,
Wrung life and pity from the softening waves?

Did they with ocean's hidden sovereigns dwell,
And sound with mermen the fantastic shell?
Did Neuha with the mermaids comb her hair
Flowing o'er ocean as it stream'd in air?
Or had they perish'd, and in silence slept
Beneath the gulf wherein they boldly leapt?

VI.

Young Neuha plunged into the deep, and he
Follow'd : her track beneath her native sea
Was as a native's of the element,
So smoothly, bravely, brilliantly she went,
Leaving a streak of light behind her heel,
Which struck and flash'd like an amphibious steel.
Closely, and scarcely less expert to trace
The depths where divers hold the pearl in chase,
Torquil, the nursling of the northern seas,
Pursued her liquid steps with heart and ease.
Deep—deeper for an instant Neuha led
The way—then upward soar'd—and as she spread
Her arms, and flung the foam from off her locks,
Laugh'd, and the sound was answer'd by the rocks.
They had gain'd a central realm of earth again,
But look'd for tree, and field, and sky, in vain.
Around she pointed to a spacious cave,
Whose only portal was the keyless wave,[1]

[1] Of this cave (which is no fiction) the original will be found in the ninth chapter of "Mariner's Account of the Tonga Islands" I have taken the poetical liberty to transplant it to Toobonai, the last island where any distinct account is left of Christian and his comrades.—[The following is the account given by Mariner.—"On this island there is a peculiar cavern, which was first discovered by a young chief, whilst diving after a turtle. The nature of this cavern will be better understood if we imagine a hollow rock rising sixty feet or more above the surface of the water, into the cavity of which there is no known entrance but one, and that is in the side of the rock, as low down as six feet under the water, into which it flows, and, consequently, the base of the cavern may be said to be the sea itself" Mr. Mariner seeing some young chiefs diving into the water one after another, and not rise again, he inquired of the last, who was just preparing to take the same step, what they were about? "'Follow me,'' said he, "'and I will take you where you have never been before, and where Finow, and his chiefs and matabooles, are now assembled'" Mr. Mariner prepared himself to follow his companion, who dived into the water, and he after him, and, guided by the light reflected from his heels, entered the opening in the rock, and rose into the cavern. The light was sufficient, after remaining about five minutes, to show objects with some little distinctness, and he could discover Finow and the rest of the company seated round the cavern. Nevertheless, as it was

(A hollow archway by the sun unseen,
Save through the billows' glassy veil of green,
In some transparent ocean holiday,
When all the finny people are at play,)
Wiped with her hair the brine from Torquil's eyes,
And clapp'd her hands with joy at his surprise;
Led him to where the rock appear'd to jut,
And form a something like a Triton's hut;
For all was darkness for a space, till day,
Through clefts above let in a sober'd ray;
As in some old cathedral's glimmering aisle
The dusty monuments from light recoil,
Thus sadly in their refuge submarine
The vault drew half her shadow from the scene.

VII.

Forth from her bosom the young savage drew
A pine torch, strongly girded with gnatoo;
A plantain-leaf o'er all, the more to keep
Its latent sparkle from the sapping deep.
This mantle kept it dry; then from a nook
Of the same plantain-leaf a flint she took,
A few shrunk wither'd twigs, and from the blade
Of Torquil's knife struck fire, and thus array'd

desirable to have a stronger illumination, Mr Mariner dived out again, and procuring
his pistol, primed it well, tied plenty of gnatoo tight round it, and wrapped the whole
up in a plantain-leaf, he directed an attendant to bring a torch in the same way.
Thus prepared, he re-entered the cavern, unwrapped the gnatoo, a great portion of
which was perfectly dry, fired it by the flash of the powder and lighted the torch.
"The place was now illuminated tolerably well It appeared (by guess) to be about
forty feet wide in the main part, but it branched off, on one side, in two narrower
portions   The medium height seemed also about forty feet   The roof was hung
with stalactites in a very curious way, resembling upon a cursory view, the Gothic
arches and ornaments of an old church." The account proceeds to mention that
according to the statement of one of the matabooles present, the entire family of a
certain chief had been in former times condemned to death for conspiring against a
tyrannical governor of the island   One of the devoted family was a beautiful
daughter, to whom the chief who discovered the cave had long been attached   On
learning her danger, he persuaded her to accompany him to this retreat, where she
remained concealed, occasionally enjoying the society of her lover, until he was enabled
to carry her off to the Fiji islands, where they dwelt till the death of the governor
enabled them to return   The only part of the tale which seemed very improbable,
was that the girl should have been in the cavern so long as two or three months   Mr.
Mariner examined every part of it, without discovering any opening, and if the story
be true, in all likelihood her stay was not much more than a fourth of the time, as the
space would not contain sufficient air for a longer period]

The grot with torchlight.　Wide it was and high,
And show'd a self-born Gothic canopy;
The arch uprear'd by nature's architect,
The architrave some earthquake might erect;
The buttress from some mountain's bosom hurl'd,
When the Poles crash'd, and water was the world;
Or harden'd from some earth-absorbing fire,
While yet the globe reek'd from its funeral pyre;
The fretted pinnacle, the aisle, the nave,[2]
Were there, all scoop'd by Darkness from her cave.
There, with a little tinge of phantasy,
Fantastic faces mop'd and mow'd on high,
And then a mitre or a shrine would fix
The eye upon its seeming crucifix.
Thus Nature play'd with the stalactites,
And built herself a chapel of the seas.

VIII.

And Neuha took her Torquil by the hand,
And waved along the vault her kindled brand,
And led him into each recess, and show'd
The secret places of their new abode.
Nor these alone, for all had been prepared
Before, to soothe the lover's lot she shared:
The mat for rest; for dress the fresh gnatoo,
And sandal oil to fence against the dew;
For food the cocoa-nut, the yam, the bread
Born of the fruit; for board the plantain spread
With its broad leaf, or turtle-shell which bore
A banquet in the flesh it cover'd o'er;
The gourd with water recent from the rill,
The ripe banana from the mellow hill;
A pine-torch pile to keep undying light,
And she herself, as beautiful as night,
To fling her shadowy spirit o'er the scene,
And make their subterranean world serene.

---

[2] This may seem too minute for the general outline (in Mariner's Account) from which it is taken.　But few men have travelled without seeing something of the kind—on *land*, that is　Without adverting to Ellora, in Mungo Park's last journal, he mentions having met with a rock or mountain so exactly resembling a Gothic cathedral, that only minute inspection could convince him that it was a work of nature.

She had foreseen, since first the stranger's sail
Drew to their isle, that force or flight might fail,
And form'd a refuge of the rocky den
For Torquil's safety from his countrymen.
Each dawn had wafted there her light canoe,
Laden with all the golden fruits that grew;
Each eve had seen her gliding through the hour
With all could cheer or deck their sparry bower
And now she spread her little store with smiles,
The happiest daughter of the loving isles.

IX.

She, as he gazed with grateful wonder, press'd
Her shelter'd love to her impassion'd breast;
And suited to her soft caresses, told
An olden tale of love,—for love is old,
Old as eternity, but not outworn
With each new being born or to be born:[3]
How a young chief, a thousand moons ago,
Diving for turtle in the depths below,
Had risen, in tracking fast his ocean prey,
Into the cave which round and o'er them lay;
How in some desperate feud of after-time
He shelter'd there a daughter of the clime,
A foe beloved, and offspring of a foe,
Saved by his tribe but for a captive's woe;
How, when the storm of war was still'd, he led
His island clan to where the waters spread
Their deep-green shadow o'er the rocky door,
Then dived—it seem'd as if to rise no more:
His wondering mates, amazed within their bark,
Or deem'd him mad, or prey to the blue shark;
Row'd round in sorrow the sea-girded rock,
Then paused upon their paddles from the shock;
When, fresh and springing from the deep, they saw
A goddess rise—so deem'd they in their awe;

---

[3] The reader will recollect the epigram of the Greek anthology, or its translation into most of the modern languages —

> " Whoe'er thou art, thy master see—
> He was, or is, or is to be "

And their companion, glorious by her side,
Proud and exulting in his mermaid bride;
And how, when undeceived, the pair they bore
With sounding conchs and joyous shouts to shore:
How they had gladly lived and calmly died,
And why not also Torquil and his bride?
Not mine to tell the rapturous caress
Which follow'd wildly in that wild recess
This tale; enough that all within that cave
Was love, though buried strong as in the grave
Where Abelard, through twenty years of death,
When Eloisa's form was lower'd beneath
Their nuptial vault, his arms outstretch'd, and press'd
The kindling ashes to his kindled breast.*
The waves without sang round their couch, their roar
As much unheeded as if life were o'er;
Within, their hearts made all their harmony,
Love's broken murmur and more broken sigh.

x.

And they, the cause and sharers of the shock
Which left them exiles of the hollow rock,
Where were they ?   O'er the sea for life they plied,
To seek from Heaven the shelter men denied.
Another course had been their choice—but where?
The wave which bore them still their foes would bear,
Who, disappointed of their former chase,
In search of Christian now renew'd their race.
Eager with anger, their strong arms made way,
Like vultures baffled of their previous prey.
They gain'd upon them, all whose safety lay
In some bleak crag or deeply-hidden bay:
No further chance or choice remain'd; and right
For the first further rock which met their sight
They steer'd, to take their latest view of land,
And yield as victims, or die sword in hand;

* The tradition is attached to the story of Eloisa, that when her body was lowered into the grave of Abelard (who had been buried twenty years), he opened his arms to receive her.

Dismiss'd the natives and their shallop, who
Would still have battled for that scanty crew;
But Christian bade them seek their shore again,
Nor add a sacrifice which were in vain;
For what were simple bow and savage spear
Against the arms which must be wielded here?

XI.

They landed on a wild but narrow scene,
Where few but Nature's footsteps yet had been,
Prepared their arms, and with that gloomy eye,
Stern and sustain'd, of man's extremity,
When hope is gone, nor glory's self remains
To cheer resistance against death or chains,—
They stood, the three, as the three hundred stood
Who dyed Thermopylæ with holy blood.
But, ah! how different! 'tis the *cause* makes all,
Degrades or hallows courage in its fall.
O'er them no fame, eternal and intense,
Blazed through the clouds of death and beckon'd hence;
No grateful country, smiling through her tears,
Begun the praises of a thousand years;
No nation's eyes would on their tomb be bent,
No heroes envy them their monument;
However boldly their warm blood was spilt,
Their life was shame, their epitaph was guilt.
And this they knew and felt, at least the one,
The leader of the band he had undone;
Who, born perchance for better things, had set
His life upon a cast which linger'd yet:
But now the die was to be thrown, and all
The chances were in favour of his fall:
And such a fall! But still he faced the shock,
Obdurate as a portion of the rock
Whereon he stood, and fix'd his levell'd gun,
Dark as a sullen cloud before the sun.

XII.

The boat drew nigh, well arm'd, and firm the crew
To act whatever duty bade them do;

Careless of danger, as the onward wind
Is of the leaves it strews, nor looks behind.
And yet perhaps, they rather wish'd to go
Against a nation's than a native foe,
And felt that this poor victim of self-will,
Briton no more, had once been Britain's still.
They hail'd him to surrender—no reply;
Their arms were poised, and glitter'd in the sky.
They hail'd again—no answer; yet once more
They offer'd quarter louder than before.
The echoes only, from the rock's rebound,
Took their last farewell of the dying sound.
Then flash'd the flint, and blazed the volleying flame,
And the smoke rose between them and their aim,
While the rock rattled with the bullets' knell,
Which peal'd in vain, and flatten'd as they fell;
Then flew the only answer to be given
By those who had lost all hope in earth or heaven.
After the first fierce peal as they pull'd nigher,
They heard the voice of Christian shout, "Now, fire!"
And ere the word upon the echo died,
Two fell; the rest assail'd the rock's rough side,
And, furious at the madness of their foes,
Disdain'd all further efforts, save to close.
But steep the crag, and all without a path,
Each step opposed a bastion to their wrath,
While, placed 'midst clefts the least accessible,
Which Christian's eye was train'd to mark full well,
The three maintain'd a strife which must not yield,
In spots where eagles might have chosen to build.
Their every shot told, while the assailant fell,
Dash'd on the shingles like the limpet shell;
But still enough survived, and mounted still,
Scattering their numbers here and there, until
Surrounded and commanded, though not nigh
Enough for seizure, near enough to die,
The desperate trio held aloof their fate
But by a thread, like sharks who have gorged the bait;
Yet to the very last they battled well,
And not a groan inform'd their foes *who* fell.

Christian died last—twice wounded; and once more
Mercy was offer'd when they saw his gore;
Too late for life, but not too late to die,
With, though a hostile hand, to close his eye.
A limb was broken, and he droop'd along
The crag, as doth a falcon reft of young.
The sound revived him, or appear'd to wake
Some passion which a weakly gesture spake:
He beckon'd to the foremost, who drew nigh,
But, as they near'd, he rear'd his weapon high—
His last ball had been aim'd, but from his breast
He tore the topmost button from his vest,[3]
Down the tube dash'd it, levell'd, fired, and smiled
As his foe fell; then, like a serpent, coil'd
His wounded, weary form, to where the steep
Look'd desperate as himself along the deep;
Cast one glance back, and clench'd his hand, and shook
His last rage 'gainst the earth which he forsook;
Then plunged: the rock below received like glass
His body crush'd into one gory mass,
With scarce a shred to tell of human form,
Or fragment for the sea-bird or the worm;
A fair-hair'd scalp, besmear'd with blood and weeds,
Yet reck'd, the remnant of himself and deeds;
Some splinters of his weapons (to the last,
As long as hand could hold, he held them fast)
Yet glitter'd, but at distance—hurl'd away
To rust beneath the dew and dashing spray.
The rest was nothing—save a life mis-spent,
And soul—but who shall answer where it went?
'Tis ours to bear, not judge the dead; and they
Who doom to hell, themselves are on the way,

---

[3] In Thibault's account of Frederick the Second of Prussia, there is a singular relation of a young Frenchman, who with his mistress appeared to be of some rank. He enlisted and deserted at Schweidnitz; and after a desperate resistance was retaken, having killed an officer, who attempted to seize him after he was wounded, by the discharge of his musket loaded with a *button* o. his uniform. Some circumstances on his court martial raised a great interest amongst his judges, who wished to discover his real situation in life, which he offered to disclose, but to the *king* only, to whom he requested permission to write. This was refused, and Frederic was filled with the greatest indignation, from baffled curiosity or some other motive, when he understood that his request had been denied

Unless these bullies of eternal pains
Are pardon'd their bad hearts for their worse brains.

XIII.

The deed was over !　All were gone or ta'en,
The fugitive, the captive, or the slain.
Chain'd on the deck, where once, a gallant crew,
, They stood with honour, were the wretched few
Survivors of the skirmish on the isle ;
But the last rock left no surviving spoil.
Cold lay they where they fell, and weltering,
While o'er them flapp'd the sea-birds' dewy wing,
Now wheeling nearer from the neighbouring surge,
And screaming high their harsh and hungry dirge :
But calm and careless heaved the wave below,
Eternal with unsympathetic flow ;
Far o'er its face the dolphins sported on,
And sprung the flying fish against the sun,
Till its dried wing relapsed from its brief height,
To gather moisture for another flight.

XIV.

'Twas morn ; and Neuha, who by dawn of day
Swam smoothly forth to catch the rising ray,
And watch if aught approach'd the amphibious lair
Where lay her lover, saw a sail in air :
It flapp'd, it fill'd, and to the growing gale
Bent its broad arch : her breath began to fail
With fluttering fear, her heart beat thick and high,
While yet a doubt sprung where its course might lie.
But no ! it came not ; fast and far away
The shadow lessen'd as it clear'd the bay.
She gazed, and flung the sea-foam from her eyes,
To watch as for a rainbow in the skies.
On the horizon verged the distant deck,
Diminish'd, dwindled to a very speck—
Then vanish'd.　All was ocean, all was joy !
Down plunged she through the cave to rouse her boy ;
Told all she had seen, and all she hoped, and all
That happy love could augur or recall,

J

Sprung forth again, with Torquil following free
His bounding nereid over the broad sea;
Swam round the rock, to where a shallow cleft
Hid the canoe that Neuha there had left
Drifting along the tide, without an oar,
That eve the strangers chased them from the shore;
But when these vanish'd, she pursued her prow,
Regain'd, and urged to where they found it now:
Nor ever did more love and joy embark,
Than now were wafted in that slender ark.

XV.

Again their own shore rises on the view,
No more polluted with a hostile hue;
No sullen ship lay bristling o'er the foam,
A floating dungeon :—all was hope and home!
A thousand proas darted o'er the bay,
With sounding shells, and heralded their way;
The chiefs came down, around the people pour'd,
And welcomed Torquil as a son restored;
The women throng'd, embracing and embraced
By Neuha, asking where they had been chased,
And how escaped? The tale was told; and then
One acclamation rent the sky again;
And from that hour a new tradition gave
Their sanctuary the name of " Neuha's Cave."
A hundred fires, far flickering from the height,
Blazed o'er the general revel of the night,
The feast in honour of the guest, return'd
To peace and pleasure, perilously earn'd;
A night succeeded by such happy days
As only the yet infant world displays.

END OF VOL. III.

BRADBURY, AGNEW, & CO., PRINTERS, WHITEFRIARS.

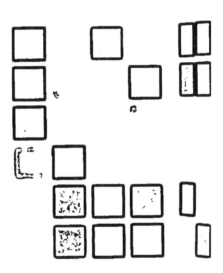

CPSIA information can be obtained
at www.ICGtesting.com
Printed in the USA
LVOW13*1410130417

530728LV00005B/19/P

9 781374 235342